Through the Periscope

SUNY series in Italian/American Culture
———
Fred L. Gardaphé, editor

Through the Periscope

Changing Culture, Italian America

MARTINO MARAZZI

Cover image: From *Time and Tide* (2000), dir. Peter Hutton. Reprinted by permission of the artist and Carolina Gonzalez-Hutton.

Published by State University of New York Press, Albany

© 2022 State University of New York

All rights reserved

Printed in the United States of America

No part of this book may be used or reproduced in any manner whatsoever without written permission. No part of this book may be stored in a retrieval system or transmitted in any form or by any means including electronic, electrostatic, magnetic tape, mechanical, photocopying, recording, or otherwise without the prior permission in writing of the publisher.

For information, contact State University of New York Press, Albany, NY
www.sunypress.edu

Library of Congress Cataloging-in-Publication Data

Name: Marazzi, Martino, author.
Title: Through the periscope : changing culture, Italian America / Martino Marazzi, author.
Description: Albany : State University of New York Press, [2022] | Series: SUNY series in Italian/American Culture | Includes bibliographical references and index.
Identifiers: ISBN 9781438488615 (hardcover : alk. paper) | ISBN 9781438488622 (ebook) | ISBN 9781438488608 (pbk. : alk. paper)
Further information is available at the Library of Congress.

Library of Congress Control Number: 2022931950

10 9 8 7 6 5 4 3 2 1

To Francesco and Bob

friends, masters

Contents

Acknowledgments ix

Introduction 1

Part I. Changing Culture

Chapter 1   A Hard Rome's A-Gonna Fall: Roman Sonnets,
            Sicilian Sulfur, and American Ballads   11

Chapter 2   Changing Culture: European Immigrants and
            New York City Literature, 1870–1940   31

Chapter 3   "Our brother Dante": Dantesque Reappropriations
            in Italian America   45

Part II. Transitional Modes of Italian American Letters

Chapter 4   All the Words That Are (Not) Fit to Print:
            Notes on the "Illiterature" of the Italian Emigration   79

Chapter 5   Questioning the Traditionalism of Italian American
            Literature   97

Chapter 6   Kings of Harlem: Garibaldi Lapolla and the
            "Grand" Gennaro   103

Chapter 7   I Am(s): Strategies of Acceptance and Denial   119

Chapter 8   Reading Robert Viscusi   129

Conclusion   141

Notes   145

Bibliography   175

Index   191

Acknowledgments

Some of these essays appeared previously in various journals and volumes. They have been revised and rewritten. I gratefully acknowledge their editors and publishers for the permission to print them again, in different forms and sometimes under different titles, as well as my anonymous readers' intellectual and editorial lucidity. Their comments were decisive in the shaping and fine-tuning of the book. For years I have had the privilege of relying on the careful grammatical and intellectual scrutiny of my friend Teddy Jefferson. My words of thanks here are a very meager way of giving back. *Grazie*. On the sources, more in detail: Chapter 2: *New York: A Literary History*, ed. Ross Wilson (Cambridge: Cambridge University Press, 2020). Chapter 3 in Dante Politico: *Ideological Reception across Boundaries*, ed. Dennis Looney and Donatella Stocchi-Perucchio, special issue of *Mediaevalia* 38 (2017). Chapter 4 partially in *Strangers in a Strange Land: A Catalogue of an Exhibition on the History of Italian-language American Imprints (1830–1945). From the Collection of James J. Periconi, with a Bibliography of These and Related Works* (New York: The Grolier Club, 2012), and *Italiano LinguaDue* 1 (2012). Chapter 5 partially in *The Status of Interpretation in Italian American Studies*, ed. Jerome Krase (Stony Brook, NY: Forum Italicum Publishing, 2011), and *RSA Journal—Rivista di Studi Americani*, 21–22 (2010–2011). Chapter 6 in *'Merica: A Conference on the Culture and Literature of Italians in North America*, ed. Aldo Bove and Giuseppe Massara (Stony Brook, NY: Forum Italicum Publishing, 2006). Chapter 7 in *Re-Mapping Italian America: Places, Cultures, Identities*, ed. Carla Francellini and Sabrina Vellucci (New York: Bordighera Press, 2018). Chapter 8 ("Breaking New Ground"): VIA—*Voices in Italian Americana* 18, no. 1 (Spring 2007). Chapter 8 ("The Substance of Chance"): *Ellis Island. Libri 1.1—4. 12* (Varese: abrigliasciolta, 2010).

Introduction

Flying high on the wings of his sophisticated magazine *Pègaso*, Ugo Ojetti—a Brahmin of the Italian cultural élite of the early twentieth century—remarked, in 1930, that "Our arch-literary literature ignores them—in fact, it has always ignored them." He was referring to all the Italians living "from Melbourne to Rio, from San Francisco to Marseille, from Lima to Tunis."

Enter Antonio Gramsci, laboriously elaborating his Machiavellian discourse on culture, politics, and hegemony. In his sixth prison notebook he culled Ojetti's observation and added his usually incisive comments. Emigration as a "socio-economic phenomenon"—wrote Gramsci—has "always" (offhandedly, the same adverb) produced "an impressive array of publications." And yet this did not translate into a creative, "artistic literature" (*una letteratura artistica*), despite the fact that "every immigrant—even before leaving Italy—bears within himself a tragedy" (*racchiude in sé un dramma*). Such a lack of attention is not surprising—continued Gramsci—, because literati disregard the immigrants' actual conditions, precisely, prior to their departure.[1] Noteworthy is the fact that neither Ojetti nor Gramsci considered the possibility of creative works produced by the immigrants themselves, or in any case coming from abroad.

Read today, this silent dialogue between two protagonists of Italian culture sounds, if not completely outdated, certainly superseded. In the last half century—if we adopt as authoritative point of departure Rose Basile Green's 1974 *The Italian-American Novel*[2]—scholarship showed a keen attention to the multifarious dimensions of immigrant culture. When it comes to the various symbolic and material modes of production of immigration, we are not confronted with an interpretive void anymore. Of course, there are always (again!) new findings, new approaches, new voices. What I find as crucial today as it was in Gramsci's time is to problematize, pointing to what he used to call the *nesso*—the connection, the relationship—, that nexus between phenomena that is grounded historically, culturally, and—paying homage to a son of immigrants, Henry Miller—existentially. Such connections fall often beyond the scope of a certified and transmissible scholarship, whose actual encounters are exorcised by dint of increasingly more intradisciplinary scholarship, in a magic circle of abstraction.

Relations, instead, figure largely at the center of the immigrant condition, which expresses itself in an unrelenting and trying dynamic between the present and the past, here and there, novelty and tradition: the dynamism of change, with its crushing challenges as well as its elating renewals. Elsewhere in the notebooks, discussing "nationalism and particularism," Gramsci offers that "explanations are perhaps coordinated."[3] I take it as a precious indication.

To an Italian intellectual, one of the huge questions ignited by an almost century-long exodus of approximately twenty-six million people toward various destinations revolves around its significance, its weight, vis-à-vis the painful and long process that brought over and then molded Italy's nation-building, the so-called *Risorgimento* and Unification, which covered, at least, the period stretching from the Congress of Vienna to the end of WWI. In another essay, I proposed to read this interplay between national formation, demographic hemorrhage, and cultural adaptation as a foundational instance of "Italexit."[4] Recognizing and appreciating the existence of societies and cultures feeding themselves on multiple belongings means reckoning with realities which we are all familiar with, but which a sobering "methodological nationalism" (Gabaccia)[5] keeps finding pragmatically inadequate to the parthenogenesis of higher learning. Such a pedagogical unease reflects the hierarchical setup whereby values are allotted according to defined borders. Forms of expression that refer to constitutive acts of movement and transformation demand, on the contrary, for the acknowledgement of an intrinsic shuttling principle, for the coordination—as it were—of explanations.

This is not to say that nations do not count, let alone the cultural structures that in a variety of ways flower and are produced within their confines. Further below, Donna Gabaccia aptly reminds us that "high levels of international migration have historically not much impeded nation-building. They may even have encouraged it."[6] Very shrewdly, Yiorgos Anagnostou puts it otherwise: "How does one dismantle identity when identity still mobilizes the public?"[7] When bowing to the diasporic trend that has been in vogue for at least the last twenty years, we should not overlook the fact that such a discourse mirrors the trajectories of the global hegemony and functions as a homoeopathic critique of Western (and prevailingly Anglo-American) power, thus consolidating, in fact, what it purports to be critically analyzing. If anything, one ought to recognize that oxymora, complexity, and even contradictions are essential tenets of the humanities borne out of a decisive condition of cultural reinvention through space and different sociopolitical entities.

My concern, in the following chapters, has been to primarily focus on a cultural—and mostly literary—panorama that operates, grows, and legitimizes itself through a constant weaving of interrelations between given traditions. These last, in turn, caught in the process, renovate themselves, put on new dresses. It is what I indicate as a *changing culture*, a metamorphic paradigm that invests both the subjects (authors and their public) and their products. Culture changes while its protagonists undergo substantial modifications.

Likewise, the changing and shuttling principle should apply to the methodology of research and to its style of presentation. To make better sense of that intrinsically movable condition, to retrieve and vindicate the "disappearance" that Kafka, in his grand American novel, marks as the defining sign of the immigrant, one might have to adopt the point of view of the periscope, bringing to focus the new through the old, and reframing the old through the unforeseeable outcomes of the new conditions. Expanding the nation(s), expanding our sense of ethnicity. Abdelmalek Sayad poignantly defined immigrant cultures in terms of the "double absence" that they inhabit;[8] I contend that, if creatively employed, a "changing culture" has the potential of reversing that void, suggesting the existence of a *double presence*, negotiating between its intense need of "homebound" traditional codes and the concurrent capacity of launching itself forward in an anticipatory mode. Especially when framed from the point of view of Old World tenets, the cultural modus operandi of ethnic cultures appears many-sided and multiverse. Lines of research that could be seen as moving along parallel paths—the dialectics among European popular cultures; the search for a usable past by American intellectuals and the rise of a distinctively modern and ethnic urban art; the exploration of Dante's cultural power and its consequences; a constant analysis of Italian American forms, with special reference to their linguistic and expressive manifestations—all of this seemed to gain in consistency as

I realized that my own scholarship found an audience moving across borders—institutional and cultural. The two nuclei this volume consists of, then—the quintessential patrimony of the Italian tradition, and the Italian American civilization—became mutually attractive foci of an ellipse, or of a system, straddling different dimensions.

I always thought that a scholar is more trustworthy insofar as s/he attempts some form of identification with the object of study. And I understand now, at the fullest divide, that to fruitfully embark on my own sentimental journey of sorts, I needed not one, but two different sets of examples, two models of guidance. Thus I had the good fortune of finding the unbinding method—methods, really, given their plural nature—in the groundbreaking works of Robert Viscusi and Francesco Durante. Their unflagging indication of a necessary scrutiny of both sides of the Italian American experience, coupled with the sheer quantity of their analyses, expanded our understanding in this field and provided a blueprint.

Viscusi—in his essays and in his poetry—kept shining new lights and testing new ideas, while very strongly advocating for a larger sense of Italian Americanness—indeed, of Italianness—one that would engage not only in the exploration of the bona fide Italian roots of yore, but also in a confrontation with contemporary Italy (a country now transformed by its own influx of inbound mass migrations). And this, as the template of a fully formed New Yorker, a city dweller with roots and branches in close proximity with the myriad faces of the metropolis. His masterpiece, *Ellis Island*, not only marks an artistic zenith,[9] but also—as it is the case—provides the most inspiring legacy through the force of its visions, rhythms, and somersaults.

Durante—as strange as it may sound—acted as the Schliemann of Italian culture outside the peninsula. He single-handedly discovered and explained the teeming world of the Italian "colonies" in the United States, thus not only giving visibility to a most articulate milieu, but in so doing also showing its "organic" quality, its structure and values, its daring stances, its creative "folly."

After their sudden disappearance, Viscusi and Durante's contribution looms large in terms of results and even more in its pathfinding nature. Taken together, their oeuvre makes clear that Italian American studies today is a privileged vantage point from which to engage in a comprehensive discussion of the "original" Old World heritage while recognizing, on the other hand, the global impact of mass migration. In particular, my studies have convinced me that it is time to analyze Italian migrations as part of an even wider—and largely homogenous—European phenomenon. It is a trite and well-known fact that Italian popular culture and Italian immigrants had to coexist, and to some extent to suffer from, on both sides of the Atlantic, the double standard of "room with a view VS. steerage class," against which *furbizia* and survival instinct pitted different strategies. Examining the encounters of actual nineteenth-century American intellectuals with the Italo-European rise of democratic demands around 1848 and beyond—like I venture to do in the first chapter—is intended to provide an antidote to such a skewed disposition.

It is also by now quite inaccurate to keep repeating that Italians scattered worldwide. What do we mean when we stress the diasporic, the transnational, the global? Emigration started in small towns and remote valleys. Italians went where there were sources of capital and jobs. And they didn't do it blindfolded. It's their lucidity that the Italian élite downplayed, resented, and fundamentally still resents. But it was one of their most precious assets, and one that it is imperative to acknowledge and confront. This awareness is precisely what distances us and our objects of study from the elaborate strategy of non sequitur that Italian literati reserved, at the height of the Great Migration, to their fellow citizens, expelling Italian migrants from memory, in obvious obedience to an isomorphism that tied together politics and sense of social standing along the lines of a self-fashioned scholarly dignity. Thus, in the masterly, acrid, dizzying historical novel *I vecchi e i giovani* (*The Old and the Young*, 1909–1913)[10]—now largely undervalued in favor of the smoother *Il Gattopardo*—Luigi Pirandello's narrator gapes with horror at a bloody massacre taking place in the town of Aragona, near Agrigento, during the revolt of the so-called *Fasci siciliani* in the 1890s. Aragona is where Pirandello's family owned the sulfur mine whose mismanagement determined the writer's lifelong financial difficulties; its netherworld was famously at the center of some of his—and of Giovanni Verga's—best short stories and—even more interestingly—of Booker T. Washington's indictment *The Man Farthest Down* (1912).[11] More to the point, Aragona being (today as a century and more years ago) a rural town with an extremely high ratio of outbound migration, it is telling that Pirandello never mentioned its outbound exodus; the same happens with nearby Milocca, both in the novel and in one of his most implacable *novelle*, *Le sorprese della scienza* (1905),[12] and later the focus of a classic study by Chicago-school anthropologist Charlotte Gower Chapman.[13] In a way this is an old story; fast forward and see how, instead, the bigger city of Ragusa and its socio-ideological slump figure positively at the center of the outbound feminist radicalism of Maria Occhipinti, the activist and writer who captured like few others the spirit of post-WWII emigration.[14] Its history needed—to put it simply—to be told in her own words. You can't expect others—not even a Pirandello—to tell you who you are, where you come from, and where you're heading.

While distancing from, and reflecting on, their place of departure, Italian migrants were shaping *their own* culture in a complex, troubled, and fascinating interaction with the new, myriad variables around them—Italo-genic signs included. Indeed, and this—again—has often been remarked, the immigrant and ethnic *landscape* would better be defined as an eye-opening, multicultural *city-scape*. For instance, from another, culturally loaded, perceptual point of view, post-WWII migration met the new craze for Italian design and taste in the Zeitgeist exhibit *The new domestic landscape* at MoMA in 1972. From then on, willy-nilly and irrespective of any actual encounter, Italian America enters more decidedly a new phase as part of a wider Italo-semiosphere. The risk, to be sure, is diluting the thick density of experience that the immigrant condition epitomized, with its baggage of tradition and sociohistorical conflict. And yet—if I read correctly the great work done in recent decades by Joseph Sciorra and Simone Cinotto[15]—there is no turning back from this reconfiguration of the Italian American sign *within* the larger stage, demands, and even histrionics of a new, totalitarian, consumer culture.

When we look at Italian America today, we operate from within this new condition of complexity, without any privileged roadmap, to scour a multidirectional network. A network determined by history, linguistically diverse, and yet identifiable, and above all, intensely experienced by real people. The point, then, is to always find new paths.

One moves forward and backward through trials and errors, but always open to new vistas; sociohistorical structures seep into one's conscience, affect the language, are transformed into acts of volition and sometimes creation that, in turn, renovate reality. Thus, landscapes and scenarios constantly move and shift—and so do the Italian American and the Italian signs, which—I think—appear now to us as demanding once more and again to pay close and sensible attention to its many voices, visions, and phenomena—especially today, in times of tedious academic conservatism, and of larger, coterminous, political exclusionary acts.

Obviously, it is not by chance that my own work on the culture of the Italian diaspora has developed, in recent decades, while Italy moved from being a point of massive departure to a "destination culture."[16] And yet literary studies (certainly Italian literary studies) by and large still show a considerable reluctance in addressing the question of the existence of a diasporic Italian culture. Instead, a full acceptance of the diasporic dimension within the literary canon should suggest new ways of looking at the Italian cultural identity, both in its historical and its present configuration. A pliable and dynamic identity characterized by cultural diversity, referring—sometimes tentatively, other times more "organically"—to a multicultural and transnational environment. A wider approach to a cultural study of things Italian challenges the conventional wisdom of an Italo-centric curriculum and opens up new perspectives in a variety of ways, while positing a more engaging cultural scenario, in light of the massive migrations presently affecting Italy, Europe, and the Americas.

If we consider the diverse and most stimulating horizons shown in the fiction of new Italian authors active in Italy and elsewhere—to name just a few, Elvira Dones, Amara Lakhous, Adrián Bravi, Helena Janeczek, Ilja Leonard Pfeijffer, and Elvira Mujčić—one is struck not only by the writers' perceptiveness, but also by the overall picture of Italy expressed in their works. A country certainly defined, by now, among other things by the incessant entanglement of different layers of arrivals. Needless to say, the creative disposition varies in accordance with the wide spectrum of interests that are given voice in every novel.

Reframed from the Italian coastline, the frontier is obviously not the old Turnerian (in the sense of 1893 Frederick Jackson Turner's) banner of an accumulative and liberating push forward, but clearly a threshold marked by too many unspeakable tragedies, the main tangible avant-garde, the new *frontiera* (in the words of an acute, militant intellectual, Alessandro Leogrande) where the First World's gloating opulence and injustice meet the new energetic thrust for liberty and stability of the dispossessed.[17] A larger consideration of this changing culture—in the United States, Italy, and elsewhere—could hopefully contribute to a better assessment of what appears today a cultural identity caught between the unerasable nations and the much more fragile, but equally unquenchable, drives of the subject. A challenge for the humanities to be, because, ultimately, it is a matter of how we interpret our role of scholars and educators in the field of cultural studies, with a strong orientation toward any product, sign, work of (artistic) creativity. A matter of whether we find soothing and somehow socially useful locking the discourse within the parameters of tradition, or instead whether we deem more congenial adopting "mobility" not as the last academic catchphrase but as an intellectual disposition corresponding to the current challenges of the global scenario.[18] Being worthy—as scholars—of the daring and searching intelligence of the migrants of yesterday and today, and therefore being "mobile" in our own studies in order to deserve interpreting those cultural metamorphoses. Never turning away from reality, and recapturing before it is too late what risks being lost and forgotten.

Italian American studies represents, in my interpretation, a privileged point of observation of this historical and cultural condition, which is still with us signaling one of the most urgent questions of today. I try in the following chapters to outline some of its contours.

Part I

Changing Culture

Chapter 1

A Hard Rome's A-Gonna Fall

Roman Sonnets, Sicilian Sulfur, and American Ballads

1

During her long and very intense stay in Rome, Margaret Fuller lived a notoriously deep intellectual, political, and personal experience. One of the more fascinating aspects of that Roman period, as it is captured in her various writings, has to do with the shrewd perceptiveness of her position not only as an outsider, but an outsider passionately taking part—not just absorbing and observing—in those very societal challenges that she dissects and presents to her American readers and correspondents. For indeed in Rome Fuller appears replenished with ideas about, and with an almost physical sense of, the surrounding Roman society. And at the same time she has it all, so to speak, engaging at full tilt with the Roman auratic charisma, without hiding the many mundane disappointments, difficulties, and irritations. She doesn't hold back: it is not a "marble faun" morbidity that pulls the strings.

What is more specific, and unique to her position, is her embrace of the Risorgimento as a revolutionary flowering where somehow transcendentalism and socialism meet and intertwine. The liberation of Rome from papal tyranny and the unification of Italy are viewed not only in practical, political terms, but also as momentous events befitting a higher concept of the soul. Freedom and justice are not abstract ideals, but emanate from the bosom.

And yet it is in my mind crucial to stress that Fuller's Rome—and more generally Fuller's Italy—is by and large very much premodern. We read it and see it on almost every page of her *Dispatches* and letters. Neither of them could be easily used as a mid-nineteenth-century handbook on the beauties and attractions of the eternal city, but it is a fact that she relishes in the spectacle of popular vitality, be it expressed in colorful processions or collective street dances (the inhabitants of Trastevere doing their *saltarello* in *Dispatch* 19[1]). The Catholic devotion for the Dead, the very Roman celebration of the sacred infant—the Bambino at Aracoeli—, the Carnival, the *moccoletti* (the feast of the tapers), the Fair of St. Eustachio, these are just some of the very lively traditions that Fuller confronts, at times more critically, but overall with a sympathetic eye.[2]

Her aim, though, is not folkloric, even less touristic.[3] In the midst of the "intoxications of joy" swarming through Rome "at the first serious measures of reform taken by the Pope,"[4] she notes a band cheering the crowd playing *Awakening of Italy*—a popular anthem of national unity penned by Italian exile Giovanni Secchi de Casali in New York.[5] The tumultuous sequence of events throughout Europe in 1848 soon invites her to bolder tones: "The news from France, in these days, sounds ominous, though still vague; it would appear that the political is being merged in the social struggle: it is well; whatever blood is to be shed, whatever altars cast down. These tremendous problems MUST be solved, whatever be the cost!"[6] What is happening in Europe provides a lesson to be sent back home:

> To you, people of America, it may perhaps be given to look on and learn in time for a preventive wisdom. You may learn the real meaning of the words FRATERNITY, EQUALITY: you may, despite the apes of the Past, who strive to tutor you, learn the needs of a true Democracy. You may in time learn to reverence, learn to guard, the true aristocracy of a nation, the only really noble—the LABORING CLASSES.[7]

The profound upheaval witnessed in Rome will lead to the ousting of the Pope and to the proclamation of the Republic. Enter Mazzini and Garibaldi. Fuller's private life—this is well known—is completely transformed by a happily requited love and by maternity. Through all of this, her dialogue with home remains open. And the plight of "the people" always figures prominently as one of the main themes. The letters express a characteristic frankness; to William Channing:

> I write not to you about these countries, of the famous people I see, of magnificent shows and places. All these things are only to me an illuminated margin on the text of my inward life. Earlier, they would have been more. Art is not important to me now. I like only what little I find that is transcendentally good, and even with that feel very familiar and calm. I take interest in the state of the people, their manners, the state of the race in them. I see the future dawning; it is in important aspects Fourier's future. But I like no Fourierites; they are terribly wearisome here in Europe; the tide of things does not wash through them as violently as with us, and they have time to run in the tread-mill of system.[8]

To Emerson, from Rieti, in the countryside, more than one year later:

> I love to see their patriarchal ways of guarding the sheep, and tilling the fields. They are a simple race, remote from the corruptions of foreign travel, they do not ask for money, but smile upon and bless me as I pass [. . .] The ignorance of this people is amazing. I am to them a divine visitant, and instructive Ceres, telling them wonderful tales of foreign customs and even legends of their own saints [sic] They are people whom I could love and live with [. . .][9]

And, from the author of *Woman in the Nineteenth Century*, this passing but revealing comment: "My poor Italian brothers, they bleed! I do not love them much,—the women not at all; they are too low for me; it will be centuries before they emerge from a merely animal life. The men too, though their sentiment is real, are in thought too much the fanfaron."[10] What is equally characteristic is the fact that such private notes seem to provide the background for a comparative analysis of searing perspicuity:

> In reference to what I have said of many Americans in Italy, I will only add that they talk about the corrupt and degenerate

state of Italy as they do about that of our slaves at home. They come ready trained to that mode of reasoning which affirms that, because men are degraded by bad institutions, they are not fit for better.[11]

I listen to the same arguments against the emancipation of Italy, that are used against the emancipation of our blacks; the same arguments in favor of the spoliation of Poland as for the conquest of Mexico.[12]

It remains that—despite the huge, historical event of the Roman Republic—the people of Rome, as Fuller witnesses them unfiltered, appear a subject whose agency—however vital—is tinged with nihilism. Their discontent gives way to bloody bursts of revolt incapable of turning into occasions of lasting change and transformation. There is no doubt that this helps to explain, too, the nineteenth-century vision of *dolce vita* and *grande bellezza* that Fuller subscribes to in her own way, finding it a conduit of spiritual and personal solace. It certainly was not lost on Fuller that such fatalistic popular wisdom meant no easy resignation and contained a truly awesome dose of poetic justice. Or at least, this is what I like to think considering the significant presence, amid the poor remains of the tragic shipwreck off Fire Island in July 1850, of two great and most explicit sonnets by Giuseppe Gioachino Belli, the supreme and cutting master of Roman dialectal poetry: *Le Pape* and *Diritto Divino*. Given their preciousness and rarity (with regard to both Fuller and Belli), it is worth quoting them here in all their poetic splendor. I adapt Fuller's longhand transcription from her papers at the Houghton Library in Harvard. Belli's versions differ in no trifling details, but is their echo in Fuller that concerns me at this point.

Le Pape (Fuller gives a title in French) corresponds to *La vita da cane*, number 2120 of Belli's last authoritative edition:

> Ah! non fà niente er papa, ahi non fà niente
> Ahi non fà niente lui, brutte marmotte!
> Accussì ve pijasse un accidente
> Come er papa fatica giorno e notte.
>
> Chi parla con Dio Padre onnipotente?
> Chi assolve tanti fiji [de] mignotte?
> Chi và in carrozza a benedir la gente?
> Chi manna intorno le indulgenze a botte?

> Chi è che conta li denari sui?
> Chi porta in petto e fà li cardinali?
> Le Gabelle, per Dio, non le fa lui?
>
> E poi la gran fatica de facchino
> De strascià tutt er giorno i mermoriali
> E mettelli a pezzetto in der cestino![13]

Diritto Divino is Belli's *Li soprani der Monno vecchio* (sonnet 360):

> C'era una volta un rè che da palazzo
> Mannò fuori alli popoli sto editto:
> "Io so io, e voi no siete un cazzo
> Sciori vassalli buggiaroni, e zitto!
>
> Io fò dritto lo storto, e storto il dritto
> Anco ve posso venne un tanto ar mazzo
> E se v'impicco no ve fò strapazzo
> Che la vita e la roba io ve l'affitto
>
> Che a sto monno chi non nasce con titolo
> O de papa, o de rè, o de Imperatore
> Quelli, non pò avè mai voce in capitolo."
>
> Poscia mannò lo boja pe corriero
> A interrogar le genti in sur tenore
> E tutti rispondieno: *è vero! è vero!*[14]

For quite different reasons, the—literally speaking—emersion of both these sonnets is very significant. *Le Pape/La vita da cane* circulated among the *mazziniani* after Mazzini himself had transcribed it in London and sent it around to Italian comrades in November 1846. This followed the publication in a monthly printed in Lausanne earlier that year by Venetian exile Filippo De Boni, who would later publish it again. We know from other sources that this typically paradoxical critique of the Pope's indolence and corruption was known even in the papal inner circle.[15] As a political satire, it certainly was instrumental to the cause of anticlerical Italian republicanism, and as such, it was later included—under the title *L'uccupazione der papa o 'na vitaccia da cani*—among the *Sonetti conservati dalla tradizione popolare* in the 1870 historical edition of

Belli's masterpiece, edited by Luigi Morandi only a few months before the last and final defeat of Pius IX marking the end of the Papal States.[16] It wasn't then by chance that Fuller was carrying the sonnet with her to America, with Belli still very much alive and largely unknown. In general—but not always—her choices tend to avoid the easy picturesque and betray a wider critical vision. Fuller's political and existential proximity to popular Italy and to the democratic aspirations of the Risorgimento make her a unique witness. And yet in many details her observations seem to overlap with those of her dear friend William Wetmore Story, whose *Roba di Roma*—a successful two-volume conversational narration of contemporary Rome—can be regarded as one of the launching pads of a touristic interpretation of Italy as rarified cradle of the arts and site of a gaudy street life. Indeed, Belli's sonnet (now with yet another title, *La Fatiche der Papa*) will make its first public appearance ever in Story's book in 1863.

Even more ideologically revealing is Fuller's transcription of *Diritto Divino / Li soprani der Monno vecchio*. To my knowledge, this scathing indictment of absolute power, with obvious innuendoes to the connection between autocratic rule and sex (see the rhymes *palazzo* : *cazzo* : *mazzo*), and between lawmaking and economic exploitation (*editto* : *dritto* : *affitto*), will not see the light until Morandi's 1870 edition, which reports it as part of Belli's popular fortune. It is to Fuller's credit that she had deemed it worthy of some serious consideration. We can only speculate as to her access to Belli's poetical lode; suffice it to say that biographical trivia attest to the poet's intimate acquaintance with the Ossoli family.[17] What transpires from Fuller's appreciation of Belli's *Diritto Divino / Li soprani der Monno vecchio* is the radical edge of her political engagement, ready to detect—behind the surface of Roman fatalism—a lucid awareness of the violence and arrogance of power.[18]

Nevertheless, such a sensibility seems to be an exception to the rule, for in other aspects Fuller's Rome and Italy show a certain kind of buoyancy that is not that dissimilar from W. W. Story's more predictable account. To be sure, Fuller—no matter how attracted by the signs of Roman culture and daily life—is always sustained by political passion. Story instead guides his reader through the amiable scenario of the aesthetic adventures of an Italophile. In Story's chock-full and sympathetic exploration of everyday Rome, even the other precious and timely quotations from Belli serve the purpose of the picturesque and the folkloric.[19] In *Roba di Roma* beggars and poor are totally objectified by the gaze of the American artist; Fuller had hardly lent herself to such blatant bouts of exoticism. On the other hand, Story's Rome, reprinted, updated, and enlarged for a good quarter century, captures with an admirable wealth of details the very same popular culture that gleams through the pages of Fuller. In an Italy where "America" is not yet a dreamland, but only a distant and unknown entity,[20] daily life and its colorful fabric made of sounds, crafts, and rituals is what sustains people's misery and fascinates the foreigner. Like in Fuller, but in much more detail, we read of games and *feste*, of street music and popular forms of poetry (*serenate, rispetti, ritornelli*, ballads like *Donna Lombarda*, etc.), of gaudy costumes and elaborate dances (*tarantella*). Everyday life is enjoyable for its improvisational creativity, yet can rely on an underlying structure of forms that makes it a living and transmittable tradition.

The vivacity of local dialects is strongly stressed by Story. The Roman dialect is only one among many in the peninsula, alongside the Venetian, the Genoese, the various Tuscan vernaculars, the Neapolitan, and so forth. The very mixed bag of *Roba di Roma* conveys "l'atmosfera irripetibile della Roma papalina, vista nelle sue celebrazioni, nelle sue abitudini, nei suoi colori e in un interclassismo, in una mescolanza di popolo e aristocrazia, di romani e stranieri quale nessun italiano si era dato la pena di ricordare."[21] In his own lofty detachment, Henry James will express a nostalgic appreciation of Story's Roman narrative, avoiding any substantial discussion.[22]

Both Fuller and Story, in different ways and for different reasons, are still witnessing an Italy culturally united and socioeconomically consistent within and despite (or perhaps precisely because of) her main territorial divisions.

2

The Unification can also be interpreted as the decade-long process that was instrumental for ushering in a more modern society, ultimately responsible of the demise of the world that Fuller and Story had been confronted with.[23] Such an upturn is at the center of the political work of an Italophile of a younger generation, the British-born Mazzinian and *garibaldina* Jessie White Mario, whose informative reports on Neapolitan poverty and the labor condition in the Sicilian sulfur mines can be read as a necessary—but also unforeseen—segue to Fuller's democratic romanticism. For it is clear to this younger *mazziniana* that freedom and independence have brought with them socioeconomic modernity and thus the end of the cohesive society of yore. *La miseria di Napoli* (1877) is a thick volume, the gist of which will be offered some twenty years later in English in an article, *The Poor in Naples*, as part of a collection of various journalists and scholars on urban poverty (the contribution by Jacob A. Riis is noteworthy for an American audience).[24]

In White Mario's close-up denunciation of the dire conditions of the lower and numerous strata of Neapolitan society, the trope of the picturesque has hardly any currency.[25] She foregrounds injustice and class divisions. The unified Italian government has blown away the ghost of the Bourbon infamy agitated by Gladstone in his famous Neapolitan letters to lord Aberdeen of 1851, but a large part of Italy still ignores the Southern question. Not by chance, White Mario is in dialogue, here, with Pasquale Villari, whose *Lettere meridionali* (1875) had powerfully established the peculiar sociopolitical discourse of *meridionalismo*. There's a new nation, to be sure, but government control implemented by the new State has meant the unknown burden of taxation, higher prices for staple goods, and the introduction of an educational system from which the people remain largely estranged: "Or la patria è creata, le mèssi sono raccolte e divise. Al popolo toccarono nuove tasse, prezzi accresciuti delle cose di prima necessità della vita, qualche scuola per chi ha scarpe e abbastanza decenti per frequentarla. Nient'altro [. . .]. Ma questa più che cristiana pazienza non può durare a lungo."[26] It was a widespread, and even quite predictable, criticism. What was less common was the level of commitment shown by White Mario in her thorough and daring exploration of the netherworld of Naples. A journey into the most appalling misery, where human degradation went hand-in-glove with urban decay, unsanitary conditions, and an asphyxiating and self-perpetuating context of violence and lawlessness. A land, "un paese dove la camorra domina,"[27] in full sight, yet ignored both by the State and the Catholic hierarchies. White Mario finds that the only exception to the prevailing strategy of total civic and intellectual apathy has come from the tireless indignation expressed in the tragic and realistic fiction of pulp novelist Francesco Mastriani, especially in his trilogy *I vermi* (1863), *Le ombre* (1868), and *I misteri di Napoli* (1869). Beggary has no romantic halo, like in *Roba di Roma*, and there is absolutely no hint at any interclass commonality. The gap between *Galantuomini* and *Lazzaroni* (the Southern lumpenproletariat) is indeed a chasm, the likes of which one cannot see *"nemmeno fra schiavi e bianchi in America."*[28] In White Mario's desperate view, this has produced the "deteriorazione della stirpe."[29] Meanwhile, emigration to the New World (Brazil, the United States, and Canada) has just started, especially from the rural areas in the East of the Po Valley (where White Mario resided), but—in the author's view—it is bound to fail because of the impossibility of acquiring land. Outbound emigration will only beget further disillusionment; it doesn't yet concern the Southern masses anyway, stuck in a predicament that—again—makes White Mario resort, in closing, to a pitiless dictum by US proslavery President John Calhoun. Indeed, Italy has failed in her mission unless—White Mario concedes—one subscribes to the American view that *"La libertà dei Bianchi è fondata sulla schiavitù dei Neri."*[30] Ten years earlier, in 1867, the original sin of slavery, based on a clear racist dichotomy, had received an unforgettable treatment in the masterly crafted novella *L'alfier nero* by the great Arrigo Boito; here the Mazzinian writer (White Mario's inquiry is inscribed "Alla memoria / di Giuseppe Mazzini / Maestro") advances—albeit paradoxically—the hypothesis of a racial reading of the Italian nation-building process.

White Mario's Southernism was further elaborated in her 1894 report on the Sicilian sulfur mines,[31] another notorious blight of Italian society, denounced in no uncertain terms by Giovanni Verga's scorching story *Rosso Malpelo* (1878) and later, with a more pronounced symbolism, in Pirandello's *Ciàula scopre la luna* (1912). Like Verga, White Mario cannot fail to bring to the reader's attention the ghastly spectacle of the *carusi*, the country urchins employed in the caves:

> Li guardai bene; i più piccini erano ragazzi come tutti i meschini che lavorano in campagna: magri, gracili, pallidi, tutti però con gli occhi rossi e gonfi. Più grandi sono, e più si vedono gli effetti del faticoso lavoro. La grossezza e la gonfiezza delle ginocchia contrasta stranamente coll'esilità delle gambe e delle braccia che parevano tutte muscolo e pelle. Alcuni avevano la spina dorsale curvata: altri una gobbetta sulla spalla sinistra. Ma erano allegri [. . .][32]

And yet White Mario is no abolitionist. Her two-month-long fieldwork is coupled by an analysis of the legal situation with regard to the questions of land ownership and labor regulations. She also considers the potential improvement brought about by new machinery, to the point of limiting herself to the mildest measures of change: a ban on the employment of women and of children under the age of twelve, but, on the other hand, approval of the night shift. The government must boost the industry cracking down on usury and reforming the bank system. As it is, the blight remains, and occasions a number of interesting observations, among which, for instance, a list of implacable curses in Sicilian and the following remark: "Risulta chiaro che fisicamente e moralmente il lavoro dei trasportatori a spalle è una schiavitù che sorpassa quella dei piccoli negri."[33] While White Mario is investigating, Sicily is swept by the social unrest headed by the socialist movement of the Fasci; only a month earlier, in the same magazine, another contributor (Enea Cavalieri) has offered a lengthy account of the revolt. What we read in the columns of *Nuova Antologia* seems to indicate that gradual reform from within is the alternative favored by the cultured élite. On the ground, though, the state of siege proclaimed by Prime Minister Crispi has unleashed a brutal crackdown, causing tens of casualties.

White Mario's position is that of an accepted and esteemed outsider, as a woman, a foreigner, and a republican; her essays follow prolonged and in-depth explorations made possible by a network of sympathetic officers and intellectuals; their publication with the major houses and journals testifies to her status as author. I find this all the more remarkable if we contrast her *meridionalismo* with the sociological work of another intellectual and outsider interested in Italian matters, Booker T. Washington, and especially with the circumstances of Washington's reception in Italy and Italian America.

In 1912, the African American writer publishes his thought-provoking *The Man Farthest Down*.[34] The book examines the conditions of the "European toilers" at the height of the Great Migration, trying to understand the causes of the mass exodus from continental and southern Europe. The plight of the "huddled masses" is framed from the point of view of one of the leading African American intellectuals, who devotes particular attention to women and Southern Italy. Six of twenty chapters deal with the Italian question; four of those six focus on Sicily, while another long one centers on Naples and its area, suggesting the hypothesis that Washington and Park's firsthand observations might have also taken into consideration previous accounts such as those by White Mario, which in many ways appear as an obvious antecedent.

As Michel Huysseune has rightly observed, Washington's pointed interest in Sicily is in part indebted to the strong awareness that Sicilian peasants, in particular, had often been employed as replacement for "black laborers in the American South." In *The Man Farthest Down*, Sicily "frequently functions as the region farthest down in Europe, the negative Other of the United States."[35] Washington's discourse on Sicily consistently adopts a comparative approach to underline the backwardness of Sicilian peasant life when considered in light of African Americans' social standing. And yet such comparative framework contains explicit critiques of any essentialist mindset: "My own experience has taught me [. . .] to distrust what I may call 'racial explanations.'"[36] Note that this statement appears in a chapter unequivocally titled *The Church, and the Mafia*, only a few paragraphs after the homage paid to Joe Petrosino, murdered by the Mafia in Palermo in 1909, the year before Washington's visit. The denunciation of the Mafia (and *camorra*) is as clear as the preacher-like indictment of the hardships of labor: "I am not prepared just now to say to what extent I believe in a physical hell in the next world, but a sulphur mine in Sicily is about the nearest thing to hell that I expect to see in this life."[37] The Catholic Church bears its share of responsibilities because "it has held fast to the old medieval notion that education was only for the few, and for that reason has done little or nothing to raise the standard of intelligence among the masses."[38] In the markets and on the streets, Washington witnesses an abundance of activity and symbolic production: he is keenly interested in, and fascinated by, the artistry and the economic relevance of the handicraft system; the ever-present images of the Virgin Mary strike him, even though he calls them "little more than fetish."[39] Overall, he comes away with an appreciative consideration for a people "at the very least, more sinned against than sinning";[40] and in reclaiming their dignity, he finds accents singularly in tune with what both Fuller and White Mario had expressed in the previous decades:

> In view of the wide differences between the people of Sicily and the Negroes in America, so far as concerns the external side of their religious life, it struck me as curious that I should hear almost exactly the same criticism of the people in Sicily, in respect to their religion, that I have frequently heard of the Negroes in America. A very large number of the popular superstitions of Sicily, what we sometimes call the folklore of a country, are very much like many of the notions that the Negroes are supposed to have imported to America from Africa.[41]

With his anti-essentialism, Washington uncovers the sociopolitical foundations of both Southern Italians' and African Americans' uprootedness and disenfranchisement while suggesting a reappraisal of their popular culture. And it is not only a matter of abstract social theory: Washington is quick to stress the role that the ongoing massive emigration to the New World is playing, forging a new, unprecedented link between the two countries and forcibly opening new paths: "Italian emigration has awakened Italy to the value of her laboring classes, and in doing so has laid the foundation for the prosperity of the whole country."[42]

Washington's travel book (indeed, all of his works) is still waiting for an Italian edition. But, as it often is the case, it is interesting to note that it elicited the attention of one of the leading artists and intellectuals of New York's Little Italy, Riccardo Cordiferro, who reviewed it in his weekly satirical magazine *La Follia di New York*.[43] Cordiferro's attack is so vitriolic as to betray the fact that it must have touched a raw nerve, certainly a personal one, but arguably also one common enough to be shared with the readers without fear of being misunderstood. Washington has "repeated the old and idiotic yarn of our *miseria*." But this is the least: it is his "comparison" between Negroes, on the one hand, and Neapolitans and Sicilians, on the other, that "does not hold, since"

> while in the last *lazzarone* of Basso Porto—under the weight of ignorance and unconsciousness accumulated during centuries of abominable secular and religious slavery—, flashes of natural geniality sparkle, and good beats palpitate and raw matter slumbers, out of which—when so needed—brave and generous men are forged, the Negro crowd is just a trifle above the animal level. Low material instincts, narrow mentality, blindness to any creative light, a clear and incurable tendency to steal, sloth, duplicity, gluttony, lust, cowardice with the strong and arrogance with the weak, a perfect amorality and a fabulous ignorance—these are the gifts for which the negro race—despised by its own American liberators—should excel over the people of Napoli and Palermo![44]

To play the card of nationalist and Southernist pride, Cordiferro sleazily resorts to racism's basest trinkets; essentialist tropes concur with and reinforce his need for denial: the state of abject poverty and economic stagnant hopelessness that has fueled his readers' flight from the

Peninsula is an "idiotic yarn." La *miseria* doesn't happen—neither here, in the "colony," nor there, that *Bel Paese* that, Cordiferro admits, has known its share of "slavery." Ideological convolutions and para-Freudian denegations heap on one another in a rhetorically charged game of hide-and-seek, rebutting Washington's dangerous claim of the common humanity of Southern Italians and African Americans, evidenced by exploitation and at the same time by their different but resilient forms of popular culture. The stakes are very high. In no way can the *popolani* from Naples and Palermo be placed alongside *i negri*. Cordiferro has very clear in mind the necessity of a positioning above the color line. It's a self-defensive (and embarrassingly sincere) strategy as mouthpiece of his community. One also should not overlook the fact that Cordiferro, albeit with a customary satirical grin, adopted for the occasion the pseudonym of "Il Turco di Ritorno" in reference to the Italian colonialist campaign against the Ottoman Empire in Lybia, warmly approved by many authors, like him, of Socialist and populist leanings (e.g., Pascoli). Seen in this light, the recent high note of his extremely successful Neapolitan song *Core 'Ngrato* (1911) acquires darker implications. That hymn to Southernist nostalgia sounds, after the fact, as part of a more complex mindset, where gestural sentimentality is but one side, and chauvinistic closure is the other.[45]

3

By the time Booker T. Washington published his exposé on European emigration, and sections of the Italian colony in New York had been disparagingly made aware of it, the other major poetical voice on the East Coast, Arturo Giovannitti, effectively burnt out, in the heat of his political battle, the best part of his fiery brand of poetry. And in so doing, he was able not simply to bridge a gap between two cultural worlds, but to wrest centuries-old forms out of a traditional mold and transform them into the conduit of a deep critical vision. Giovannitti's poetry marks a crucial passage in the transformation—through emigration—of Italian popular culture in America. Critically appreciated by Fuller in the words of their greatest poetical demiurge, Belli, exotically observed by the Jamesian W. W. Story—and later denounced for their abject poverty by both White Mario and Booker T. Washington—the Italian lower classes had crossed the Atlantic in droves, carrying with them a stratified and complex cultural heritage. Now, through emigration, they had reached a new awareness and were ready to express it poetically, declaring their new identity. They were looking back and at the same time moving on, speaking a new language and engaging in new relationships. In his highest artistic creations, Giovannitti draws on unmistakable Italian forms to "sing" the tragedy of past and present conditions. He confronts the impossibility of return, and through his poetry he creates—or tries to create—a new home, both for himself and for his new public. Bilingualism played a crucial role in Giovannitti's poetics, one that bespeaks his almost heroic, titanic striving for dialogue and change, but also one that proved too difficult to sustain creatively and individually over the years. Nevertheless, the major extant texts of his art carry with them a meaning that reverberates beyond the time capsule of pre-WWI sociopolitical activism.

Nenia Sannita appeared in the front page of *Il Proletario* (the weekly newspaper of the Italian Socialist Federation) on July 29, 1909, marking the anniversary of Italian King Umberto I's murder at the hands of Gaetano Bresci, the anarchist who had previously emigrated to Paterson, New Jersey. The title, in fact, is followed by the caption "(In Memoriam)"—content-wise, the most significant variant of a poem that the author will subtly rewrite in his later collections. The parentheses make clear that the final exhortation to "stab our good king" (*roncola il re*) must be interpreted quite literally. The poem, then, is—even from the editorial layout—the centerpiece of a collective celebration of the regicide, viewed as a political act that finds its explanation in the drama unfolding in the seven stanzas. In the *Nenia* (the *Samnite Cradle-Song*), Giovannitti is revisiting the form of the popular ballad. Both lines and stanzas, though, present deliberate metrical irregularities; likewise, while rhymes are deftly adopted, they do not follow any predictable pattern and often resort to easy echoes using morphological desinences. The vocabulary is at the same time plain and "rural," that is, rich in words that are specific to country life. The overall effect is one of a careful reconstruction of reality—of a traditional world beset by social and environmental hardship, and eventually made unbearable by class injustice. In the last strophe, the repressive institutions come to the fore, embodied by the king "With all his princes and barons" and by the bishop.

The narration is sustained by a singsong rhythm, resting on a minute web of repetitions and adversatives. This is a long lullaby, which—irregularly, again—opens and closes its segments with refrains that allude to a sweet baby talk. Its best moments convey a fusion of harshness and tenderness. The fictional context, in fact, is one of a young mother talking to her only son, an infant who is the addressee of this radical bucolic poem, where Giovannitti demystifies a landscape of cultural and political stasis infusing a sense of sepia-toned dejection and materialistic matter-of-factness. It is a mute dialogue, where—one is tempted to infer—the baby is the stand-in for the actual readers, for the immigrant crowd and its poet. That speechless baby boy has listened to his mother, grown up and emigrated, and perhaps even returned home to take revenge. Between mother and son there are the words of a ballad and the new, huge, historical reality of emigration. Consequently, the venerable form of the ballad receives here a new interpretation, at once more desolate and rebellious: it asks for an extra-literary closure while textually inhabiting a bilingual territory. Giovannitti soon re-presented it in English in his first collection of poetry, *Arrows in the Gale* (1914).[46]

Meanwhile, his persona had become the object of a cause célèbre, following his incarceration in winter 1912 as a consequence of the Lawrence, Massachusetts, strike. With perfect timing, the *International Socialist Review* of March 1912 proposed his articulated analysis of the Italian colonialist campaign against Lybia, in which Giovannitti read that military effort as the other side of the sociopolitical and economic predicament at the roots of the massive outbound exodus from Italy. Then, in the September issue of the same magazine, with Giovannitti still in jail, there appeared *The Walker*—also later in *Arrows in the Gale*—which launched his reputation in American letters.[47]

The Walker is a powerful prison poem, whose charged immediacy cannot belie its rhetorical debt toward Whitman. Not only is it Whitmanesque in its option for a rhythmic prose, energetic, forward-going and yet doubtful; its Americanness is also the dramatic result of an accomplished transnational education. As Sebastiano Martelli has pointed out, the young Giovannitti had moved his first steps at a college in Campobasso (then part of the Abruzzi region), whose principal, Luigi Gamberale, was the Italian translator of *Leaves of Grass*.[48] In a way, Giovannitti's prison experience acted as the catalyst of his diverse background and contributed to the credibility of an essential prophetic voice, moving ahead through images, shards of thoughts and impressions, daydreams and obsessions. The urgency avoids the bombast that elsewhere engulfs the poet. The thrust ahead is as implacable as it is emotionally moving:

All the sounds of the living beings and inanimate things, and all the voices and all the noises of the night I have heard in my wistful vigil.

I have heard the fearsome moans of him who bewails a thing that is dead and the sighs of him who tries to smother a thing that will not die;

I have heard the stifled sobs of the one who weeps with his head under the coarse blanket, and the whisperings of the one who prays with his forehead on the hard, cold stone of the floor;

I have heard him who laughs the shrill, sinister laugh of folly at the horror rampant on the yellow wall and at the red eyes of the nightmare glaring through the iron bars;

I have heard in the sudden icy silence him who coughs a dry, ringing cough, and wished madly that his throat would not rattle so and that he would not spit on the floor, for no sound was more atrocious than that of his sputum upon the floor;

I have heard him who swears oaths which I listen to in reverence and awe, for they are holier than the virgin's prayer;

And I have heard, most terrible of all, the silence of two hundred brains all possessed by one single, relentless, unforgiving, desperate thought.

All this have I heard in the watchful night,
And the murmur of the wind beyond the walls,
And the tolls of a distant bell,
And the woeful dirge of the rain,
And the remotest echoes of the sorrowful city,
And the terrible beatings, wild beatings, mad beatings of the One Heart which is nearest to my heart.
All this have I heard in the still night;
But nothing is louder, harder, drearier, mightier, more awful than the footsteps I hear over my head all night.[49]

Here, too, as in the *Nenia*, Giovannitti plays with an effect of orality. *The Walker* is a modern epic, organized in segments akin to *laisses*: but while the cradle-song strove, "politically" and formally, to be superseded in order to refute the unbearableness of the nature and history therein depicted and versified, here we are confronted with a much larger—masculine—breath. The subject's loud voice vies with the surrounding silence; the "I" seeks, through his pensive epic, to reach out to his inmates, in the common dream of freedom. The ballad of the past has given way to a multitudinous prose-poem that lives in the present. Accordingly, this is a work that Giovannitti never turned into Italian—something of an anomaly in his production.

What instead seemed to be working in *that* now distant present was a "poetics of global solidarity."[50] *The Walker* announced the actual release of Giovannitti and his comrades from prison; two years after its publication in *Arrows in the Gale*, Carl Sandburg, in his *Chicago Poems*, paid a curios homage to the Italian American colleague with another prose-poem, *Onion Days*: "MRS. GABRIELE GIOVANNITTI comes along Peoria Street every morning at nine o' clock [. . .]."[51] *Chicago*, Sandburg's opening, eponymous poem, is iconically and rhythmically resonant with Giovannitti's lines: "CHICAGO // HOG Butcher for the World, / Tool Maker, Stacker of Wheat, / Player with Railroads and the Nation's Freight Handler; / Stormy, husky, brawling, / City of the Big Shoulders: [. . .]."[52] And in turn, Giovannitti's later hymn "O *Labor of America: Heartbeat of Mankind*" sounds strongly similar:

> Welcome, dark, fierce cities, daughters of volcanoes,
> hearths and matrices of the new world—
> Duquesne, Homestead, Calumet, Buffalo, sleepless and
> tortured and flint-faced.
> And you, Braddock, fevered with an endless
> contemplation of the Satanic glow,
> And you, Pueblo, titan-limbed, monster biceps
> bursting in the almighty effort of gestation and
> agony of the implacable fecundity of our
> ferocious industry.
> And you, McKeesport, mountain-ribbed, and you
> Akron and Youngstown, rubber-thewed, washing
> your stolid blank faces in your rusty creeks,
> And you, astraddle the Styx and the Acheron,
> Pittsburgh, wrathful resting grave of
> spent meteors, gateway of Hell,
> All ye, unhallowed grails of the last eucharist of sweat,
> Welcome to the home of Labor, the last stricken
> Archangel,

> For your resurrection has come.
> Detroit has its hand on the lever,
> Gary maneuvers the brakes
> and Chicago, feeder of the world,
> Rules the switches of the two-fisted earth.⁵³

There is definitely an *air de famille* circulating within these communicating vessels. Such sloganizing creativity received an authoritative consecration in 1919 when Louis Untermeyer included Giovannitti in his critical anthology *The New Era in American Poetry*, alongside Sandburg but also Frost, Lindsay, Amy Lowell, Masters, Pound, H. D., and others. The poet from Southern Italy was thus inducted into the American modernist Pantheon.⁵⁴

In my mind, the passage from the *Nenia* to the *Walker* epitomizes a wider cultural drama, which has social as well as formal implications. It also signals, among other things, the transformation and adaptation of venerable literary schemes. Giovannitti is anything but naive: his choice of language, in matters small and big, is obviously deliberate; and I contend that when we add his voice to the larger chorus put together by Untermeyer, some echo of that "New Era" might have still been heard at the distance of a few decades.

Not by chance, I think, the young Bob Dylan, for instance, was a fervent admirer of Carl Sandburg and aspired to be considered an heir to his poetry. At least there seems to be a certain similarity between the passage from *The Walker* quoted above and the third strophe of Dylan's *A Hard Rain's A-Gonna Fall* (1963), which famously includes the lines "Heard ten thousand whisperin' and nobody listenin' / Heard one person starve, I heard many people laughin'."⁵⁵

Hard Rain's incipit and dialogical exchange are borrowed from the Anglo-Scottish ballad *Lord Randal*, which in a number of "regressive" studies Giovanni Bronzini documented as having a wide European and American dissemination.⁵⁶ In fact, the first occurrence of its Italian equivalent, the *Avvelenato*, dates back to the first half of the seventeenth century. Bronzini lists thirty-six different Italian versions, including one from the Abruzzi (where Giovannitti was born and raised); other major European reworkings are attested in Hungarian, German, Danish, Swedish, and Dutch. Numerous are the variables in the British Isles, where *Lord Randal*—in a variety of forms and titles—is documented from the second half of the eighteenth century, with an American life, in New

England, that is traceable even earlier, in the first half of the same century.[57] Dylan freely adapts the initial scheme but immediately enlarges it and strengthens the overall message, bringing the ballad to disquieting heights in a dazzling succession of anaphoras, alliterations, synaestesiæ, and other rhetorical figures, ultimately expressing allusive political and racial undertones. He pays respect to the source and transforms Lord Randal into a Cold War apocalyptical ballad that is entirely his own.[58] He keeps the poison motive but makes it recede into the final enumeration and tones down the familial sketch.

Even a scant philological overview is enough to dissuade from going any further in a comparative analysis.[59] What I think may be still worth considering is the condition of remote cultural kinship somehow resurfacing in those peremptory "I [have] heards," especially if we imagine Dylan moving freely between the Nenia and The Walker. In both ballads (Nenia and Hard Rain) a mother speaks to her son. To be sure, there is not a direct relationship between the Italian song of the Avvelenato and Giovannitti's compositions, although through them the Italian American poet undoes the ballad and eventually rearranges the narrative in a non-stanzaic, modernist pattern to make sense of the larger undoing and rearrangement that he strives to give voice to. This undoing and reshaping of the ballad-form is another element that both Giovannitti and Dylan have in common. On the other hand, The Walker contains no prophecy, mired as the poet is in the depth of his captivity; Hard Rain is assertive in tone, although the answers are deliberately oracular, because "black is the color [and] none is the number." The Avvelenato and Lord Randal share a robust cultural root; Nenia, The Walker, and Hard Rain, much closer in time and space, less so. And yet both the prison poem and Hard Rain are culturally predetermined in such a way as to suggest a displacement followed by an emboldening realization. Giovannitti relies on Whitman to express the inquisitive solitude of the rebel-migrant; Dylan relies on European folklore to express the thrust of a new prophecy. In both poets, the lines have a strong, almost physical quality and need to be read as in dialogue with a "real" audience. Consequently, the word composition, the balladry, has undergone a visible change too. Familiar, regular cadenzas have been powerfully restructured and modernized, highlighting the centrality of the poetical subject. The poet and his poem are as much the message as the actual content of what is being said. In both cases, the old voice of the European peoples, with their rhythms and wisdom, has been washed over—like those Roman sonnets of sanguine intelligence, miraculously saved from Fuller's shipwreck and Belli's self-deprecation. In the New World, the ballad has acquired new forms to adapt to new situations and convey new meanings. But there is not, as in Europe, a romantic, or a classic, whole any more, expressing a collective and shared conscience. In America, reality is bewildering, at times cruel, almost always indecipherable; it's its tension, more than anything else, that the poetical voice wades through.

A hard Rome has been falling and falling again, without completely disappearing. European motives reappear arranged and signified anew, recognizably or subliminally, in both cases poetically compensating for the social and ideological complexities littering the history of transatlantic relationships. Hawthorne seems to have uncannily foreseen this when, in *The Blithedale Romance,* the fictional Fuller (Zenobia, a veritable revenant) addresses the fictional author (Coverdale) in these terms: "Ah, I perceive what you are about! You are turning this whole affair into a ballad."[60]

Indeed.

Chapter 2

Changing Culture

European Immigrants and New York City Literature, 1870–1940

Here is the powerful incipit of a rather overlooked novel set mostly in New York during the First World War:

> Arnold Levenberg, junior partner of the wealthy firm, "Levenberg Brothers and Company," Manufacturers of Handkerchiefs, had been visited by a haunting dream.
>
> The world was in the throes of a devastating epidemic—a sort of black plague. On a single fateful day, all New York had died out. He alone had been spared. He was certain of that. All New York was dead; he was the only living being.
>
> There he was in the street—to be more exact, in his own street, one of the Seventies near Madison Avenue—yet at the same time he could see the entire city in panorama: lower and upper Manhattan, the Bronx and Brooklyn, East and West, elevated railway and subway. All was hushed in the stillness of death.
>
> It was a day in Spring, yet all outdoors seemed half-concealed behind a veil of mist. It was like a Sunday dawn in a lonely lane of a little town.
>
> He was heartsick and wretchedly sad. What was he to do in this solitude?

> He hit upon the idea of walking to the Grand Central. Perhaps trains would be coming in from other cities bringing living people. Then the certainty assailed him that the rest of the country, too, had succumbed to the plague. The whole continent was dead, from pole to pole, from San Francisco to New York.
>
> All dead. He alone had survived. The only living person on the continent.[1]

A comprehensive look at the New York literature of European immigrants invites us—among other things—to rethink in aesthetic terms the interaction between the psychic and the sociohistorical. As is always the case, the historical exodus into the United States from the second half of the nineteenth century to the implementation of the Johnson-Reed Act in 1924 proved to affect its protagonists as a totalizing experience: it filtered from the daylight travails into the unconscious imagination and left its mark on practically every aspect of human life. David Pinski's novel *Arnold Levenberg* testifies to this, as it were, at a genetic, linguistic degree, beyond the cinematic ghosts of its hero. In fact, the author composed it in his native Yiddish as *Der Tserissener Mentsch* (The Torn Man)—and, in this form, he would never see it published, only to have it later translated into English. This is a fitting example of the opportunities and difficulties faced by a "changing subject," with *subject* meaning both the agent and the topic.

Only since the 1970s has a growing body of scholarly work made it possible to familiarize oneself with the overall picture of the peculiar phenomenon of an American literary ethnicity that played a significant part in the "creation of ethnic selves."[2] In turn, a closer look at the literary dimension of the Irish, German, Scandinavian and Dutch, Italian, Jewish, Polish, Greek, and other components of New York raises the question of the specificity whereby immigrant authors, or second-generation authors with a strong immigrant background, related to and portrayed a city—and a city like no other—such as New York. Their direct involvement meant the adoption of a distinctive point of view that previous chroniclers simply could not display, despite all their acumen and intense trafficking with the various and sundry layers of urban life.[3] The astonishing, almost tyrannical presence of this particular metropolis in post–Second World War Western culture, and especially visual culture, suggests that we are dealing with one of the master tropes of our current imaginary.

And indeed, the European immigrant experience, captured in its heyday, contributed in a variety of ways to such a mythopoeia, expressing early on and from within the voice of the "transatlantic century."[4]

At the same time, we should keep in mind that we are not here in search of hidden treasures, but rather of the testimonies of a larger cultural event—that is, the coming of age of a particular form of urban modernity, grindingly shaped by ethnic and socioeconomic diversity and disparities. Mass immigration fostered in the New York of that period the almost perfect concentration of the three classical dramatic unities of time, place, and action, thus giving evidence to an epochal change that was at the same time external and internal, sociopolitical and existential, and whose effects are palpably present in the immigrants' literature. The massive global inflows from Castle Garden and Ellis Island happened because of, and coincided with, a tumultuous industrial, economic and capitalist thrust, causing a gigantic urban growth. To be sure, this was a phenomenon of obviously global dimensions, which concurred and vied with the aggressive nationalistic mindset of the time and became an active element of a push-and-pull dynamic. Indeed, "in a multitude of ways each immigrant culture articulated group identity as national identity, and enforced the idea that this national identity entailed a lasting commitment to certain cherished loves and hatreds."[5] At the same time, the immigrants' negotiation with their sense of national belonging intersected with growing American nativism and "fear of the city":

> At the outset of the twentieth century, the city occupied a suspect place within the wider continental United States. It was seemingly a city populated by foreigners, without the requisite "American" singular identity; the residents of New York were seemingly tied to their previous homelands, cultures, religions and possibly possessing radical political sympathies which could unsettle the Republic.[6]

Ethnic, urban villagers were rapidly and forcibly transformed into a population of consumers. Their literature, by and large, vented the circadian alternation of resistance and exhilaration in front of such an unforeseen social and existential upheaval. Thus, narratives of consumerism coexisted, or were at the same time narratives of resistance to consumerism, creating, in both cases, "further opportunities for disillusionment and irony."[7] Appropriately, James Sullivan's *Tenement Tales of*

New York updated the Dickensian mold, projecting it onto a multiethnic stage where a "Slob Murphy" was juxtaposed to a tragic "Cohen's figure," and the story of Luigi Barbieri the fruit dealer preceded the closing of the circle—"*A Young Desperado*"—the linguistic portrayal of an Irish boy through his brogue.[8] On the other hand, ethnic art itself adopted modes and tropes of mass entertainment. "Fun" (and the lack thereof) was a much sought-after quality in the immigrants' stories. The rise of an American political satire and furthermore the distinctly urban comic strip likewise proves to be closely related to European and/or immigrant sources, as testified by the German and Austrian origins of Thomas Nast and Joseph Keppler—founder of *Puck*—and by the Irish air of characters such as the Yellow Kid. And a recurring trait of New York ethnic literature is the plethoric abundance of light verses.[9]

The stage of the metropolis intensifies such characteristics: it conflates, confuses, and congests. The city experience, as seen through its literary and written traces, becomes internalized. We witness a sort of urbanization of the mind, or what we could refer to as the systemic formation of a *city-self*. New York literature provides evidence of the fact that its immigrant cultures (in this case, its historical European components) forge new identities in an unprecedented, new urban environment.[10] The "city-self" is a transitive disposition, or mode, whose phenomenology one comes across at practically every step. It plays itself out clearly when the stories tell us about generational conflicts and (often simultaneously) about the impending, almost classical curse and reward of the job. The city is indeed a lived-in set of conflicts, labor, necessity, and dreams of success, or dreams of an impossible stasis and peace. We witness the birth of a peculiar form of Western sensibility, pointed out by German philosopher Peter Sloterdijk when he talks of the inevitable embrace of "stress and freedom."[11] The urban self comes of age as New York grows more and more like the epitome of the Western modern city of contrasts.

Take for instance a masterpiece of realism such as Abraham Cahan's 1917 *The Rise of David Levinsky*: here the arch-American mantra of success and happiness is articulated in such a way as to disprove itself. The socialist champion of Yiddish culture, Cahan, flawlessly adopts the nineteenth-century novelistic pattern and transforms its inner positivism into an aporetic parable of loneliness. Accumulation meets sentimental deprivation. Overall, its characters express the clearest political awareness of their economic condition and of the American scenario: "Meyer went on with his argument: 'What is a man without capital? Nothing!

Nobody cares for him. He is like a beast. A beast can't talk, and he can't. 'Money talks,' as the Americans say.'"[12] Similar parables of social ascent and personal dissatisfaction infuse a peculiar New York taste of inextricable buoyancy and despondency in two other great works by Jewish American writers: Anzia Yezierska's *The Fat of the Land* (1919) and Samuel Ornitz's *Haunch Paunch and Jowl* (1923).[13] But the opposite is also true: Sara, the narrator and protagonist of Yezierska's 1925 exquisitely touching novel *Bread Givers*, unshackles herself from the grip of her father, moves out, and, as a single young woman in the city, has a rather active, although not entirely full and satisfactory, personal life. Socially, though, she is far from fulfilled.[14] When funneled through a social and existential scenario fraught with contrast and uncertainty, realism becomes the conduit of disenchantment and at the same time of a characteristic skeptical humor.

The best examples of this fiction deliberately work around stereotypes but avoid being predictable by portraying their main characters as full of doubts and even contradictions, and their actions as nuanced rather than one-sided. To be sure, it is also a matter of perceptiveness and artistry: witness a slightly later Italian American novel, Garibaldi Lapolla's 1934 *The Grand Gennaro*.[15] Here, the tragedy of the hero, a hardworking Calabrian turned East Harlem ragpicker and wealthy businessman, is part *David Levinsky* (with an explicit homage to the Jewish American master) and part *Cavalleria rusticana*. It is a robust and fascinating story, but in a way it already sounds derivative and dangerously close to an "ethnic" paradigm.

The fact is that an immigrant literature often runs the risk of flattening the representation, of being simplistic. The challenge is that of elaborating a personal voice while retaining the strength of a radical specificity, courting typology without ever fully embracing it. One is called to move, as it were, between solipsistic subjectivity and accumulative descriptivism—two hypothetical extremes that, in a way, we find hinted at on both sides of our chronological arc in two outsiders' views: in Antonín Dvořák's 1895 suggestion that there is indeed a "good" voice on the streets of Manhattan and, at the other end of the spectrum, in the 1939 praise of Brooklyn in James Agee's *Brooklyn Is*, an extreme form of modernistic objective correlative applied to an entire borough.[16]

Can we at least try to sketch a New York literary soundscape—a New York "urban sentence" (*phrase urbaine*), in the words of French author Jean-Christophe Bailly?[17] Much of New York immigrant literature plays itself out on the street level and shows to have eyes and ears fully equipped to absorb the diversity of the environment. This was all the more apparent when the city and its inhabitants still coexisted with a most active harbour. Here is South street in an almost virtuosic passage from one of the masters of Irish American literature, Edward Harrigan:

> Coal barges, ships, schooners, sloops, lighters, steamers and vessels of all kinds load and empty their cargoes at all the piers which line the river from Whitehall to Corlear's Hook. The heaviest draught vessels are usually berthed at the piers lying between Fulton Market and the upper sectional dock floating at the foot of Clinton street. The noises of steamboat whistles, puffing of tugs, rolling of trucks, steam hoisting machines, the cries of workingmen and truck drivers, the clanging of the calkers' shrill mallets, ship carpenters' and iron workers' tools, together with innumerable other sounds of industry, keep the old street alive with a constant din. This falls to a dead silence at night, when South street is deserted by the workers and only a few drunken sailors may be seen at times rolling along on their way to their ships, singing snatches of the songs which they had heard in the music hall and dance houses, where, when Jack's ashore, he spends the better portion of the night.[18]

The sounds of the harbor dissolve in the various voices of the city. And clearly, these last ones are signs of linguistic identity and diversity. Noting the arrival of "Latin races," Harrigan points out:

> The commingling of the children of these people with the children of the English, Irish and native born has developed a jargon that twists our language into a dialect only matched by that spoken by the costermonger of London [. . .] Languages mingled. The Gallic intonation blended with the soft Italian, and contrasted with the guttural German.[19]

The stress on sounds and languages indicates just a section of a multisensorial panorama that covers every aspect of perceptual experience. Immigrant art—literary or otherwise—gives form to the senses in a context where the coming together of cultures meets the prosthetics of modernity, enhanced by urban density. Trains, cars, electricity, telephones, and so forth are all recurring presences. The sensory experience can thus become part of a new instrumentality that, in turn, modifies the environment.[20]

By the same token, New York immigrant literature appears equally concerned with giving voice to the subject, which is most revealing in terms of a "city-self" attitude. In the New York Yiddish poetry of the times, this is simplified by the interplay and rapid succession of a loosely connected group of socially conscious authors (the "sweat-shop poets") and of a more structured school of introspective lyricists (the post–First World War *In Zich* poets). The opening of a signature poem like Morris Rosenfeld's *In the Sweat-Shop* captures with absolute poignancy the crisis of the ego—more than threatened by the alienating forces of the exploitive lines of production.

> The machines in the shop roar so wildly that often I forget in the roar that I am; I am lost in the terrible tumult, my ego disappears, I am a machine. I work, and work, and work without end; I am busy, and busy, and busy at all time. For what? and for whom? I know not, I ask not! How should a machine ever come to think?
>
> There are no feelings, no thoughts, no reason; the bitter, bloody work kills the noblest, the most beautiful and best, the richest, the deepest, the highest, which life possesses. The seconds, minutes and hours fly; the nights, like the days, pass as swiftly as sails; I drive the machine just as if I wished to catch them: I chase without avail, I chase without end.
>
> The clock in the workshop does not rest; it keeps on pointing, and ticking, and waking in succession. A man once told me the meaning of its pointing and waking,—that there was a reason in it; as if through a dream I remember it all: the clock awakens life and sense in me, and something else, I forget what; ask me not! I know not, I know not, I am a machine![21]

As Rosenfeld's case should make clear, New York immigrant literature is not some postmortem academic reconstruction, but for the best part the product of an organic, stratified, and teeming culture, with its diversified audience, its militant critics, its producers and publishers and scholars. This is particularly true for Yiddish literature, and long before two successful anthologies of short stories and poetry edited by Irving Howe and Eliezer Greenberg in the 1950s and 1960s.[22] Rosenfeld's *Songs from the Ghetto* came out in 1898, translated by Leo Wiener, teacher at Harvard and author the following year of an indispensable *History of Yiddish Literature*. Meanwhile, in 1891 and 1898 Alexander Harkavy completed the first Yiddish-English dictionary. Many of the same authors, Rosenfeld and Cahan included, will then be introduced again only a few years later in the classic ethnic travelogue *The Spirit of the Ghetto* by Hutchins Hapgood.[23]

These were the golden decades of foreign-language journalism and theater in the United States, and especially so in the tristate area. The four major Yiddish dailies of the time (the *Jewish Daily Forward*, *Wahrheit*, *Morgen Journal*, and *Tageblatt*), totaled more than 455,000 copies in 1914.[24] The Italian-language *Progresso Italo-Americano* and *Corriere d'America* could boast a combined printing close to 200,000 copies and exemplified a typical New York convergence of big interests in publishing and construction on the one hand (the long-lasting empire of the Pope immigrant family, urban developers, and owners of the *Progresso*) and "colonial" effort of the motherland on the other (in this case Italy, and more specifically the powerful interest group of the Milanese daily *Corriere della Sera*) in securing the profitable market of its outbound huddled masses.[25] The German-language *Staats-Zeitung* (founded in 1834 and still running) had a circulation, around the First World War, that also went well beyond 100,000 copies: at the turn of the twentieth century, it vied with the almost equally successful socialist *Volkszeitung* and with Hearst's *Morgen Journal*.[26] The *Polish Morning World* (*Nowy Świat*), with a prestigious roster of Polish intellectuals, along with a number of other Polish papers, catered to the approximately 200,000 Poles living in New York around World War I.[27] And the two major Greek voices, *Atlantís* and *Ethnikós Kýrix*, promoting their share of popular literature, had a combined circulation that at the time easily surpassed that of any Athenian daily.[28]

A similar, quantitative approach can be applied to the very active scene of the ethnic theater flourishing in the Lower East Side and on the Bowery, but also on Broadway and in Brooklyn. One title above all, Jacob Gordin's *The Jewish King Lear* (1892), remained in the repertoire for a good thirty years. "At the turn of the century, eleven hundred performances were given annually (in Yiddish) before an estimated two million patrons."[29] And again, there was also a very significant production and activity by Irish, German, Italian, and Polish authors and companies.[30]

A rather obvious observation suggested by such big numbers is that immigrant literature could at least theoretically rely on, and address itself to, a wide readership within each ethnic community, and the same constant dynamic between allegiance to the past and adaptation to the New World operated in the columns of the press and on the pages of the literati—not only that, but it was shared by the nearby communities and thus intensified the process of Americanization. It was a constant, daily process of mutual offer and exchange. In the 1880s, under the editorship of Udo Brachvogel, the German-language *Belletristiches Journal* could boast an impressive circulation of more than seventy thousand copies;[31] the Italian American *Follia di New York* (founded in 1893 by the Sisca family) held high for a century the venerable tradition of dialectal poetry of the peninsula, with its characteristic gusto and sentimentality; and thanks to the tireless intuition of Abraham Cahan, in 1906 the *Jewish Daily Forward* launched a direct line of communication with its readers in the daily feature "A Bintel Brief," soon to acquire an almost legendary status as the voice of the Jewish diaspora, based in New York but scattered everywhere.[32]

Bernard Martin has calculated that at least sixty-five novels of "popular" quality appeared in Yiddish before 1898.[33] This is confirmed with the timely observation by the linguist and historian Leo Wiener (1862–1939): "The amount of many-volumed so-called novels that they have produced is simply appalling."[34] The 1890s also saw the serialized production of the so-called Homer of Little Italy by the pulp fiction Tuscan writer and journalist Bernardino Ciambelli (1861–1931), a prolific author of urban "mysteries."[35] An early account of Ciambelli's fame among Italians of New York is in a 1906 eye-opening evaluation of immigrants' reading practices by Norman Duncan:

> "*La Trovatella dei Cinque Punti?*" cries the keeper of the bookstore in Mulberry Bend. You nod your wish to possess that work—or, *I Delitti dei Bosses*; or, *I Misteri di Mulberry*; or, *I Briganti Americani*: whereupon the smile grows broader still.
>
> "Ciambelli!" with a gesture expressive of infinite space. "He great-a man!"
>
> With what distraction, then, has Bernardino Ciambelli provided the people of Mulberry Park, that he is so beloved? With a whirl of intrigue and adventure and passion—a series of New York police novels, from the Mulberry Bend point of view.[36]

Even works of much more lasting repute like *The Rise of David Levinsky* moved their first steps in the columns of the press—in Cahan's case, partially serialized in *McClure's* as *The Autobiography of an American Jew* (1913). An intellectual of strong ethnic background like H. L. Mencken (1880–1956) showed a very clear awareness of this phenomenon, both in his tireless linguistic work (emphasizing, in the fourth edition of *The American Language*, 1936, the influence of "Non-English dialects") and as an editor of *The American Mercury*, promoting both immigrant and African American writers.[37]

This massive evidence of collective cultural activity did not tame, of course, the existential trials at stake, which expressed themselves most peculiarly, in New York and elsewhere in the United States, in a variety of "divided" modes, as in the juxtaposition of the autobiographical memoirs in German *and* in English of German American Senator Carl Schurz (1906–1908);[38] in the virtuosic but also bookish bilingualism of the revolutionary Italian American poet Arturo Giovannitti (decadent and aulic à la Gabriele D'Annunzio in his poem *La città incredibile*, 1915, but Whitmanesque in its English rendition, *New York and I*);[39] in the almost chilling distancing of his immigrant past in the success story of Dutch American journalist and publisher Edward Bok (longtime editor of the *Ladies' Home Journal*), who writes about his "Americanization" in a third-person narrative and talks about "two persons" (1920);[40] in the generational gap that feeds David Pinski's fiction;[41] and especially in the deep psychological crisis at the center of Ludwig Lewisohn's tellingly titled *The Island Within* (1928). Taking his cue from this novel Allen Guttmann aptly wrote about Lewisohn as being "in a sense, the Jewish writer as Prodigal Son,"[42] which certainly applies to the fate of the protagonist, brilliant psychologist Arthur Levy, graduated from Columbia, estranged from the Eastern Jews of downtown, until—after the divisions of the First World War, the failure of his marriage to a Gentile Elizabeth, and the breakup of his family—he confirms his earlier realization that "the mechanism of the Jewish anti-Jewish complex was precisely analogous to the mechanism of insanity."[43]

The immigrant condition of crisis is certainly hard to express and communicate. It is unquestionably one of the chief tenets of its literature, whose nuances pervade the whole ethnic spectrum.[44] One of the standard songs of the Neapolitan songbook, *Core 'ngrato*, is an impeccable tale of Latin unrequited love, and at the same time a purely New York product (crafted and customized for the voice of tenor Enrico Caruso), to the point that it can be read as a complex, almost subliminal metaphor of the interaction between the two cultures. In a moving game of make-believes, the trope of Mediterranean melo is seemingly reproduced lock, stock, and barrel in the New World.[45] A completely different trajectory is testified in the fascinating bilingual New York memoirs of Italian American painter Martino Iasoni, which have remained unfinished and partially unpublished, in part since it is so difficult to confront oneself with the impossibility of a return to the country of origin, and thus with an unspeakable future.[46] In prose, in poetry, on the theatrical stage and, obviously, in the daily lives of the immigrants, bilingualism and multilingualism play a defining role: it is a social trait which radically affects the individual, with a special incidence within the family. Writers and artists cannot help resorting to it in an effort to express their condition. For example, the quasi-Dickensian tale of a Southern Italian shoe shiner of Prince and Spring street, *Peppino il lustrascarpe*, was published in the 1880s by its author, L. D. Ventura, in Italian, English, and French.[47]

The theme of a deeply distraught inner division is recurring and, apart from its rather predictable linguistic aspect, can be expressed in a variety of tones. In the immigrant experience, "speaking in tongues" is often the conduit for self-irony. This is the staple of Mr. Dooley, the witty character created at the turn of the century by Irish American writer and journalist Finley Peter Dunne—a very popular mouthpiece of Irish Americans' common opinion, or rather opinions. Such is the implacable attention lavished on the most current urban trivia by the heavy brogue of this everyman.[48] In the 1880s and 1890s, in the regular columns "written in a Hessian (sometimes Saxon) dialect, [. . .] fictional German-American narrators who clung to their ethnic customs commented humorously (and always negatively) on life in the modern American metropolis—German cousins to Finley Peter Dunne's widely syndicated Mr. Dooley."[49] A fictitious Madame Because attended tens of satirical performances of the German American and German Jewish theater on Union Square and on the Bowery, providing an example of "performing spectatorship."[50] Meanwhile, real German-speaking audiences crowded the ethnic musical (self-)parodies by Adolf Philipp and the more upscale productions by Rudolf Christians.[51] In the hands of Neapolitan actor Eduardo Migliaccio, a similar mask of ethnic self-consciousness, Farfariello, acquired almost devilish dimensions: playing not on double, but on triple entendres (Italian, Southern Italian dialects, and English), the immigrant author and performer transformed mimesis into self-reflecting and gestural mimicry, poking serious fun at modern America and the greenhorns' backwardness—a black humor that saves no one.[52]

Education and self-education represent another defining and familiar feature. And here again, immigrants appear to be facing different choices—mainly, either an institutional pedagogy or the rough-and-tumble street life of the neighborhoods. In both cases, growing up requires by necessity meeting and negotiating with the other in terms of gender, ethnicity, and age. And yet, as Karen Majewski has stressed for Polish American literature, "only infrequently [. . .] are Polish immigrants in personal relationships with Americans."[53] Not by chance, it is at school on the Lower East Side that the Irish meet the Jews in Myra Kelly's *Little Citizens* (1904)—pretty much the same kids fighting in gangs, learning about sex as exploitation rather than tenderness, and committing a bevy of misdemeanors as in Mike Gold's *Jews Without Money* (1930).[54]

Living in the city is so absorbing because it coincides at the same time with the formative years *and* with the blossoming of a new, in-between identity. Such is the intensity of some (the most accomplished) among these works that, curiously enough, it is as if New York itself shied away. Most of the time the stories remain focused on the neighborhoods and are confined, almost trapped, in a cluster of streets. It would be hard to recall a unified vision of Greater New York, of the metropolitan area. And this happens despite the fact that the Great Migration of those decades did contribute to a substantial new start for the city, as Burrows and Wallace have most convincingly shown.[55] The system of mass transportation and the subways are hardly used in this fiction and poetry. Human contacts still take place in more familiar surroundings—the streets, stoops, staircases, rooftops, crammed apartments, shops, and workplaces. Landmarks and monuments are noticeably rare; no skylight and few bridges for these busy New Yorkers,[56] hardly any outings to Central Park,[57] and no trips to Harlem (a must for foreign intellectuals), unless you actually live there. "New York, my city, O stony cradle! O dirty fatherland! Place of my deepest, oldest friendships, in whose earth sleep my father, mother, brother and dear friends, you were never to me the tourist's gaudy postcard!," waxes sentimental Mike Gold, reminiscing about his "Jewish Childhood in the New York Slums."[58]

What matters is still very direct and immediate; there's a physicality that is part and parcel of the sweeping personal trajectory at the center of it all. The literature of the immigrants attaches a particular importance to the present and repeatedly concentrates on life as it unfolds.[59] New

York emerges as a knot of affection. To put it another way: through this literature, one can trace a vivid diagram of a collective empathy with the city—an empathy fed by a love-and-hate relationship and therefore deeply enmeshed with one's biography, affecting minds and bodies with unprecedented thickness.

Three masterpieces might provide some final evidence. A fortuitous coincidence had two of the strongest Jewish novels set in New York published the very same year: *Call It Sleep*, by Henry Roth, and *Summer in Williamsburg*, by Daniel Fuchs, both out in 1934.[60] The year 1939 saw the publication of Pietro di Donato's *Christ in Concrete*.[61] As it is always the case with masterworks, these three exceed any strict categorization. They also share the fact of being the first, and unsurpassed, novels of young authors describing in their fiction very defined ethnic environments. So many are the big and small points of contact mirroring each other that one would wish for a rigorous parallel reading.

The three novels succeed in being highly original, multifaceted, and representative of the feverish relationship between individuals (especially the young, even preteen, main characters), an immigrant milieu, and the larger urban context. They signify what Werner Sollors, in a number of seminal studies, has referred to as "ethnic modernism."[62] In all three of them, the tongue can be assumed as a pivotal conduit of sociability and emotion. Language figures eminently as a macro-sign of novelty, reflecting hardship and gains. It has a quasibodily evidence. Moreover, sounds, sights, materials, odors and tastes, skin touches, and sexual drives stimulate and overlap, suggesting three multisensorial and concurring portraits of the city. It is as if New York emerged as the synthesis of an organic process of growth, as a sort of hyperorgan that mirrors the troubled coming of age of the male protagonists. The creation of a "city-self" here is all the more convincing because we, the readers, are confronted not only with human characters, but also with the city "selfying" itself, defining itself through words, images, and intellectual as well as material self-expressions.[63]

The immigrant content of the stories stresses the multiple and contrasting nature of these self-portraits. These three New York "selfies" from the 1930s are all brilliantly site specific (the Lower East Side for Roth; Williamsburg for Fuchs; an unnamed tenement district for di Donato), but at the same time they powerfully reverberate, staging dramas and relationships that go far beyond New York, and touch, indeed, the fundamentals of life: the love between a mother and her son, the adolescent urge for comradeship and erratic action, the tragedy of orphanage, not in a Dickensian sense but in a fully developed, ruthless capitalist metropolis, where God and/or Christ eyes distractedly from above an accumulation of concrete that the very same people build with their hands, pay for with their rent, and even die for as anonymous martyrs of labor.

> And now, high up a million miles into the sky, God sits in His trundle on a big cloud. He looks absentmindedly about, the beard long and very white, the flesh of His face gnarled because it has been such a very long time, such a very long time. And now He peers down, and for a moment His gaze rests again on Williamsburg, and He says to Himself, how are things going on down there, I wonder. And He looks. We must forgive God for His apathy; it has been a hot summer and He is a little tired of us, we never vary the show. So He sniffs to clear His nose and He returns to the task.[64]

Ultimately, the immigrants' New York provides, in its strongest representations, a condensed view of humanity, in its cyclic wholeness and historical materiality—a diverse but very solid aesthetic formation, and something different from both a "diasporic" and a "minor" literature. A corpus that is as self-centered as it is nationo-phobic: urban, ethnic, plural, and one; with a tendency to unshackle its creations from canonical filiations; developing its own manifold poetics. Playing on its multisensorial density as well as on its multilingual and multicultural richness and confusion, their city appears as the obvious antecedent of our globalized and ubiquitous New York, but with a grittier, darker, and somehow more saturated (one could say a more "organic") figure.

Chapter 3

"Our brother Dante"

Dantesque Reappropriations in Italian America

Quasi-Italian American

There is something to be said about the presence of Dante in Italian American letters and culture. And just *saying* that "something," saying that it is there and it is worthy of a critical discourse, might prove to fulfill a significant part of the overall meaning of Dante among Americans of Italian descent. In fact, Dante's position within Italian America is so obvious, and even in some way so predictable, that it is quite simply not very much considered. It is as if it is so taken for granted—especially by educated people and scholars—that it goes unnoticed, which is a telltale paradox. This unconscious strategy of effacement seems an introjection of the much wider removal experienced by Italian Americans both in the United States and in Italy. It functions—Dante's removal, or bracketing—as a homeopathic remedy that stimulates and readies the larger Italian American social body to its comfortable marginality. But this is made possible by the fact that Dante as a whole—his texts, his "figura," the aura of his authority—has had a long history in North America, to the point that, as a cultural pawnbroker, he has acquired a quasi–Italian American status. Identifying with Dante implies legitimizing the history and existence of an Italian American culture and providing its experience with a radical narrative of searching and foundation, liable to be used both as an existential compass and a shared, collective patrimony.

A (yet another) sign of Dante's inexhaustible depth, but also of the pliability of Italian American culture, is the fact that the allegorical journey and the towering stature of the poet could and can adapt to totally different historical conditions, forging a somewhat plausible dialogue between fiction and reality, between a God quest and a harsh economic pull. Dante and his encyclopedia are reinterpreted by an "exiled" people on the move—diverse, divided among themselves, inquisitive, dissatisfied, driven by a concomitant need of consent with the surrounding American society and its many social and ethnic components. Dante's dreams, which structure the ascent to Purgatory, also authorize the immigrants' dreams, their social and quite real Purgatory. The poet's centrality is the blueprint for a new, hard-won, unprecedented individualism.

To a certain extent, what there is of Dante amounts to debris. Accordingly, I make reference mostly to his literary traces. But traces and debris are not due to the old age of our sources; rather, they constitute the by-product of a huge ritualistic banquet, so to speak, where the veritable roots of Italian culture have been served, appropriated, metabolized. It would be imprecise, though, to consider the Italian American Dante as the transatlantic counterpart of a Dante-as-we-know-him in Italian popular culture, because the cannibalization of Dante in the Little Italies and beyond developed in the peculiar context of American Dante studies and of Dante's constant American fortune; the Italian American Dante always retained a distinct Italian *American* character. Far from being mere leftovers, this debris instead points to the larger, coherent picture of a dignified, self-adjusting civilization. Its relevance, to be sure, resides precisely in the echo that it is capable of producing, all the more when it eschews a strict scholarly circulation and makes a connection with the intense, real-life immigrants' experience. An expression such as "the Italian American Dante" acquires, thus, its proper meaning, anachronism notwithstanding.

Da Ponte and the Promptings of the Dante Club

Dante acquired slowly a proper Italian American dimension, his first appearances something of a footnote to the literary militancy of the glorious and legendary Dante Club. It might be an overstatement to extol the scholarly virtues of Pietro Bachi, Pietro D'Alessandro, Luigi Monti, and Vincenzo Botta, wayward representatives of the Risorgimento between Boston and New York from the 1820s well into the next century. It is a well-known fact that Longfellow, while working on the first complete American translation of the *Commedia* (1865–67), was teaching at Harvard to students instructed in the subtleties of Dante's *volgare* by Pietro Bachi, whose post would be taken over by Monti, brother-in-law of Thomas W. Parsons (whose *First Ten Cantos of the Inferno* had been printed by W. D. Ticknor in 1843, preceding Longfellow's version). This was a tightly knit circle of literati indeed, part of a larger community of Brahmins and assorted Italophiles. A thorough chart of their various achievements related to the study and diffusion of Dante would prove quite intricate and rich in such overlappings. The pattern is one of second-rate Italian intellectuals (oftentimes, by necessity, self-appointed intellectuals) ancillaries to crucial figures of the Cambridge and Boston area, Harvard being the magnet in most cases.[1]

While this seems to be the prevailing setup, one could at the same time try to delineate the thin thread of a counternarrative. If the bona fide American Dante is a product of "lungo studio e grande amore" (long study and great love) (the evidence for which rests not only in the inauguration of a notable lineage of translations, but also in scholarly works—see the establishment, in 1882, of the journal *Dante Studies*), the earliest Dante brought over to North America by Italian writers betrayed, not surprisingly, a higher degree of familiarity, even of confidence. Dante is referred to self-ironically by Lorenzo Da Ponte in his "scherzo poetico" (poetic joke) *Alle mie sorelle* (composed in the mid-1820s) as the first guest of his "Picciola navicella . . . . Della dolce favella [Sweet tongue's . . . . Small boat]," vessel of a "magazzino [warehouse]" where "vendo dal mattino / Fino che il sol si corca. / Vendo parole, è vero."[2] Da Ponte's largely autobiographical *Storia della lingua e letteratura italiana in New-York* (1827) confirms that, in the 1820s, translations from the *Inferno* were the staple of the librettist's teaching of the Italian language.[3]

Ten years later, in 1835, Da Ponte's élan was curtailed by the more modest Pietro D'Alessandro into the aptly dejected mood of a victim of Romantic poetry, the political and artistic avant-garde of peoples who are yet to come: "Cui, l'alternarsi de le umane cose, / Vittime poscia condannava a trarre / Sciagurata la vita a frusto a frusto / Esulando raminghi."[4] This is the clearest instance of an empathic quotation (from *Paradiso* 6.141) in a poem littered with traces of Foscolo and Parini and interspersed with minute Dantesque lexical borrowings.

A close, topical reading of a very different sort is the one offered, in the sixth centenary of Dante's birth, by Vincenzo Botta, who, in his *Dante as Philosopher, Patriot and Poet* (1865; reprinted in 1867 and 1887 with the title *Introduction to the Study of Dante*),[5] provided a very ample précis, rich in quotations from Cary's version, and notable for its political bent (Botta was also the author of *Discourse on the Life, Character, and Policy of Count Cavour*, delivered at the New York Historical Society in 1862). In keeping with a secular and patriotic reading of Dante already made popular in Britain by Foscolo and Mazzini, Botta

> made Dante a precursor of liberalism and Italian nationalism and the prophet of Italy's political unity and independence.... Having become a good American, Botta went so far as to suggest that in *De Monarchia* Dante "anticipates in some measure the plan adopted by Washington and his companions in the Constitution of the United States," and that therefore Dante was a true democrat in the modern sense of the word.[6]

Truth be told, the soil had already been tilled, as it were, and Botta could well have been aware of it: the comparison between Dante and Washington had been proposed, in passing, by the "founding Father" of Italians in the United States, Filippo Mazzei;[7] while for a Ghibelline and anti-papal Dante, there sufficed other oft-referred sources—Foscolo, again, and Rossetti;[8] Renan and Henry Clark Barlow. However, not everything fell into quite such an intricate cobweb: around the same period, one of the first scholarly pieces on Dante by a student of Italian descent was a lengthy review of Parsons's translation penned in 1868—not so unpredictably—by an anonymous contributor to "Catholic World."[9] By this time, such articles of Danteana snugly positioned themselves more or less within the coordinates of a well-educated international culture, poised between the literary interests of the Bostonians and the heartier accents of the Italians, for whom Dante at the same time confirmed and soothed the bitter divisions of the Risorgimento. It is a necessary antecedent of a story that will soon follow, veering toward a different use of this totemic author.

La colonia di Dante

In the first decades of the twentieth century, as participants in the Great Migration from southern and eastern Europe began to settle and make roots, we witness a clear divarication in the approaches to Dante, depending on the social and intellectual milieu of origin. While the academic industry strengthened and professionalized itself, deepening and specializing its searches, there rose the new, refreshing, and enthusiastic Dantism of Pound and Eliot, for whom Dante functions as a source of poetical radicalism and is a genial inspiration for their critical, creative interpretation of modernity. But from our point of view, what needs to be stressed is that neither way of reading the old master leaves any mark on the culture produced by the "huddled masses" funneled through Ellis Island and other ports of entry. And a culture they did produce, quite enmeshed in the signs of yore and at the same time very receptive of a certain contemporary scene. Dante, for instance, can be used comically, to mail back to the sender–with a vengeance–the accommodating rhetoric of the Italian "colonies" as unproblematic sites of conventional patriotism. When Pascoli published his *Inno degli emigrati italiani a Dante*[10] in July 1911, the satirical weekly *La Follia di New York* joyously seized the opportunity and for the next four months printed (often on the front page) mock op-ed pieces, vignettes, and *terze rime* daring to ridicule both the pomposity of the Italian literary celebrity and the messy plans to send a bronze statue of Dante from Milan to New York.[11] Two of the main contributors to the magazine—the novelist Bernardino Ciambelli (aka "Pin"), the most prolific novelist of Little Italy, and the poet Riccardo Cordiferro, pseudonym of Alessandro Sisca, identified here as "Cor.," "Corferreum," or "Eisenherz"—managed to concoct a lively hodgepodge of cheap criticism stretching superficially from Trento (site of the huge 1896 Monument to Dante by Cesare Zocchi) to the New York branch of the Società Dante Alighieri, from Giolitti's opportunism to the mounting rhetoric of anti-Turkish propaganda (which would be sealed, in due time, by Pascoli's famous last speech, *La grande Proletaria si è mossa* [1912], infused with a typical brand of colonialist populism). The *idées reçues* of the ruling class are duplicated and contested with the light vulgarity of gossip journalism. What is noteworthy, though, is that the witty intellectuals of the Little Italies show a complete and shrewd awareness of the trap that, in the name of Dante, various institutions of the motherland are about to set: such an awkward operation is turned on its head, so to speak, and the object-Dante shipped with great danger in the hold ends up being held in customs.[12] What was meant to be an easy symbol of patriotism, brandished in the mystifying context of a conventional colonialist and capitalist war, becomes a common good that nobody wants to pay for: "Io che son de l'Italia onore e vanto /

debbo star qui nel fondo d'un vapore, / dopo che più di un mese ho sempre pianto /. . . ./ E così il vate de la nostra gente / si rassegna a restar ne la Dogana, / qual merce giunta qui nascostamente."[13] This is a rather bold way of representing Dante in a comic register in order to poke fun—via the "monumental" Dante—at the eternal conformism against which a certain stratum of Italian immigrants had "voted with their feet" by opting for new shores.

A much more bitter take on Pascoli's definition of a "colonia di Dante" was elaborated in 1912 by the amateur sonneteer Achille Almerini, a medical doctor based in New York whose short cycle of six sonnets by the same title would be rescued from oblivion by the literary taste of Giuseppe Prezzolini, who reprinted it in his *I trapiantati*.[14] The approach here is totally negative and critical: Almerini's is the caustic view of a member of the educated professional class who is forced to make do with his ignorant and cheating clientele, placed under a linguistic spotlight functional to his peculiar version of a *satira del villano* (satire of a peasant), not devoid of various ethnic slurs:

> Qui, più ci hai *morgheg* sul *rialestèta*
> più *isi* tu diventi *prominente*,
> e più *isi* ti fanno *president*
> le società, più sei analfabeta.
>
> Con l'amicizia poi d'un pezzo grosso,
> *politiscia*, *bartenda* od avvocato
> da *Mistar so and so* diventi un *bosso*;
>
> poi ti fanno il banchetto, tal e quale
> come da noi lo fanno al deputato,
> e ti mettono in coppa del giornale.[15]

A similar attitude would only be exacerbated later by the rallying of the Italian American majority under the banner of fascism: in the second sonnet of the cycle, *L'italianità coloniale*, one of the incipits is peremptory: "Dante non serve; nessun sa chi sia. / Cristoforo Colombo serve a poco. . . / Meglio Marconi! La radiofonia."[16]

One of the chief points starts to emerge: just as in the "certified" field of Dante studies—in Italy, in the United States, and elsewhere—so too within the much narrower limits of Italian America, with its peculiar orientations, it would be an inane exercise to try to reduce to a shared consensus the many different voices of this New World Dante, often modulated by a single writer according to changing critical landscapes.

Poets of Justice: Bartoletti and Giovannitti

Such seems to be the case, for instance, for the personal appropriation by a forgotten minor bard of the Italian immigrant proletariat, the self-taught Umbrian miner Efrem Bartoletti. His use of Dante spanned a forty-year period (from the 1910s to the 1950s), and it varied over time. In keeping with the main facets of his muse, it spells a leftist credo and a traditional poetics, and it is always expressed in an aulic Italian. Fundamentally, Dante's presence emerges as a sign of a quest for justice, both moral and political; Dante, directly or indirectly, is the master who facilitates coming to terms with the personal and social exploitation suffered by the immigrant workers; not only that, but as a literary creator, he functions as the poetical matrix on which a new "proletarian" poetry can be modeled.

Nostalgie proletarie, Bartoletti's first and most interesting collection, published in 1919 by the Italian-language imprint of the I.W.W. publishing house, opens with a programmatic and self-referential sonnet where the "Versi d'angoscia, rime di dolore [Verses of anguish, rhymes of sorrow]" of the very first line ring out, in the last two tercets, a percussive "Noi nascemmo a luce spenta, / noi 'l grido siam de la sepolta gente [We were born with the lights out, / we're the cry of the buried people]"[17]—with a half-concealed echo of *Purgatorio* 3.132, and, more in general, a recourse to Dantesque iconography. Here, the images of darkness and burial refer, in a poignant re-semantics of trite metaphors, to the actual condition of the ore miners in the Mesabi Range of Minnesota.

In *Il Mattino del Minatore*, another sonnet, a similar interplay sounds both more explicit—almost tragically naked and desperate—and more covert, less inclined to blatant quotations. Once again, the poetical spark is set off in the final tercets, which condense the dire, real trajectory of this new everyman:

> . . . al fumigante . . . angusto foro
> del sepolcro de' vivi m'incammino
> penoso e mesto. L'anima ferita
> piange il suo fiero e tragico destino.

> E dico: Ecco la trista alterna vita
> del minator; discendere al mattino
> e non saper se a sera àvvi un'uscita.[18]

The rhymes are elegantly and densely derivative, a sign more of poetical memory than of humanistic *imitatio*; but there is little doubt that the existential simile (the moving sentence that opens with "anima ferita") confers further strength to the description. The first *terza rima*—"m'incammino . . . destino . . . mattino"—resonates with crucial passages, especially from the *Inferno*: "'mpediva tanto il mio cammino /. . ./ Temp'era dal principio del mattino" (1.35–37); "Qual fortuna o destino /. . ./ e chi è questi che mostra 'l cammino?" (15.46–48); "con questa orazion picciola, al cammino, /. . ./ e, volta nostra poppa nel mattino" (26.122–24).[19] But it is obvious that Bartoletti's "vita," in such strong position, is attracted and absorbed, so to speak, by the previous "m'incammino," in a fragmented retelling of the incipit of the *Commedia*, made more harmonious and in a way authorized by the rhyme with "uscita" (cf. *Purgatorio* 7.130–32—with its similar syntax—and *Paradiso* 7.104–8).

In his later verse production, Bartoletti continues to show a strong attachment to forms and meanings of a clear Dantesque imprint, although he tends to narrow the focus of his usage of them. Bartoletti frequently pays homage to *terza rima*, which he must have admired also in the popular "visions" of Vincenzo Monti (see Bartoletti's "Il vascello della morte" [Dante's Vessel], which introduces the character of Ulysses, and his unpublished "La Ridda delle Ombre" [The Shadows' Round-dance], dedicated to Giacomo Matteotti's widow).[20] Conversely, we encounter a number of formulaic quotations: from *Inferno* 5 in "Per le nozze d'un amico" (For a Friend's Wedding); from the "political" canto *Purgatorio* 6 in his later poems tinged with antifascism, such as "Venticinque luglio, Espiazione" (July 25th, Atonement), and with an interesting concern about the dangers of American democracy in his "Sulla morte di Re-Pesce" (On the Death of the Fish-King), a parable about Huey Long. Even vaguer traces are found in the prolonged "metaphysical" song "Nel Sogno D'oltretomba" (The Dream of the Afterlife).[21] A more direct but well-articulated homage to Dante motivates two significant pieces, "In morte di Giovanni Pascoli" (For the Death of Giovanni Pascoli) (1912) and "L'Invettiva di Dante" (Dante's Invective) (1921).[22] The former poem, in *terza rima*, bemoans the death of "Lui che attraverso l'alto mare infido / con Colombo e Alighieri sovra un sol legno, / esuli erranti, a quest'estraneo lido / scorti n'aveva" [He who across the treacherous sea / on the same boat with Columbus and Alighieri, / erring exiles, to this foreign shore / escorted us]. Far from the demystifying satires of *La Follia* and Almerini, Columbus and Dante are summoned as ennobling guarantors of the life-changing journey. Bartoletti finds in Pascoli a brotherly voice who understood the social and political claims of the immigrant workers: "Lui sol ci disse, ci chiamò fratelli" [Only he named us, and called us brothers] in rhyme with "ribelli" [rebels] (ll. 37–39). "L'Invettiva," also in *terza rima*, is, rather, an almost unbearable showing-off of performative erudition. As far as we know, its author left it in the columns of the local political press (under the pseudonym "Etrusco") and wisely decided not to reprint it in volume. In "L'Invettiva," a born-again Dante, at the height of the political turmoil that shook the peninsula during the so-called *biennio rosso* (1919–20), laments with a highly rhetorical vocabulary, drenched in Danteana, the violence, divisions, and uncertainty dominating every aspect of life, "ché ovunque imbestia la ferocia umana / tra quei che un muro ed una fossa serra" [Because human cruelty rages everywhere / among those within a single wall and moat]. The mission of poetry has been distorted by D'Annunzio, "colui che, vate del piacer, s'ammanta / d'un patrio vel che omai di sangue gronda, / tal che l'Arte ne arrossa tutta quanta" [He who, prophet of pleasure, shrouds himself / in a patriot's veil by now dripping with blood / so that Art blushes entirely]. The Dante-character can only deliver his invective and, irate and scornful, retreats into an Inferno that is more familiar and therefore even dear to him. Still, he threatens: "al novo Sol tornerò a schiuder gli occhi; / e a sciorre il carme universal, eterno / d'amor fraterno, d'equità e di pace, / conforto ai buoni, ed ai malvagi scherno" [In the new Sun I'll come back to open your eyes; / and to unloosen the eternal, universal poem / of brotherly love, of equality and peace, / relief to the good, scorn to the evil]. Dante, then, personifies the wishful thinking of a full civic and cultural reawakening, rather than being a companion, a hero larger than life, or a political prophet speaking in tongues (or rather, in his own highly connoted tongue).

Issues of linguistic and literary allegiance figure prominently in the history of the relationship between Dante and the culture of the Italian diaspora; still, we lack rigorous philological studies that could lead us to a finer assessment of its contours. This is particularly the case for the most prominent poet of the first generation, Arturo Giovannitti, whose heyday dates from the 1910s. An accurate understanding of his rich poetic output would demand a thorough examination of the many Italian- and English-language magazines and papers that, especially during the first three decades of the twentieth century, benefited from his contributions. It can be argued that we would reap a rather consistent crop of Danteana, all the more when Giovannitti "institutionalizes" himself in the role of tribune of the ethnic trade unions, without renewing any of the accomplishments of his first collection, *Arrows in the Gale* (1914). In fact, before the late 1930s the role of Dante in his work does not go beyond the obvious and the anecdotal.[23] It is only after the fully autonomous collection *Parole e sangue* of 1938 that, under such an unmistakable title, we are able to detect a rather foreseeable dose of Dantean elements: *terze rime* first of all (in *A mia madre*; *Il cenacolo*; and *Sogno del forzato 9653*) and later the very freely Whitmanesque "A Dante,"[24] an extemporized exhortation in first-person plural to a "Padre" Dante who is in direct communication with God ("ora che tace Gesù [Now that Jesus is silent]"), author of "vangeli dell'ira e della riscossa [gospels of anger and revenge]," and the inspiration for an ill-defined "progenie guerriera [warlike offspring]"—a rhetorical comrade, in line with much of the bombast encumbering a not irrelevant chunk of Giovannitti's poetry. His erudition gambles on the validity of the allegorical mode: in "Tre Donne Intorno Al Cor Mi Son Venute" (Italian title, but verses in English), the three women represent the main sources of inspiration for the poet's soul, namely, Revolt, Poetry, and Death.[25] Additionally, the *terza rima* functions as the conduit for the topic of a "real" inferno, to wit, the corrupt locale of Little Italy: a theme at the center of *Malebolge*. "Mulberry Street" even has the audacity to evoke the redeeming arrival of a "Hound" (the *veltro*?), savior of immigrants who cherish the name "America." Its *explicit* is: "America, no word of glowing fame, / Nor even the eternal name of Rome // Beats faster in their bosom than Thy name."[26] Enter, via Dante, an unprecedented New World nationalism. This is understandable, because as the first generations deepened or loosened their ties with either country in the interwar period, even an icon of traditional *italianità* such as Dante could, when necessary, be adopted as a banner of a new kind of *italianità*, winking at the rising template of "my country, right or wrong," a troubling platitude for a large part of Italian Americans, uncertain as exactly to whom they should have committed themselves. Dante becomes then, in the 1920s and 1930s, a rather contested ground within the Italian American community.

Nationalist Dante. The Last Spoof:
Le Avventure di Dante in America

Nowhere is Dante's contestedness more apparent than in the preposterously huge efforts lavished on Dante by a bizarre character, the "colonial" journalist Luigi Carnovale. His campaign for the celebration of the sixth centenary of Dante's death proved to be *so* generous as to convey a sense of wackiness. More than a literary or cultural symbol, in Carnovale's hands Dante turns into a pawn in a gigantically ramified game of networking. The goal is, once again, to proclaim the primacy of Italy and its people, an old adage that receives a new sheen by its current displacement. Carnovale's promotional campaign is structured as an out-of-kilter drama. First, Dante's virtues are extolled at the Chicago Literary Club by a chorus of distinguished American professors: a young Ernest Hatch Wilkins, the venerable Theodore Koch, and Kenneth McKenzie. Then comes the proposal of a Dante Memorial Day, to be celebrated throughout the United States on September 14, 1921, and the munificent idea of two gifts to be presented to the main American cultural institutions "by the Italians of the United States of America":[27] a life-size bronze statue, and Dante's complete works. Despite the alleged devotion to the master, and the reverence paid to the precious Hoepli edition of the Trivulziano 1080 codex (a copy of which would be sent to the White House, to then-president Warren Harding), the wording of the initiative is infused by the usual vapid banality and shows an embarrassing flaw in its gross misquotation of the poem:

> Gl'Italiani sparsi negli Stati Uniti d'America—gl'italiani esuli—osserveranno il 14 settembre 1921 religiosamente: con un intenso ed austero raccoglimento del pensiero e dell'anima; coll'íntimo, col tacito ma saldo proponimento di ispirarsi e conformarsi sempre, in tutte le contingenze della vita, alle purissime e purificatrici virtù di Lui, del "Ghibellin fuggiasco," il quale, mendicando la vita a frusto a frusto
>
> > "ben tetragono ai colpi di ventura
> > e della sua sciagura,"
>
> scrivendo il divino poema ed esalando l'anima giustamente sdegnosa lontano dal *bello ovile*, rese tanto sacro e glorioso l'esilio.[28]

This sounds like praise of the uncommon Italians who, like Dante, sanctified exile. In due course, though, the scheme acquires the characteristics of an unwitting farce: a bevy of individuals (among which an assorted Who's Who of the growing Italian American middle class) and institutions pledge their backing, but only an insufficient minority reach for their wallets. The master plan, more or less, fails, and Carnovale—not so unwillingly—remains at the center of the stage with a few faithful friends. Almost three hundred copies of Dante's *Commedia* and complete works will nonetheless find their way into US libraries; the weird chronicle of such a gargantuan project would also find room on the shelves.

Still, Carnovale's quixotic enthusiasm might be considered less laughable than it first appears, as it shares with other manifestations of Dante's cult a distinctive interest in visible action. It should not be overlooked that the same year as Carnovale's tome (1924),[29] the Italian community of North Beach in San Francisco inaugurated the new church of Saints Peter and Paul (destroyed by the 1906 cataclysm), which sports on the façade, in block capitals, the solemn incipit of the *Paradiso*: "La gloria di colui che tutto move / per l'universo penetra, e risplende." A Catholic priest resident in town, Albert R. Bandini, would shortly afterward provide an Italianate and aulic translation of the poem in *terza rima* (1928–31).[30]

Meanwhile, in *Le Avventure di Dante in America*, V. A. Castellucci repeats and exhausts the "colonial" subgenre of satires of Dante visiting Little Italy.[31] From many different points of view, though, the structure is here unusually robust and multilayered. Not by chance, it is subtitled <u>Poemetto</u> *Satirico Umoristico*. In fact, a big part of Dante's trip from Boston to Washington is told, mostly by "Virgilio Plubius" [sic], in a *terza rima* that is alternated with prose narrative. The satire is quite wide-ranging and reinforced by a solid grid of literary references. We may add to this a pervasive linguistic sensibility, which peppers the tale with an almost virtuosic exhibition of "Italglish." The references span from "Gesovele Carduccio" (Giosue Carducci) to "Sor Gigi" Pirandello, with only passing mentions of Giusti, D'Annunzio, Papini, and more incisive characterizations of Vincenzo Monti, "Mario" Scartazzini (a clear nod to the Swiss Dante scholar), Torquato Tasso, and Vittorio Betteloni. But the spirits are particularly enflamed by figures much more connected, on the one hand, to the Italian American experience and, on the other, to Dante's cult: during the visit to New York, we read the praise for its "colonial" novelist, Bernardino Ciambelli, who "rivelò tanti misteri / che la *ghenga* fu presa da paura, / abbandonò di fretta quei quartieri / e altrove andò cercando la ventura."[32] Later, we hear the bitter irony of his castigating one of the princes of Italian journalism, "Gigi" Barzini, who, unable to adapt to the corrupting embrace of "colonial" petty maneuvering and the bloodthirsty and money-grabbing Mafia activities, had to abandon his post at the ambitious and short-lived *Corriere d'America*. Finally, Dante's scorn lashes the popular Tuscan sonneteer Venturino Camaiti, who had acquired fame around the sixth centenary of the poet's death with his *La Divina Commedia esposta e commentata in cento sonetti fiorentineschi umoristici e satirici* (1921).

Virgil is cast as a sweetly ridiculous but faithful figure: he impersonates the Italian immigrant who has earned his meager income "un po' maneggiando la *sciabola*, un po' *pedolando* col carretto di banane, e un po' aggiustando *sciocchese* di *second-end*."[33] He guides the poet not only through the "colony," but also across an America marked by economic depression ("*Lucca . . . lucca* quanto *pipolo* è in fila nella *bred-laina*")[34] and ethnic diversity. The Italian immigrant has to curtail his sense of primacy, confronting a linguistic Babel (when Virgil and Dante ask for an interpreter at the Berlitz School in Boston, the question is "Olandese, Rumeno, Slavo, Yeddish, Polacco o Turco?")[35] and the disquieting presence of the color line (on the train, the poet's attention is aroused by a "figlio di Etiopia [coi denti d'oro e col giubbetto bianco]").[36]

Dante's visit to this "otherworld" is quite far-reaching: it expounds with witticism on comparative food habits, thanks to a flamboyant Neapolitan waiter; it offers a scathing criticism of the violent feuds devastating the community when the official parade in Dante's honor—opened with the customary Roman and Fascist salute—is wrecked by a bomb in downtown Manhattan; and most of all, it aligns itself with a century-old European tradition (particularly active in Italy until at least World War II) of moralistic judgment toward what were perceived as the free mores of liberated American woman. It is noteworthy, though, that Dante is increasingly portrayed as incapable of unshackling himself from his severe and clearly ridiculed views:

> Gridar vorria: O depravate genti,
> di regale beltà fu Beatrice,
> che corto avea il piè, perfetti i denti,
> d'angeliche sembianze, inspiratrice

> di pudiche virtù; non trasparenti
> le vesti avea che cuopron la matrice;
> modesta e candida, coi dolci accenti!³⁷

However, all the while, his Italian American fellow travelers appear to embrace a more realistic attitude: "*Tu-dei*, a ben ragione, non s'adatta / la donna a lavorar da vivandiera," and "s'appresta il *fild* elettorale."³⁸ The narrator, after all, has an eye open to the modern beauties of the metropolis: "Annotta. New York, di sera offre al poeta uno spettacolo straordinario per l'effetto magico e sorprendente di luci e di colori inverosimili, che s'incrociano, si frantumano in scintille, in prismi, in strisce, in serpeggiamenti: ardono, fiammeggiano, s'agitano in un brulichio luminoso di lettere."³⁹ But the pendulum keeps swinging back and forth, and eventually both Dante and Virgil concur: "il paesano deve rimanere 'paesano.' "⁴⁰

A satire without straightforward irony, *Le Avventure di Dante in America* recapitulates the genre with a sort of cerebral and complex parody, caught, as it were, between opposing motives. Socially shrewd, it is highly metaliterary and metalinguistic as well; it is also in some way self-consuming, feeding on its own "mean" intelligence. It is indicative that it does not really incite a follow-up.

In the First Italian American Novel: Lapolla and di Donato. Plus: Dante, Prophet of Mussolini

In the same year as the publication of Castellucci's poem (1935), in accordance with the vitality of a decade that witnessed the rise of a national figure such as Fiorello La Guardia, mayor of New York City, with all that entails in terms of biculturalism and bilingualism, one of the great novels by a second-generation Italian American, *The Grand Gennaro* by Garibaldi Lapolla, inaugurated a refreshingly new way of dealing with the avatars of the culture of origin. With utmost narrative and aesthetic maturity, Lapolla exhibits a different stance. Dante is totally objectified in Lapolla's novel; he is used as an element of color, needed in order to focus better on the attitude of one of the characters, thus providing a finer picture of his attachment to the Old World. References to Dante are few (only three), but they do not go unnoticed; they are always and only introduced in association with Davido Monterano, a minor but not irrelevant figure through whom the narrator castigates the unsuitability (half arrogant, half ingenuous) of a lower-middle-class, parochial Italian, entrenched behind "his famous poet" in a disastrous strategy of denial of the surrounding modern metropolis. The external narrator is almost ruthless in underlining the inappropriateness of Davido Monterano's quotations from Dante, interjected ad lib "no matter how incongruous or far-fetched."[41] But his misquotations, insofar as they distort with a fair degree of innocence the letter of the *Commedia*, are an ironic wink at the far more troubling phenomenon of linguistic displacement: those cut-up lines are like a life raft in the ocean of a new language. Quickly, Davido (or, rather, his family) must adjust and find an occupation: Dante comes to the rescue and soothes the wounds of his ego; the misquotations can provide an opening motif for a passage whose English flaunts—as Ballerini and Chiappelli shrewdly argued years ago—"una luminosità inconfondibilmente italocroma":[42] "'Surely we are busy . . . or *per dillettanze over per doglie* [sic],' he smiled as he misquoted the famous exile. 'Like Dante, whether it be pleasure or pain, we work in bitterness who tread a foreign shore.'"[43]

The very nobility of Dante and his cult give way to a tragically ridiculous act, yet it should be noted that Dante *is still there*, "no matter how," as we have seen. Such dissonant contradictions happen at a most uncertain hour and express only part of the picture. Little Italy, in the mid-1930s, was the site of quite a lot of unabashed, through-and-through fascism; among the paraphernalia, a black-shirted Dante would not be amiss, perfectly consonant as he was with the popular prophet hailed up and down the peninsula as a staunch proponent of the Impero. Bonifacio Grandillo proposed exactly this, with arguments so close to the ones pointed out in recent studies that he may be considered as a true representative of a first generation consistent with the mindset of the longed-for motherland.[44] Grandillo (who dates his Preface "Brooklyn, 10 aprile 1936") concurs with Pope Pius XI (duly quoted in the epigraph) in seeing the providential meaning of Mussolini, who is literally interpreted as a Godsend, a "messo di Dio." Not only that, Mussolini was sent from Heaven to save Italy and humanity, announced in fastidious detail by two veritable prophets: Saint John the Divine and Dante: "Il Duce Benito Mussolini è preannunziato col numero enigmatico 666."[45] The hefty pamphlet elaborates and strives to corroborate its thesis in the course of nine chapters, followed by an appendix tellingly titled "La Lupa Dantesca: L'Inghilterra" (Dante's She-Wolf: England). Grandillo drums with deadpan seriousness into his Italian American reader (the book was published by the noted S. F. Vanni imprint on Bleecker Street) the seemingly self-evident truth of the correspondence between the prophecy in the Apocalypse and the life and figure of Mussolini. Numerology and cabbala are pervasively misused:

> Questo 9, dunque, è il numero propizio a Mussolini, ed infatti si hanno:
> 9 lettere nel cognome: Mussolini.
> 9 vocali in Duce Benito Mussolini.
> 9 lettere in Predappio. . .
> Le parole Italia, Impero, Romano, contengono 6 lettere ciascuna, perciò 6, 6, 6. . .[46]

And this is only skimming the surface. Obviously, the Veltro couldn't be born anywhere but in Predappio (halfway between Feltre and Montefeltro); the "cinquecento dieci e cinque, / messo di Dio" (*Purgatorio* 33.43–44) is one and the same with the new Duce. Dante relished similar correspondences between letters and numbers when expressing his Imperial political program (*Paradiso* 18's "diligite iustitiam"); and because Veltro, DXV and "messo di Dio" are three, Mussolini is analogically linked to the Trinity.

It is fascism per se that is foretold by the Apocalypse's "prima bestia" (first beast): the cult of Rome, the political program of Renovatio Imperii, the huge public works, the Ethiopian campaign, the adoption of such symbols as the Eagle and the Fasces, and the Corporate State—all these historical realities were alluded to by precise passages from the Apocalypse.[47] Following similar premises, the outrageous finale is almost a no-brainer:

> Perciò come Iddio coll'Impero Romano preparò il mondo alla venuta di Cristo, così, forse, per l'avvenire col movimento iniziato da Mussolini prepara il mondo al ritorno di Cristo sulla terra. Lo sarà? Il tempo e la storia ne saranno testimoni e giudici.[48]

How widespread reasonings of this tenor were in the Italian American community is hard to tell; one should probably not exaggerate in either direction. Still, it is telling that the author (probably the homonymous Molisano—an immigrant from Molise—registered at Ellis Island in 1911 and 1920, who donated a rare, inscribed copy of his tract to the New York Public Library in 1937)[49] could find, in a time of tense relations between the two governments, a well-disposed publisher in S. F. Vanni, a prestigious institution of the literary colony of downtown Manhattan.

Fathers and sons were, at the same time, still cohabiting—sociologically speaking, first and second generations under the same roof. But looked at in terms of Danteana, the picture might prove to be not quite so sharp. Along the many conflicting and merging currents of such an absolute masterpiece as Pietro di Donato's *Christ in Concrete* (1939), the ground keeps moving and shifting. Dante is there, too, once again: he shimmers and fluctuates, almost inadvertently, among the bricklayers from the Abruzzi who form the chorus of the tragedy. As a "real" figment of their imagination, he appears only sporadically; but in a story based on a modernist and working-class reading of Christ's Calvary, on a *sacra rappresentazione*, if you will, played out on the scaffoldings and in the poor tenements of New York, one may surmise that Dante's *Commedia* fulfills a higher concept. In fact, di Donato must have felt that Dante's journey was deeply and idiosyncratically congenial to the mentality of many of his characters and narrators. One can more effectively map this out by paying respect to di Donato as *author* in the fullest sense that he deserves to be considered. In *Christ in Concrete*, the plight of the characters weighs on the whole story, bringing to the fore moral and one might say metaphysical issues that, according to the dominant ethos, tended to be couched in religious terms. The novel deals with God, justice, love, death, grief, and responsibility as much as it deals with mortar, extreme cold and heat, food, blood and piss, companionship, and solidarity. At the center of it all looms a forbidding godhead, a "Job" of almost biblical or Hesiodic overtones. Paul—arguably the main character—is no prophet and is quite deliberately a contrarian; still, through his eyes we perceive the materiality of a hunger for understanding and the unquenchable necessity for personal growth. Inasmuch as Paul has autobiographical traits, he also expresses a Dantesque thrust for spiritual as well as material betterment and metamorphosis that will continue in the later installments of di Donato's oeuvre. Meanwhile, at a more common level, Dante can, once again, provide some local color for a rowdy depiction of Little Italy.

Deep into the phenomenal "fiesta" of chapter 4, Annunziata, the seemingly illiterate young *mater* and widow *dolorosa*, resorts to a proverbial Dantism. It is a sudden flare that conveys, in a nutshell, the resentful fatigue of a doting mother. Her brother is finally getting married, and he requests, nicely but firmly, to have her by his side. Neighbors agree: it's high time to leave and go to church for the ceremony—too bad if the kids aren't ready yet. Annunziata's thoughts begin:

> Where had the children left their hats and coats? Who would hold whose hand and tend so that there would not be imbroglios and fracas and then it would be said that one did not know how to bring up one's children—ah but children were made to let the heads of their mothers go scattering—woe-woe but why were they born straight from Malebolge and Devil came they and parents were wracked and ruined for them—No, O blessed Jesu-Giuseppe e' Mari, excuse these rabid thoughts—I know not what I say.[50]

It must be said that, invoking the Holy Family, Annunziata repeats the same words muttered by her husband just before being choked to death by concrete at the beginning of the novel. *We* know, *she* does not; it is a chilling version of a "lessico famigliare" (family lexicon).

Later, at the height of the wedding banquet, unbridled by symposial mirth (food, alcohol, music, sensuality), the "ladies persuaded Maestro Farabutti to perform." Pun, obviously, intended.[51] The guy launches himself—and drags others—into an unforgettable chauvinistic tirade:

He placed himself near the window. Then flinging his arms wide:

> "We are Italians! Know you what that means? It means the regal blood of terrestrial man! Richer than the richest, purer than the finest, more capable than an-y! an-y! race breathing under the stellar rays of night or the lucent beams of day!—"
>
> [. . . .]
>
> "—and in the sacred realm of Arts the children of Italia beautiful have achieved the celestial heights—for are not Michelangelo and Raphaelo our own? Cellini!—"
>
> "It is understood. . ."
>
> "—our brother Dante Alighieri who has scribed all that need be read—"

"Ah yes," mused Orangepeel-Face Mike profoundly, "the *Comedy Divine* is said to contain all the verities mundane and spiri-tual. . ."

"—the bravest warriors! and—"

"Right!"

"We are the glory of Rome, *the* culture! By us the rest are scum! And it is the duty of us great Italians to—."[52]

What to make of that inevitable and embarrassing pride? The narrator and his author won't let such a question drop. Indeed, this is only the beginning of di Donato's Dante.

Tusiani and Ciardi:
Flight from and Adherence to the Letter

In the meantime, much before di Donato resumed his own quest, any Italian American sense of aggrandizement received a decisive blow from World War II. A "fiesta" such as di Donato's, if not unthinkable, would have been inappropriate in terms of representability in the 1950s. Meanwhile, after the war, thanks to the magisterial readings of Charles Singleton, American Dante studies attained a literary and epistemological sophistication capable of influencing generations of future scholars. At least two important Italian Americans, Joseph Tusiani and John Ciardi, accepted the challenge and embarked on a long and rather idiosyncratic commerce with the medieval master.

In Tusiani's case, a summary list of his tireless Dantes should suffice to comprehend the difference of his approach, at once more literal and faithful, much rounder, and more direct, but also more allegorical. Tusiani has written two novels about Dante in contemporary settings—one in Italian and one in English; his scholarly contribution has covered extensively Dante's poetry and the poetry of Dante's age, with the translation of all of Dante's lyrics and of a substantial selection of Duecento and Trecento poetry.[53] Furthermore, his unfailing productivity as translator has begotten a successful précis of the poem for the benefit of the young: *Dante's Divine Comedy: As Told for Young People*. Two novels, extensive translating activity, and a candid prose bowdlerization of the *Commedia*, all from the second half of last century, attest to more than fifty years of loyalty to Dante in completely different registers and genres. What keeps all of this together is an unwavering treatment of Dante as source of cultural, ideological, and literary authority beyond discussion. Such a disposition leads to intensive creative (in the novels) and re-creative work, which is admirable and surprising per se, but can often border on mawkishness and ingenuity. Even when Dante returns to present-day Italy (whether from Purgatory or Paradise) and engages in current and relevant debates about politics, the sciences, literature, public education, or private morals, as in the otherwise daring constructions of *Dante in licenza* (1952) and *Envoy from Heaven* (1965),[54] his role is one of a protracted deus ex machina, a fixture of the Western and indeed Catholic world. Dante as a character may well go through an exhilarating variety of contemporary phenomena, showing his comical unfitness or severe righteousness, but in fact, as a fictive element, he is always flung abstractly from outer space. Underneath the surface of the sugary timelessness there lies an unflinching, programmatic Catholic and Roman orthodoxy whose contents (by definition repetitious and dogmatic) would demand to be seriously dismantled were this something other than an account of literary and cultural history. Respect for the author's serious beliefs suggests, instead, that such acritical orthodoxy is not to be taken seriously, but rather as a narrative gimmick, almost as an extended joke. I am aware that this is not, of course, the *intentio operum*. Tusiani's main goal, by all evidence, must be recognized in his transparent autobiographical effort to give vent to a pious morality (sexophobic, to be sure) and to a Cold War sociopolitical mindset concerned with the rise of a secular culture and in particular of the then-menacing Italian Communist Party. Tusiani does not conceal that *Dante in licenza* is a straightforward novelization of a propaganda piece commissioned by the missionary order of the Padri Comboniani based in Verona.[55] *Envoy from Heaven*, built and written with more maturity and nuance, nevertheless relies structurally on the pattern of a procession, having Dante regularly lectured to by a series of Catholic personalities and icons of Italian culture: angels, Church fathers, Mother Cabrini, Saint Thomas Aquinas, Michelangelo, Machiavelli, and others. The prevailing mode is one of prolonged dialogue, contrived and stilted. One wonders, again, about the extent of the reception that books like these could obtain, a full generation after the already trying satire of *Le Avventure di Dante in America*; on the other hand, the recognized commercial success of Tusiani's later Dantism—*Dante's Lyric Poems* and *Dante's Divine Comedy:*

As Told for Young People[56]—is not hard to understand. The subtlety of his poetic translations has been amply and justly pointed out; an aspect that needs to be stressed is certainly his metric and harmonic sensibility, well refined by his multilingual poetical practice. Here, Tusiani works on firmer ground and offers his art to an audience that largely extends beyond that of Little Italy. In particular, the experiment of a Dante "Told for Young People" deserves attention for its conversational qualities and its ability to deliver, without banality, a "storyline" like that of the *Commedia*. Some of the same childlike rhetorical directness that in the novels sounded far-fetched here helps to convey, with the required ease, the peculiar décor and high messages of Dante's journey. Whereas the novels' implied reader was someone well acquainted with Italy and Catholic culture, the subsequent work is a popularization that widens readership, although, one should add, with a distinct classroom taste. Finally, the Italian Americanness of Tusiani's Dantism ends up having more to do with the personal detail of the author's identity than with what is being said in the texts; the Italian American intellectual and artist is "simply" an ambassador better equipped and more motivated than others to interpret parts of Dante's complexity. Such, at least, seems to be a widespread view if one just glances at the large number of Italian Americans within the crowded field of Dante's American scholars and translators. In particular cases, such as Tusiani's, the implications and ramifications of this rapport deserve specific attention.

Another crucial instance of this deeply personal cultural knot concerns John Ciardi and his successful version of the entire poem in imperfect *terza rima*. The fact that the completion of Ciardi's endeavor was endorsed by John Freccero's *Introduction* to *Paradiso* confirms, in my view, the *longue durée* of a shared involvement, the mere existence of which reveals the deep influence of ethnic feel. With the passing of time and generations, the organic imbrication of Italian America and Dante has transformed itself rather rapidly into a more diluted, more symbolic disposition—and at the same time has been specialized almost professionally. And with the waning of actual physical neighborhoods, the merging via Dante of similar shared dispositions can function as a sign of a new ethnic consciousness, of an "imagined community."

This is by no means the manifestation of some vague and undefined sense of belonging, as Ciardi's literary and linguistic engagement demonstrates. His choice of Dante and his deliberate championing of a "natural" and expressive translation that could convey the thrust of orality indicate the exact opposite of detached lip service to the source. In his "transposition"—Ciardi famously stated in his 1954 *Translator's Note*—he "labored . . . for something like idiomatic English" in order to come close to the quality of the "spoken tongue" of Dante's language, a "common speech . . . made perfect."[57] One could expect that precisely a poet of Ciardi's background might dare to consider himself up to the task, having grown up surrounded by an Italian "tribe" in the Boston area in the 1920s and 1930s (the opening section of his *Selected Poems* is titled "Tribal Poems") and then having struggled (generally successfully) to assimilate into the Wasp literary élite. The existential weight of the linguistic condition in an immigrant culture—a condition beset by silence and forceful adaptation, by keen attention and sense of loss—finds luminous expression, not by chance I think, in the collection published only one year after the completion of *Paradiso: Lives of X* (1971). In "Epilogue: The Burial of the Last Elder" (which seals the *Selected Poems* as well), Ciardi gives powerful expression to a *topos* of Italian American letters,[58] writing a moving and insightful tribute to one of the "last ones":

> . . . He was the last where none
> could sing the yokel cadence of his mountain—
> not dialect but defeat, a tribe's long waste
> from father stones it could no longer read[59]

The long devotion to translating Dante, apart from its artistic and utilitarian merits, should also be seen in this light, as a contribution in a father-and-son framework, a way of reclaiming a language, an "unknown tongue." As the *canticas* were being published, Ciardi expanded his *Translator's Note*, adding deep and personal reflections on the topic:

> [W]ords consist of much more than denotation. Every word has a certain muscularity. That is to say, it involves certain speech muscles. Certainly any man who is word-sensitive is likely to linger over the difference between the long-drawn Italian *carina* and the common, though imprecise, American usage "cute" when applied to an attractive child. The physical gestures the two words invite are at least as different as the Italian child's good-bye wave ("*Fa ciao, carina*") with the palm of the hand up, and the American child's ("Wave bye-bye")

with the back of the hand up. The very difference in ethnic concept between two peoples moves the words about in their mouths. As I once wrote in a poem I am not moved to cherish particularly but whose point remains:

> My mother facing a day in Avellino
> Tasted it: *una dolce giornata*.
>
> My wife's mother in Protestant Missouri
> Judges it: *it is a good day*.[60]

On May 1, 1965, on the occasion of the seventh centenary of Dante's birth, Ciardi delivered (after J. Chesley Mathews and Francis Fergusson) the last of three lectures on Dante at the Library of Congress in Washington, DC: *The Relevance of the* Inferno.[61] It is a precious gem of an essay by a writer not inclined to publish—at least, not at such length—his scholarly musings. Because of his nature, neither academic, nor explicitly "essayistic," it has not gone down in the Dantean record, yet its intellectual intensity is deserving of attention. We would give it away by trying to summarize it; let us just mention that its palpable personal engagement is never couched in "ethnic," or Italian American, terms. The individual history of the poet-translator is totally silenced here; given the overall poignancy of the speech, one can hardly lament its absence. Yet that silence is somewhat puzzling, and from our point of view, it does speak volumes. One cannot help but think it a half-concealed suppression, and a price to be paid to be accepted at the literary heart of the federal government. The masterly deftness of the delivery bespeaks the by-then "natural" outcome of a decade-long cultural adaptation to America.

A mention should be made of another kind of translation, the highly expressive tour de force by Nicola Testi, a minor but consistent figure of the Italian-language literary underworld, who, toward the end of his life, published in Florence with the prestigious Vallecchi publishing house an *Inferno* "in vernacolo pugliese [in the vernacular of Puglia]" (1958). This is a meticulous rendition of the poem in *terza rima*, laboriously crafted. Testi was a resident of Trenton, New Jersey, like another dialectal poet, the Roman Alfredo Borgianini; Testi had emigrated in 1906 and could boast of a number of poetry collections, both in Italian and in dialect. His version of the *Inferno* (double-checked against the corresponding English versions by Longfellow, Sayers, and Ciardi) represents a dignified result, if compared with the amateurish nostalgia of his own poetry. Tusiani, in his preface, effectively captures one of the motives, and preconditions, for Testi's success: "Chi è lontano dalla lingua viva della Patria, traduce, voglia o non voglia, quasi come sognando, al contatto con ogni nuova parola appresa, con ogni sfumatura impensata e impressionante della lingua non sua."[62]

Ferlinghetti. Di Donato, Parts 2 and 3. *Underworld*

Nineteen fifty-eight was the year in which a far more acclaimed poet made a breakthrough in American letters: Lawrence Ferlinghetti, with *A Coney Island of the Mind*. About halfway into this slender group of "illuminations," in a section that is in dialogue with great masters of the past, Dante figures in a prominent, negative opening:

> Not like Dante
>   discovering a <u>commedia</u>
>   upon the slopes of heaven
> I would paint a different kind
>   of Paradiso
> in which the people would be naked
>   as they always are[63]

The everyday, libertarian quality of Ferlinghetti's imagination conjures up a quasi-cartoonish version of Dante's morals with "alternative" credos, always expressed in contrastive terms. It is still a Dante "of the mind." Twenty years later, one of Ferlinghetti's most celebrated poems, "The Old Italians Dying" (1979), provides a deceivingly tender, noncommittal variant in which the illustrative quality of the images, by dint of repetitions, succeeds in mimicking the fatigued loyalty of the old Italians (and their poet) to that impressive incipit from *Paradiso* 1 imposing itself at the heart of one of the farthest Little Italies, in San Francisco, overlooking the infinity of the Pacific. The "unfinished" business of it all keeps resurfacing in the poem, evoking the eternal cycle of life, which feeds on death. Dante and his magisterial lines here become sovereign catchwords; the "old Italians" are another symbol of everyman and his fall. The capital letters remain up there, on the façade of Saints Peter and Paul, and are Dante's. Down at street-level:

> You have seen them
> every day in Washington Square San Francisco
> the slow bell
> tolls in the morning
> in the Church of Peter & Paul
> in the marzipan church on the plaza
> . . . .
> You have seen them sitting there
> waiting for the bocce ball to stop rolling
> waiting for the bell
>   to stop tolling & tolling
> for the slow bell
>   to be finished tolling
> telling the unfinished Paradiso story
> as seen in an unfinished phrase
>   on the face of a church[64]

Dante cannot possibly be a Beat, but even a Beat poet can measure up to his lesson. The (objective and subjective) Italian American quality of the entire setting clearly provides something other than mere circumstantial evidence.

Let us return to the East Coast to follow our thread in not-so-dissimilar territories. We left di Donato before World War II, and we tried to point out the intensity of his Dantesque evocations back then. Now *Three Circles of Light* (1960), the irresistible prequel to *Christ in Concrete*, presents a structural frame that is admittedly indebted to Dante, thus suggesting the deep intertwining of religious and literary values, which is necessary if one is to look ahead and aspire to redemption. When Geremio, the father, fell from the scaffolding and choked to death by ingesting concrete, he left the inferno of capitalist America and ascended to Heaven. Both at the very beginning (the *Prologue*) and at the very end of the novel (chapter 25) one reads:

> Mother whispered: "Your father lives where there is neither heat nor cold, nor hurt nor want. He dwells blissfully in the aura of the Rainbow within the Three Circles of Light, which is the vision of our Lord, and in that oneness of wish and will with God Who Himself is Love. Your father wants me to give his kisses to his loves."[65]

Narratively speaking, the reappearance of the same sentence means the closing of a circle. The "vision of our Lord"—di Donato explains in a 1991 interview—corresponds to "the face of God at the end of the Divine Comedy; if you will recall, she was called Beatrice. He was expecting to see a figure like a man, three rainbows irradiating. So I symbolized each circle—one was the job, one was the home and the other was the church, religion."[66] This is a striking personal interpretation of the "tre giri / di tre colori e d'una contenenza [three circles of three colors and of one circumference]" and of their reflection "com'iri da iri [like a rainbow by a rainbow]" of *Paradiso* 33.116–18. We have already noticed how Annunziata, the mother, had surprisingly commended to Dante the minutiae of her difficult widow's state. She does it again here, confiding in the ascension of her unfaithful husband ("the genial, grinning, behorned satyr") to Heaven. Dante (who is not explicitly mentioned) is the author of the arch-Christian narrative, subject to a devout reading by a nonliterate young mother, which helps her to make sense of a life and a lifestory. God as Love will overcome death. Mother Annunziata spells out her faith in a new Christ, the deceased husband, in direct communication with God, via a more-or-less veiled Dante. Dante, then, is instrumental in a redemption that also means, once again, acceptance of America. And it is particularly telling that this happens through the mother rather than the son.

Di Donato's ambitious last project, *The American Gospels*, published posthumously in 2011, was immediately withdrawn from the market for legal reasons. Luckily, a handful of copies are in circulation. It is foreseeable that a present-day novelization of the Gospels in American dress, by such a committed Italian American personality, will offer material for our overview. In fact, Dante keeps making appearances here and there among the four radically contemporary Gospels in which four different "hues" of Christ (Red, White, Yellow, and Black: an American Indian, a young Communist, Madam Ho Chi Christ, Black Angela Christ) spread the good news. In *The American Gospels*, di Donato expresses his audacity at full tilt: vast, verbose, rambling, viscerally antinarrative, the I-"narrator" strives to shout his quest for salvation at the "United States of Totalitaria."[67] At times, the soapbox speechifying attains a furious and lucid grandeur; elsewhere, the reader (if not the narrator himself) risks losing the plot—except that losing it is also part of the challenge. Dante is only one of the myriad ingredients, to be sure: but the squareness of his poetry and thought provides solace and inspiration in crucial instances. He is a poet, a prophet of love, a dialectical thinker: all elements in great esteem in the new Gospels. Retracing Dante's footsteps, it seems, could already provide a promising new start:

> J. C. began to address the mob. His poise was sure. He said, "Brothers and sisters dear, I was anticipated by the Prophets and Kings. I was suggested by Aristotle. Dante Alighieri spelled out the dialectics of my moral imperatives and he lyricized the anatomy of my love philosophy." He suddenly thought of something—he boiled over and shouted, "Generation of vipers, ye have Zerox machines for the souls! Not your contemptible Dictators in Washington but you are the cause of putrid evils! Your leaders in D.C. are only the scum upon the cesspool that is you![68]

Dante's inspirational force reaches its acme later when a "sacred madness permeated me. . . . How does one carnally penetrate God and not be consumed by the infinite radiation of the Maiden-Godhead's orgasm?"[69] The full communion, fleshly and spiritual, with God, pictured as a very attractive Asian woman, is in some way reminiscent of the immaculate orgasm that is alluded to in the rhymes and narration of the closing sequence of the *Paradiso*. Di Donato also describes a holy vision, unspeakable pleasure, then silence: "A heavy honeyed somnolence wafted me on the trip of trips high over Jerusalem. . . ."[70]

The Fourth Gospel (which includes a "sightseeing" trip to Hell, 102ff.) departs at least fragmentarily from the previous experimental prose and plays around with the scheme of the *terzina*, albeit unrhymed and completely irregular metrically. But the footprint is there, as it is at the very end with the Wagnerian epilogue of *The Veneriad*. Venusberg abuts on a last female epiphany, a Jewish girl, a "perfect splendorous beauty" resurrecting "from the Nazi ovens," and named Stella. Stella—and "love" (the very last word of these Gospels):[71] a fitting repetition of Dante's distant prophetic model.[72]

In the Hands of Tosches and Viscusi

We have entered, by now, a completely contemporary scene. It is a scene shared by blatant occurrences of Danteana—in popular fiction and movies, to wit, Dan Brown's *Inferno*, Matthew Pearl's *The Dante Club*, and, for instance, a movie thriller like *Se7en* by David Fincher (1995)[73]—and by a sophisticated, eye-opening, unprejudiced new American school of Dante scholars whose pace, if anything, foreign colleagues strive to match.[74] And still, despite the by-now stabilized transformation of the physical ethnic communities into airy and disconnected networks wishfully connected by memories, or sometimes interests and accomplishments, there seems to remain a residue of attention and longing for an author and symbol of unremitting global stature, a residue we could label as Italian American. Dante is probably the one banner that is so driven into the history and the culture of the peninsula of origin as to be practically impossible to wrest away and entrust—sentimentally speaking, at least—to *someone else*. Two among the finest and most intelligent writers of Italian descent, Nick Tosches and Robert Viscusi, have offered examples of such an attitude, interpreted with a dark bent in the first case, and in an epic-elegiac mood in the second case.

Nick Tosches's 2002 novel *In the Hand of Dante* appears to temporarily wrap up with a stroke of mind-blowing inspiration, but after long strides of narrative self-indulgence, after a series (actually, and fittingly, a triad) of sprawling stories connected and disconnected by some blistering wounds, dreams, and evil deeds, "made in Italy." In fact, the novel comes third after *Power on Earth* (1986), an investigative portrait of the Mafia- and Vatican-banker and criminal Michele Sindona (Tosches's family is of Sicilian descent, from the Arbëreshë-Albanian minority), and *Dino* (1992), a biographical masterpiece devoted to Dino Paul Crocetti, aka Dean Martin, son of immigrants from the Abruzzi (Tosches is a long-time music journalist).[75] The story of the discovery of the *Commedia*'s original manuscript (attributed to a Sicilian Albanian priest working in the Vatican library) fires off an international imbroglio at the center of which is an ultra-narcissist narrator named Nick, equally committed to a lust for "broads," big bucks, and high culture. Somehow, Dante the poet and Dante the mysterious author of the lost and invaluable manuscript can represent a worthy alias for the narrator's ego. The plot progresses, juxtaposing here and there, now and then, in a somewhat predictable and showy structure, the preening of Nick's rough-and-tumble, streetwise persona and his more sober, erudite traits, focused on Dante's creative and philosophical search and on Gemma Alighieri's position. On the side, there are mobsters, librarians, and dealers of various sort. Eventually, dissatisfied with his own oeuvre, both for its too-stringent formal apparel and because of an inexpressible need for a higher, more all-encompassing concept of God, Dante will sail to Gazirat Malitimah (Arabic for the small island of Marettimo, off Sicily's western shores) to meet an Islamic sage befriended at the Sorbonne by a Venetian Jew, Jacob, a late source of extramundane inspiration; Nick, quite mundanely, will instead strand himself on another tiny island in the Caribbean, living off the piecemeal selling of the manuscript.

A half-century after Tusiani's novelistic forays, it is as if Tosches followed the lead of that first-generation Italian American. One could not imagine two more distant intellectual figures: Dante clearly fulfills in both cases, however, the unintentional role of cultural binder, worked and reworked through the force of extensive fictional reimagining. Once again, Dante acts as the go-between of the two worlds, and, even in an affected end-of-the-millennium writer-*maudit* such as Tosches, ushers in a renewed experience of love, in his case for an appropriately named Italian Giulietta, who inspires this valedictory passage:

> There are those whom I love and who dwell within me. Some of them I have abandoned long ago. Others long ago have abandoned me. Yet they dwell in the love within me.
>
> There are others, whom I never have abandoned, and who never have abandoned me.
>
> When my second death, my true death is near, I will bring them to me.
>
> For so long, the souls of others sustained me as much as my own soul did.
>
> God, how I long now for them.[76]

And so we are come—"giunti"—"a l'occidente [to the West]," but to a world that is hardly "sanza gente [without people]"; what remains, at least temporarily—the "rimanente" that had driven Ulysses westward—is a scenario that may be less tangible, but is inhabited by dreams and ghosts and memories still somehow connected to an origin whose cultural and linguistic matrix, whether we like it or not, has been to some extent spelled out by Dante in his oeuvre. The old master had radically interpreted *that* journey, Ulysses's journey, as an unredeemably sinful act. I suspect that elements of that attitude may be accounted for among the few properties shared, contradictorily, by Italians and Italian Americans, although neither of them would admit it, of course. But since the actual demise of the first epic wave of the

Great Migration, we have reached, after an entire century, a territory closer to silence and invisibility, analogous to a (collective) unconscious, expressible through forms of aesthetic creativity rather than through the firmer grip of a sociopolitical engagement. The latest metamorphoses of Dantean discourse, then, are to be found, for instance, in poetic traces and metaphorical allusions. It may sound like a feeble echo, but it is probably the deepest and most convincing one: it is a "rimanente," however troubled, of that long and definitive journey unwittingly predicted by the one whom Italians call "father," and whom di Donato's workers addressed as "brother"—Dante.

In a way, the Florentine poet could well be admitted into the Pantheon of "Buried Caesars" that Robert Viscusi has eloquently unearthed and explained over more than thirty years of imaginative and influential scholarship, analyzing Italian American culture—mostly through its literature—and pointing out the powerful anthropological traits that Italian immigrants and their descendants brought over and elaborated on the other side of the Atlantic, often arriving at an unprecedented and unforeseeable awareness—at one time removed, expelled, ignored, and/or despised—of precisely their Italianness, whatever that meant. And *whatever* that meant, it could no longer be contested by those who had stayed behind. In fashioning his acute, steely, consequential work of cultural self-empowerment, Viscusi—not by chance—critically reinterprets his Roman origins, without any hint of chauvinistic neo-fascism, but also relies on the Dante-demiurge of *De vulgari eloquentia*, appropriately revered as a powerful keepsake "according to Grandpa."[77] This is no watery nostalgia, but rather rigorous cultural philology, for an award-winning American writer who writes and "lives" "English as a Dialect of Italian"[78]—an essay complemented by the one that follows: "*De vulgari eloquentia*: Ordinary Eloquence in Italian America."[79] The linguistic and the literary are compounded in a quasi-Vichian reading in which historiography is just the flip side of epic thinking: "Italian literature has so absorbed Dante that it employs allegory as part of its normal mode of operation. Italian American literature as well has adopted allegorical methods to its narratives of its own meanings and purposes."[80] It does not take long to perceive that Viscusi is at the same time a fiery literary critic and an essayist laying the ground for his own work. In fact, his sweeping Whitmanesque poem *Ellis Island*, finally published in 2013 after various partial anticipations, contains among its multitudes some epiphanies with a Dantean accent. It is an epic that has just been launched into the future, and therefore suggests a cautionary reading. I may be somewhat carried away in my interpretation, but, among the experiments in *terza rima*, of a total of 624 sonnets, there are six, arranged in three pairs (10.4 and its correspondent 43.9; 10.9 and its correspondent 43.4; 10.11 and 10.12).[81] Numerology itself is a supreme tool in Dante's hands (Tosches's Dante also muses on that, by the way), although I may well be mistaken in this particular case. And yet, when we read one of the most fascinating, Sonnet 10.12, one cannot but notice that almost every line contains and resonates with a term, an image, or a thought on which, centuries earlier, Dante had stamped his seal: "glow," "sand," "gaze," "pleasure," "dreams," "command," "fear," "sail," and others. As faded as it may look, the seal appears to be still there, at an oceanic distance, designated by interlocking rhymes:

10.12

> a glow may rise when tides fall very low
> and sunset slides across the glassy sand
> the glaze upon your gaze appears to grow
> until the sky has colored sea and land
>
> when pleasure has its purple in the mind
> your dreams assume the charter of command
> and all you see you see you have designed
> though things you meant to save you seemed to waste
>
> and used to lose the things you meant to find
> what most you feared you frequently have faced
> around the world you sailed your broken heart
>
> forgetting all you had by now displaced
> but subtle shifts of current change the chart
> the ocean is a restless work of art[82]

As I have tried to show, Dante has been from the very beginning an authoritative—possibly the most authoritative—imaginary companion in that most real of all journeys.

Part II

Transitional Modes of Italian American Letters

Chapter 4

All the Words That Are (Not) Fit to Print
Notes on the "Illiterature" of the Italian Emigration

It is a truism that we are defined by our culture (whatever, precisely, "our" means in this predicament) as much as a, or "our," culture needs us to represent it. And language is a fundamental, genetic component of that inextinguishable relationship. Using, and one might even say creating, the Italian language for the first time in recorded history, the "poet" Dante (creationist metaphors and etymologies abound here) gave a highly personalized account and interpretation of this knot. In his mind (an erstwhile Italian mind), it was, after all, a family matter, ultimately having to do with love, or rather with the fiery passion pulling a man and a woman together. Our physical existence is the effect of a union that is set up by spoken words, that is, by language. Language figures preeminently as a cause of our bodily being: "This vernacular of mine was what brought my parents together, for they conversed in it, just as it is fire that prepares the iron for the smith who makes the knife; and so it is evident that it has contributed to my generation, and so was one cause of my being."[1]

Such was the situation in the Middle Ages, at the outset (the Origins, as they are commonly referred to in Italian studies) of Italian literature. In turn, the origins of an Italian ethnic culture in the United States have been alluded to in somewhat similar terms by Salvatore Scibona in his intense and multivocal novel *The End* (2008). In this case, one could say that in the beginning was the end: an old Italian woman, who emigrated for love from the Roman countryside to Ohio in the 1890s, seals the epic with a stream of consciousness that reads like a letter to her beloved. Many things and thoughts pass through her mind, including the following: "Here is what we call a mother tongue. Think of the physical tongue of your mother. Think of your father's kisses on that tongue and how the kisses precede you into the world. / My dear, I have never heard spoken since a word in my mother's tongue. My darling, I forsook it for the promise of you."[2]

Tongues, kisses, spoken words cut through a mighty knife belonging to the extralinguistic dimension of mass migration. A tsunami sweeping away people's lives, transporting them elsewhere, metamorphosing their culture and inner being with the energy of a centrifugal force. Local histories, global economies, wars and persecutions, risks and dreams, poverty and opportunity, uprooting, distance, crushing toil, circadian cycle of hope and despair—and language, "our" language, caught in the midst, clenched to as if it were a raft, a complex system of cyberlogic daily dismembered and benumbed, striving to somehow reconfigure itself. From the rather abstract plane of linguistic research, scholars ask themselves such endlessly stimulating questions as "How Languages Are Born—or Made" and "How Languages Disappear."[3] But real life and real spoken words precede—at least from the point of view of personal histories—the cultural landscape rapidly refashioned by the Italian American communities on the other side of the ocean.[4]

As a historian of the literature of Italian immigrants to the United States and elsewhere, I have read and come across many thousands of pages of material published under the most different circumstances.[5] Collectively, they represent a gigantic written monument of Italian immigrant culture. Linguistically speaking, they entertain a dynamic relationship with the surrounding territory of the language spoken in a context of emigration. "When reading Italian American writers, we need to observe the ways in which traditions both American and Italian, both oral and literary, function in their narrative constructions."[6] It is undeniable that especially early immigrant autobiographies were imbued with the characteristics of orality, yet my position is somewhat more questioning. I don't necessarily see these two dimensions—literacy and orality—as communicating vessels; sometimes they operate likewise, but in my view they refer to distinct domains of individual and social experience. Moreover, the actual and obvious weight of the oral dimension can by and large be inferred from written sources, so that if and when we discuss orality, it is as if its improvisational dynamism has been muffled and long gone already. Nevertheless, its vitality gleams even through whatever written documents we have available. These are fragile sources, better conveyed by some form of sound recording and/or visual reproduction. Some among the shrewdest early observers of the Italian "colonies" worldwide (Amy A. Bernardy, Giuseppe Prezzolini, Renzo Nissim, etc.) concur in their keen attention to the fleeting traces of the pliable, unheard-of, innovative use of the venerable Italian language in the new contexts of immigration. The language of Dante combusts with the different materials of the many distinct Italian dialects and with the languages of arrival—be they English, but also Spanish and Portuguese (in Latin America), French (in and all around Paris and the French Midi), and later German. Bernardy even fantasized, as early as 1911, about the day when the future historian will have the full catalogue of the colonial written documents at his or her disposal—a *corpus inscriptionum* (much alike the one that scholars of ancient Rome religiously leaf through) made of street signs, posters, flyers, commercial ads, and the like.[7] Living in years that are ushering us into a predominantly digital reconfiguration of the public word, we might be better equipped to consider the relativity and fragility of the written word vis-à-vis the lived multiplicity, the ever-shifting adaptability, the idiosyncratic expressiveness of the actual tongues of the immigrants. In the instances where the spoken words had actually been transmitted through the medium of writing (often in private correspondences), they retained much of the spontaneous immediacy of their real accents, allowing to glimpse into a field of emotional, human forces at the same time raw and irreplaceable.

The study of emigration invites us, by definition, to cross the borders. European languages are often viewed as coextensive with national states, and therefore vehicles of national identity. Migratory dynamism complicates our conventional wisdom and challenges such a view. For instance, even before the proclamation of the Italian Kingdom in 1861, a consistent part of the Italian-speaking, rural population of neighboring Switzerland looked for a better living in other parts of Europe and in North America. The West Coast of the United States became a major pole of attraction for its Alpine laborers, whose future loomed problematic because of limited agricultural opportunities, insufficient cattle, the restrictions of too-closely-knit family networks, and the general hardship of a life spent in a forbidding mountainous environment.[8]

Sometimes even a simple alphabetical character can suffice. That's where *littera*-ture comes from, after all: letters and any written document, either mailed back to the motherland or just plainly and carefully composed in longhand. Two examples: Giuseppe Leoni's simple and elegant big painted sign on the wall of his stone house in the small village of Verscio, fewer than ten kilometers inland to the north of Lake Maggiore (figure 1), marked his proud homecoming. Giuseppe, a return immigrant, limited himself to writing down his full name in large capital letters, adding only his arrival point and the source of his acquired wealth. The painted sign on the entrance wall of his house is a strong proclamation of success, attached to its tangible result, and a self-evident declaration of an identity that is spatially and chronologically defined by his migratory experience. The phonetics highlights the Italianness of his American dream: despite the supposedly intense period spent in the remote West and the equally committed effort at establishing the geography of his *nostos*, he adopts with the utmost clarity the grapheme *gn* commonly used in Italian for the palatal sound /ɲ/: "Califorgna," that is something in between the reproduction of the actual sound and a writing that could be labeled as hypercorrect. That "gn" sign is a sort of minimal cultural and linguistic slip: it visualizes in a way acceptable to an Italian-speaking person the foreignness of a not familiar name.

Spoken-written words.—Let us start, then, by trying to briefly sketch how Italians used and/or "inscribed" their spoken language in the United States. The corpus of the immigrants' epistolary literature represents an

Figure 4.1. Mural inscription, Verscio, Switzerland.

enormous and inexhaustible body of evidence. Postcards sent in both directions can sometimes dramatize the relationship between the verbal and the iconic; the recto is as important as the verso; further layers of tenderness, self-vindication, and mischief can also be extracted if we consider the distance between the sender and the addressee, and the imbalance between their different levels of knowledge.[9]

Severo ***, a resident of the Lower East Side of Manhattan, mails a few lines to his friend Florinda Zatti in Civiasco, a village of North West Piedmont, on New Year's Eve, 1901. The verso of the mailing card bears a touching photo of Third Avenue at Cooper Square, with Cooper Union to the left and the Third Avenue El in full motion, speeding north and south (figures 2A and 2B). Underneath it, commerce and human traffic. Severo has marked a cross on the upper right of the Avenue, next to where he lives on East 11th Street. He refers to the "terza avenida," betraying a familiarity with Spanish: after all, a "Carlo" who is close to both correspondents has decided to "restare di nuovo a Barcelona" (= again, keep staying in Barcelona), despite the fact that "io avreba stato molto contento che avesse venutto dove in poco tempo potteva guadagnare molto danaro" (= approx. I wood had had very happy that he had cum where in a short time he cood earn much money). The orthography presents quite a few misspellings; there are also some mistakes (like in "avreba [i.e., "avrebbe"] stato," instead of "sarei stato") due to his recourse to a not too familiar mode; some forms reproduce "correctly" the dialectal pronunciation and grammar (anca te = "anche tu," i.e., you too; poi = "puoi," i.e., you can); above all, it is fascinating to observe that there is not a single punctuation mark (but proper names are duly signaled with capital letters, except for the above mentioned "terza avenida"), as if such a brief message was meant mostly in its continuous entirety, almost like the prolonging in ink of a fast and fact-laden street conversation, and thus as if it was not concerned with internal prose rhythms and logical hierarchies. Once it starts with the formulaic salutation, "Cara Florinda," it proceeds in an uninterrupted flow all the way to Severo's signature and address, followed by the only minuscule, but visible, period.[10]

Is Severo, "il tuo sempre amico" (your always friend), Florinda's fiancé? It is tempting to think he might have been, although if he was, some sign of a stronger commitment probably would have leaked out. As far as we know, we can only say that he is ensconced downtown,

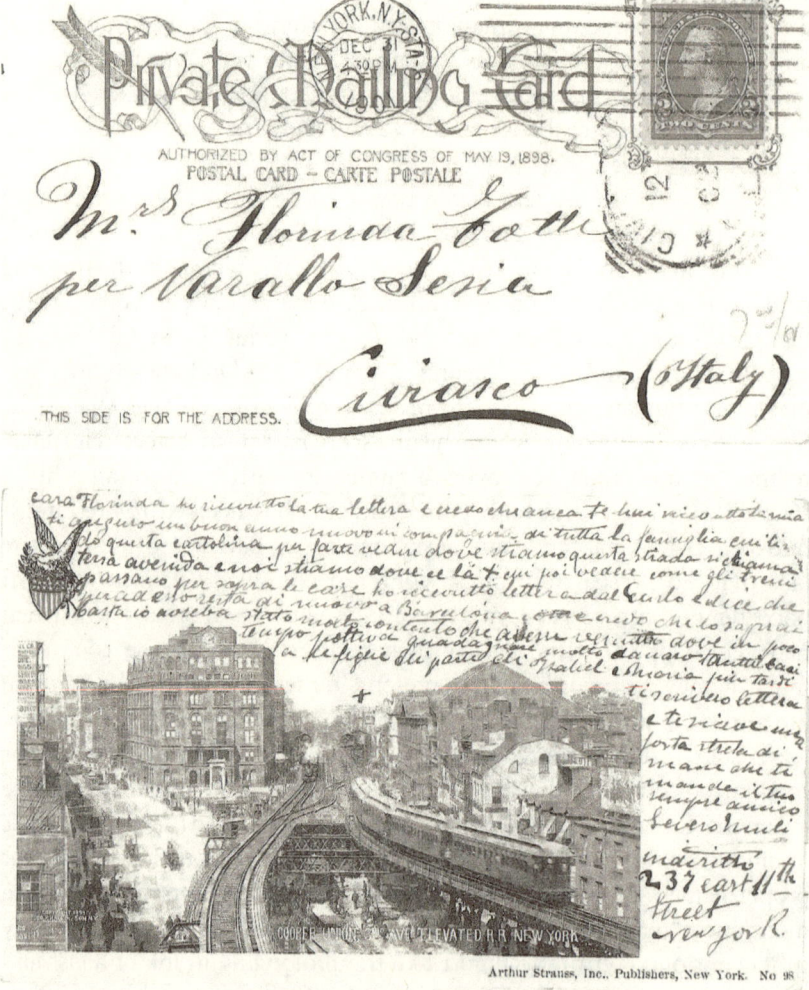

Figure 4.2a and 4.2b. Postcard from New York to Civiasco, Italy, 1901.

bewildered by modern urban bustle, and that he is very aware of the economic opportunities around him. He sends wishes on behalf of a couple of fellow countrymen, N*** and Maria; he keeps in touch and promises a letter in the future. He addresses his female friend with the intimate "you" form. He most probably left Italy (after a stint in Barcelona?) for economic reasons, leaving his relationship with Florinda at an uncertain standstill. She needs to be reassured, but he can't (or doesn't feel he can) seriously commit himself. His card has an energetic pull but manages to waddle in a typically masculine airiness. Here is an atom in the very middle of American capitalism at the beginning of the twentieth century. His shout back to his familiar hilltown[11] must have been read with a mixture of puzzlement and pride, hope and concern. What was this guy actually saying? What was going on in his mind? Are we (and she with us) witnessing the slow formation of a linguistic fault line?

The spoken word is subject to interpretation just like any other. Examples like the one above are not that dissimilar to the spirit of what scholars of Italian American history consider the master narrative of the Italian immigration to the United States, the autobiographical account of Rosa Cassettari,[12] where the contagious alertness of this Milanese peasant turned Chicagoan informer to the benefit of the local school of sociology in many instances lets us glimpse into a performative enactment of her bilingual identity. Rosa's words, no matter how filtered by the professorial editing of her interlocutor Marie Hall Ets, usually resort to Italian bits when at their most spontaneous or emotional. Whenever we hear her speaking Italian, albeit in a flash, we sense that we are entering a particularly charged territory of her memory. And, above all, it is the interplay, the negotiation between the two codes, that really counts: it's the movement back and forth. There is not *one* language on one side and *another* language on the other side; rather, there is a conscience that operates linguistically on a moving ground.

Back to California for another pair of epistolary messages, at the same time stripped to the bone and containing a fair degree of elusive, even deceiving imagination (figures 3A and 3B; figures 4A and 4B). The postcards containing them were part of a consistent batch, mostly from the 1920s and 1930s, addressed to various centers of Eastern Liguria. Ligurian communities are well documented from Buenos Aires (La Boca) to San Francisco. These two colored postcards—probably sent with other items—claim to have been mailed from California.

Someone is writing to an aunt back in Italy (figures 3A and 3B). That someone shows a nice handwriting—clear, slightly flowery, learned and practiced in years of school. There is a feminine touch to it. It's a simple elegance. A young boy is just learning to read and write at the Lincoln Grammar School, in Madera, near Fresno. And he is so good that he can even try his hand at some Italian: he grabs his pen and movingly writes in

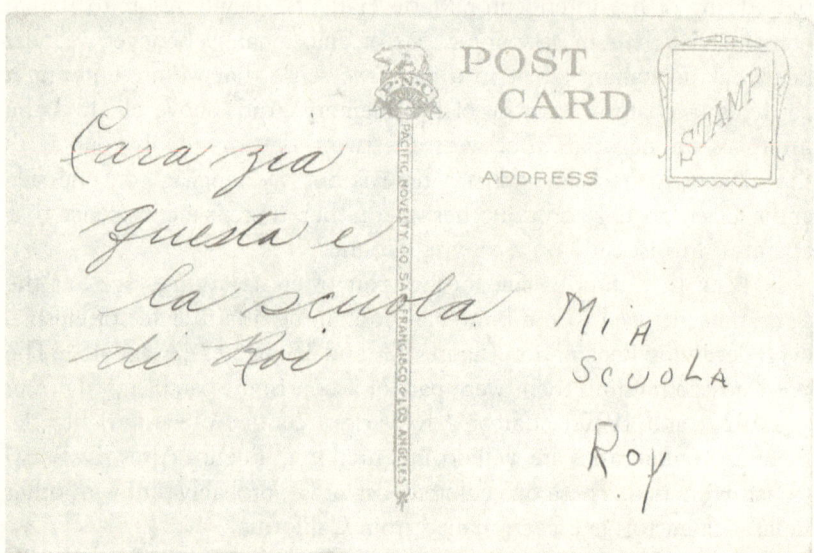

Figure 4.3a and 4.3b. Postcard [from Madera, California, to Italy, 1920s–1930s?].

block capitals the simplest, caption-like piece of news: "MIA SCUOLA," plus his name, "ROY." The elementary use of syntax seems to indicate that he is mentally translating from his native English or striving to write under dictation or both, because he omits the definite article, obligatory in Italian. His name is not an Italian name. Where does it come from? Maybe he is the son of a marriage between an (Italian) immigrant (woman) and an American (man). Maybe the son of two immigrants of different origins, or of two Italian immigrants opting for an Americanization. In any case, an American name was chosen. And the mother, who has such a clean handwriting style, Italianizes it, with a minimal but blatant misspelling: "ROI." Not only: interestingly enough, in neither card does she bother marking the accent on the third person singular of the verb *to be*. Her *is* is not once, but twice the simple vowel: "e" instead of "è." It is quite a bit disconcerting, considering the general flair of basic but good education and the respective positions in this small family drama.[13]

And there is even more if we turn to the second card (figures 4A and 4B). Here we find another quick description of the immigrant's daily condition. She says they have a garden and that it is covered with snow. But it really is a scam: the Ligurian auntie can probably be fooled quite easily. The deictic "questa" is deliberately misleading because it purports to associate the supposed garden and a pristine scenery from Yosemite National Park; here again is an elementary blunder, that is, the quite cacophonous lack of gender agreement between adjective and noun: "questa [. . .] giardino coperto." Such grammatical errors add up. They're *so* basic and seem so much in contrast with the surrounding nicety that one is tempted to guess that it is the mother who is actually American (hence her flawed Italian) and that the Italian aunt could in fact be related to her Italian immigrant husband. Except that it would still be striking that a mother misspelled the name of her child and an American showed a lack of familiarity with the letter *y*. Is it possible for a mother to be ignorant of her son's first name? It is not easy to come up with satisfactory answers. Roy is proud of his American *y* and his American school; we are induced to think that he speaks the (new) local language and recurs to Italian mainly within the family circle. Wherever we turn, we find ourselves captured inside this small drama of motherly love and deceit, of tenderness and pretentiousness, made bigger by the participation of Roy and made all the more plausible by the aunt's distance. Her expected ingenuity is not that different from our cluelessness.

"*Authorial*" *writing*.—Immigrant writers transport such a dynamic to a different, one could say a much higher, degree. I am referring here more

Figure 4.4a and 4.2b. Postcard [from Madera, California, to Italy, 1920s–1930s?].

in general to a conscious use of artistic expression. That is, writers, artists and intellectuals can be more effective to the degree that they tap into the shared needs and codes of their community. Their creativity can show up on a page, on a canvas, on a stage. The more perceptive observers of the time were quite aware of this:

> But the ill-clad Italians, with their odious pipes puffing out mal-odorous smoke, who crowd into the dramatic stable

yard and make the atmosphere within the old mule shed unbearable to all save themselves, do not go there for vulgar vaudeville or cheap variety. You would not expect it, and it is hard to believe when you see it, but these ignorant, untutored men, who labor with their hands all day at the worst work in New York, flock to the Star [the Star Theater at 101 Union Street, in South Brooklyn] to see the highest of Italian drama attainable here. They flock there every night and listen enthralled at the words, written centuries ago by the immortal Tasso, the Italian epic poet, who, together with his father, Bernardo Tasso, contributed some of the best of Italian epics. [. . .] The Star Theater is a dirty place to go: it is filthy and sickening to the sight and senses, and one sees men there who surely never wash. Yet with all its dinginess and dirt; its bad odors and mean looking men, it is worth a visit, and if one is of the people of the Italian quarter and doesn't object to the smoke and grime and understands the Italian language, it might be worth enough visits to cover at least a canto of "Jerusalem Delivered."[14]

This full reenactment of *Jerusalem Delivered*, performed with marionettes at the Star Theater of Brooklyn in 1899, is a bold statement. What was happening was the conscious appropriation and reuse of styles, languages, and stories passed down through the centuries along the Italian peninsula and elsewhere. To different degrees, all the major voices of the Italian American communities crafted their stories and poetry transporting the homegrown tradition to the new shores. Such a modus operandi was risky but inevitable and necessary to win approbation and consent; repetition had to go hand in hand with openings.

In the 1922 *Memories* by another Italian-speaking Swiss laborer, Dante Righetti, one finds the transcription of a poem by his older brother Pompeo, he too active on a farm in California. His *Canzone del mungivacche* (*The Milker's Song*), composed sometime around 1900, is an example of personal and creative popular poetry that probably never made it to the page and thus was confined to a small group of relatives and assorted acquaintances. It is overflowing both in its illustrative and its metaliterary and metalinguistic capacity. So much for the naiveté of popular culture. Here it is, in a tentative translation.

The Milker's Song

Nowadays in this new century of ours,
What with so much industry, and progress
There's no job, and no profession,
Which cannot boast its song.
Even the tailors, the hairdressers,
Shoeshiners and waiters,
While they're busy working,
The glories of their art are singing.
And yet none I know, the noble
Milker's art ever sang!

When the cock's morning song
Across the valleys sends its echoes
Swearing and yawning do I
Get out of my poor pallet.
And while stumbling, in the dark,
I put my trousers on,
My worn boots, my hat,
Grinding my teeth, I chew the refrain:
"In this world, no job is worse
Than the milker's job!"

I get onto my horse. The sky's freezing
My ears, nose, hands and face.
The North wind blows, the night's dark,
But hey! these are trifles.
Into the woods, down by the hills
I push ahead, behind the cows.
Sometime, as I'm passing under a branch,
New Iscariot, I get caught:
"A sadder life—then I shout—
Than a milker's just there isn't!"

When the one-legged stool I buckle,
It's like being a martyr for the Holy Faith;
Whether week-, or holidays,
Be there wind, rain or storm,
Let the thunder roar, and lightnings dart—

Never ever is there a truce for he who pulls the tits!
Like someone sentenced to jail,
Always he's on call, day and night.
In this world, no job is worse
Than the milker's job!

Can't comfort me, a sip
Of old *grappa*, of a good wine—
A bit of water with tea, or coffee,
I'm ready to drink, if there's any.
I am forced to repent,
With abstinence, without sin!
O well, cry I, in a few years' time
The bum's art will I practice.
But then, resigned, happy and serene
My muscly arms I wave.
And with the gurgling of the white humor
The milker's song I tune.

But all things considered, this craft of mine
It's not indeed to thrash away,
'Cause some cents shower down
In this crumpled purse of mine.
And when on my workers' hands
Some yellow gloves I put, on top of calluses,
With a nest-egg full of shining
I sport the air of a boss
Even bankers and grand lords
To the milker raise their hats.[15]

(In questo nuovo secol, d'adesso
Con tanta industria, tanto progresso
Non c'è mestiere, nè professione
Che ancor non abbia la sua canzone.
Persino i sarti, i parrucchieri,
I lustrascarpe ed i camerieri
Mentr'occupati son nel lavoro
Cantan le glorie dell'arte loro.
Ma niun ch'io sappia, cantò sinor
La nobil arte del mungitor!

Quando echeggia per le convalli
Il mattutino canto de' galli
Fra una bestemmia ed un sbadiglio
Scendo dal povero mio giaciglio
E mentre al buio, tentoni
Mi vò infilando i pantaloni
Gli stivalacci ed il cappello
E fra i denti, mastico il ritornello:
"A questo mondo, mestier peggior,
Non v'è di quello del mungitor!"

Monto a cavallo, il ciel m'agghiaccia
Orecchi, naso, mani e faccia.
Tira aquilone, la notte è oscura,
Eh! sono inezie.
Dentro a boscaglie, giù per le chine,
Mi spingo in traccia delle bovine.
Talvolta ad un ramo passando sotto
Resto impigliato, nuovo Iscariotto;
"Vita più triste, io grido allor
Non vè [sic] di quella del mungitor!"

Quando s'affibbia il monopede
È come un martire di Santa Fede;
Giorni feriali o dì di festa,
Vi sia vento, pioggia, tempesta
Rimbombi il tuono guizzin saette
Mai, non c'è tregua pel tiratette!
Qual condannato alla galera
È sempre in ballo, da mane a sera.
A questo mondo, mestier peggior
Non v'è di quello del mungitor!

Non mi conforta, un sol bicchierino,
Di grappa vecchia nè di buon vino,
Acqua di thè o di caffè
Son pronto di berne, quando ce n'è.
Sono costretto coll'astinenza
Senza peccato, far penitenza!
Ma pazienza, esclamo, fra qualche annaccio

Farò il mestier del Michelaccio,
Ma poi, rassegnato, lieto e sereno
Le nerborute braccia dimeno.
E col gorgoglio del bianco umor
Accordo il canto del mungitor.

Ma infin dei conti, quest'arte mia
Non è poi proprio da buttar via,
Poichè fà piovere qualche quattrino,
Nell'aggrinzato mio borsellino.
E quando copro con guanti gialli
Le mie manacce, piene di calli,
Con un gruzzolo di quel lucente
Assumo l'aria d'un prominente
Sino i banchieri ed i gran'signor
Fan da cappello al mungitor.)

Even from the translation one can recognize the solid structure of six stanzas made of ten lines each, organized in five pairs of rhyming couplets, with the exception of lines three and four of the third stanza. The fifth stanza presents an additional couplet. The rhymes get lost in my English version, as does the irregular succession of meters made of mostly nine, ten, or—classically, to an Italian ear—eleven syllables. Each final couplet in each stanza has a strong rhyme, stressed on the last syllable; in fact, stanzas two to four end with a refrain, and all stanzas, in the original, close on the thematic word—*milker* (*mungitor*).

Righetti deliberately mixes, sometimes juxtaposes, poetical, literary images—and words or elements that are far more realistic: *sbadìglio* (*yawn*) rhymes with *giacìglio* (*pallet*). But this happens at every level: with the use of phonetical details (*de'* = *of*), of poetical forms (*niun*; *vò* = *none*; *I go* [instead of more common "nessun," "vado"]), and of the omnipresent, lyrical use of syntactical inversion. The hard plight of the milker's life can be elegantly expressed through periphrases such as *bianco umor* (*white humor*, i.e., milk) or easy ellipses (*di quel lucente* = *full of shining*—"money" implied). Certain passages (stanza 2 above all) remind of famous episodes of Italian poetry (Parini, Foscolo)—and one could perhaps even point out, in stanza 4, a direct quotation of Leopardi's *dì di festa* (*holidays*, "festive days"). Such nods to the poetical tradition coexist with clear traces of a Catholic culture and education (*New Iscariot*; *a martyr for the Holy Faith*), but also of popular folklore (*il mestier del*

Michelaccio = *The bum's art*). Overall, it is a cleverly crafted composition of self-assertion, dedicated to an unjustly vilified manual job. It draws a parable of hard labor and well-deserved wealth, adopting the liberating stance of a first-person narrative. Thus, the literary veneer does not risk being misunderstood as the awkward residue of the old bucolic genre. This is clearly neither Virgil nor Robinson Jeffers nor an early Robert Frost. It's a worker's autobiographical song, grittily harmonious—in such a way that might not have been possible on the steep Alpine pastures. A very refined and at the same time almost expressionistic example of what Fred Gardaphé has poignantly called "illiterature."[16]

Reassure and dare is the emblem of an immigrant art that is at the same time popular, multilayered, and ephemeral. Pulp fiction lived side by side with the diabolically intense skits of the vaudeville multilingual theater of Eduardo Migliaccio, aka Farfariello. The romantic potboilers by Paolo Pallavicini, embellishing the life of a mostly imagined Italian middle class in California, were at some point in such demand as to appear in the columns of the colonial newspapers in San Francisco, and at the same time to be printed by major publishers back in Italy. Arturo Giovannitti, the first great bilingual Italian American poet, poignantly called *The Cage* (eloquent title) "a poem of rotting tradition and living men."[17] He had composed it on a Sunday, in 1912, unjustly detained in Salem Jail; and its first publisher had been *The Atlantic Monthly*—just like a decade later Pascal D'Angelo, author of *Son of Italy*, was to be read both in *The Nation* and in the New York–based nationalist monthly, with strong Fascist leanings, *Il Carroccio*.

Italian immigrant artists can count on a public attuned to their culture. This is not surprising, because they are well and truly part of it, being for the most part immigrants themselves, largely self-taught, and more often than not used to doling out a meager living with an assortment of jobs. Gigi Damiani, aka Simplicio, a leader of the hyperactive anarchist subterranean network, can flaunt his familiarity with the real common ground of most Italians at the time, the language of the opera, when he inserts in an otherwise virtuosic but rather inane parody of Fascist opportunism three joyous and sonorous lines like the following: "Addio banchetti, addio ragazze belle, / e facili guadagni, / 'clamori e canti di battaglie addio!' "[18] ("Farewell banquets, farewell fair girls, / and easy money, / 'farewell shouts and songs of battles!' "). That is, he is quoting from the Arrigo Boito's free adaptation of Shakespeare's *Othello*[19] for Verdi's opera, one of his late masterpieces. It is telling that Shakespeare is served to an immigrant public (striving to unshackle it from its torpid social and political conformism) through the mediation of Verdi and Boito. Can you be more aptly bicultural than this?

Such a playful and sophisticated intertextuality affects at different levels the creativity of immigrants' art and constitutes an indispensable prerequisite if we want to approach without naiveté the varied and adventurous world of the immigrants' publishing world, in both its commercial but also cultural components.

Publishing.—Arrival point. When you publish, you decide to go public. And in so doing and being, you forge a public. What was previously an intellectual operation that required recognition as a hypothesis now tests itself in front of a real audience. Your public is no more a double of the mind but a real paying entity, and, on occasion, it votes with its feet. A substantial level of mutual linguistic understanding is paramount, and so is a close relationship with the territory. If your public has a high degree of returns, both physical and imaginary (if daydreaming and being informed about the motherland remain a staple of everyday life), then you should also consider stretching as much as possible your activities, in a variety of ways, on both sides of the Atlantic.

More plainly, the appearance of an Italian American publishing world means that an Italian American public is born, that is, acquires the consciousness of being such. Italian Americans existed before Frugone & Balletto, before the Italian Book Company—Società Libraria Italiana, before New York's *Il Progresso Italo-Americano*, San Francisco's *La Voce del Popolo*, and stores like E. Rossi on Mulberry and Mott; but such ventures testify to a new raise of status and self-confidence. The same linguistic and expressive phenomena that we have tried to exemplify above now make it into print.[20]

There's a difference between being a native speaker (no matter how traumatized or energized by the encounter with a different culture, depending on a myriad of variables) or writer (using and/or abusing tradition)—and, on the other hand, making your appearance on the social stage, becoming a read item, metamorphosing into an author. Books do that. You may still be halfway between a god and a jester, but your voice doesn't just produce a narcissistic echo any longer: the publisher bets on its response and its recognizability. The name above the title is now, potentially, a beacon for a community.

The histories of the Italian American publishers (and there were, literally, hundreds of them up to the 1970s, scattered all around the United States) are replete with big and little facts, with acrimonious bickerings, with grand or petty failures (and, less often, successes), with opportunistic schemes and political feuds. Taken collectively, they can represent, in some way, a metaphor of the entire Italian immigrant culture. Italian publishing in the United States started, in the mid-nineteenth century, in the fiery climate of the Italian Risorgimento and soon expanded and adapted to the gigantic wave of immigrants from the peninsula (arriving in steerage class with other hundreds of thousands of Southern and Eastern Europeans). While always, by necessity, open to both worlds, from the 1920s they also increasingly showed signs of interaction with the surrounding linguistic landscape. Simply put, the English language takes over more and more newspaper columns as we get closer to the outbreak of World War II: not only do "English sections" begin appearing as a rule on the last page, but Italian American authors venture into bilingualism, book publishers print volumes in both languages, and typical "American" products, such as the comic strip, quickly eschew the short, goofy Italian translations. Newspapers like the *Corriere d'America* look American (see their elegant use of pictures and the overall layout of its pages) way before their Italian counterparts in the peninsula. And after WWII, a New York magazine like *Divagando* anticipates Mondadori's *Epoca* in imitating, at least superficially, the graphic design of *Life*.

On an individual level, the authors of the Italian American community show more and more their keen attention to a close rapport with their audience. "Publishing," that is, mingling with the public, is for them, literally speaking, an essential dimension of their popular activity. That is why, especially until WWII, these two dimensions (authorship and publishing) represent, in the Italian American world, almost two communicating vessels. They mirror and strengthen one another, following the trajectory of a generation that had come of age in the years of the Great Migration, between the end of the nineteenth century and WWI. So Tresca and Giovannitti rally the "ethnic" crowds of the unionized workers; Migliaccio/Farfariello cheers the undifferentiated spectators of the neighborhood theaters and, later, of local radio station listeners; and newspapers of all orientations show an unfailing devotion to the most diverse products of "colonial" literature (fiction, poetry, op-eds, even drama). And as it had rapidly formed with strong homogeneous characteristics, so that same culture will gradually but inevitably disperse from the 1950s on, to be replaced by new ways of being "public," and eventually turn its back on the Italian language.

Chapter 5

Questioning the Traditionalism of Italian American Literature

If you read the most recent entry for the word "Italian-American" in the *Oxford English Dictionary*[1] you would, I think, be impressed by the breadth of ground covered in about twenty lines. Ten are dedicated to the adjective and nine to the noun. The definition touches, no matter how sketchily, on the historical, social, ethnic, political, artistic, and—sure enough—criminal aspects of the Italian American experience. As a result, the entry offers a rather reliable mirror of the prevalent attitudes of bona fide Americans (with just a little help from their British friends) toward those newish citizens making their way from the Old World. This is also why I find on the whole that these mirror images are justified in reflecting stereotypes too, at many levels.[2]

It is worth focusing our attention on a curious and in a way ennobling instance of name-dropping. This is the case of the 1938 quotation culled from the Federal Writers' Project's historical volume *The Italians of New York*,[3] which refers to the "many popular novels on Italian-American themes" composed by a writer named Ettore Moffa. Now, this sounds as close as we can get to an authoritative recognition, provided by an institutional body like the OED, of, precisely, the popular culture produced by first-generation Italian Americans. Typically enough, this recognition is an oblique and basically inadvertent one, even more so because the real name of the writer, Moffa, conceals the telltale pen name, Italo Stanco, under which he had made his fortune in the *colonia* since the 1910s. A halfway homage, in other words, and a quotation that demands explanation. The OED entry poses a challenge: what do we—culturally, historically, politically—mean by "Italian American"? Is there, *really*, a link between turn-of-the-century italophone Italian Americans and contemporary Italian Americans? Between Italo Stanco, a movie like *Big Night* (also quoted), and Camille Paglia? Even if we can't think of one, I am convinced that if we really want to write a history of Italian America, we must try to establish a connection between such elements.

In other words, has there ever been a common ground, and/or a common narrative, in the cultural productions by Italian Americans since the last decades of the nineteenth century? Was there one *then*, and is there one, *now*? And a more insidious question—is there a tried-and-true culture that we can distinctly label as "Italian American"? Or, how did the individuals that we brashly lump together as emigrants elaborate their forced dialogue between two very different societies? What was symbolically and mentally their way of coping?

The Italians who came to the United States certainly had a very strong sense of tradition, even of a literary tradition. They knew it and cherished it. Their average low level of literacy did not prevent them, in the least, from using, reusing, and reproducing even the classics. A very conscious rewriting of Tasso, for instance, is to be found at the beginning of the third *canto* of Antonio Andreoni's *Passaggio*:

1

O musa, tu che di caduchi allori
ne circondi la fronte in Elicona,
e solo tu che in fra i beati cori
hai di stelle immortali aurea corona,
tu spira al petto mio felici ardori,
tu rischiara il mio canto e tu perdona
se il canto che io ne vo per cominciare
come tu brami non verrò a formare.

2

Sentiste, amici, nel canto passato
la mia campagna fatta nell'estate;
ma or quella dell'inverno ho incominciato:
bisogna che anche questa voi ascoltate,
e sentirete quello che ho incontrato

> se bene attenti tutti state;
> e il tutto vi dirò come poss'io
> e con l'aiuto dell'eterno Iddio.⁴

Andreoni's "passage" adapts the venerable mold of the chivalric poem to evoke his years of harsh toil on the railway tracks of the Midwest. His emigration to the United States (from the Lucca region, in Northern Tuscany) dated from the early 1900s; the poem would then be composed around thirty years later, after his return to Italy, and it testifies the persistent popular fortune of the narrative octaves, ready to be used—lock, stock, and barrel—for the epic tale of migration. It is true that Andreoni is an example of return immigrant, but even if we consider the rich, indeed impressive, body of literature produced by first-generation Italian Americans, the diversity of themes, plots, and diction shows only one side of the story. The other reveals a conscious appropriation and reuse of styles and languages passed down through the centuries along the Italian peninsula and elsewhere.⁵ For instance, the "popular novels" mentioned by the OED were a conflation of central European motives exploited and brought to success by Eugène Sue and Conan Doyle, to name only a few. All this points to an obvious familiarity with the staples of Italian and indeed European cultural debate and its main aesthetic results, both high and low. Novels, autobiographies, novellas, variations on the *commedia dell'arte*, and poetry were composed according to the golden rules of the most exquisite and even trite rhythms. When we try to recollect the pieces of the personae of those Italian Americans, there is little doubt that they were moving along the lines of a quite definite tradition—and that they were making use of it not only referentially, objectively, but also *ritualistically*. One could just think of how opera—from Verdi to Puccini's "Western" *La Fanciulla del West*—was eagerly absorbed almost verbatim inside and outside the *colonie*, representing a common ground between popular and sophisticated forms of art, indeed between America and Italy. Singing the *arie* by heart was, within the arch-Italian code of familistic religion, a proof of command, on the part of the *tenori-patres familias*, which demanded admiration and respect. It is not by accident that Caruso became an icon a century ago; his regular contribution of drawings in *La Follia di New York* was further proof that he functioned in a variety of ways as the mouthpiece of the community.

To be sure, a tradition is not, or should not be, by itself, synonymous with conservation. On the other hand, it would be hard to disagree that, by employing tradition, Italian Americans showed off their obedience to one of the chief tenets of *italianità*. Their strategy could be interpreted as a message thrown back to the peninsula, almost like the response of the underdog. "You don't consider us as Italians anymore because we left, and betrayed national unity? Well, we are going to show you that we know where we came from, that we respect the rules of the past and follow the teachings of the masters."

In turn, as the use of traditional mores (in the arts but not only there) defined and strengthened their sense of identity, first-generation Italian Americans were almost unwittingly transforming such identitarian practices into a form of defensive ideology. At the same moment that tradition was stiffening into rigid traditionalism (fully blown, just to give an example, in the poetic vocabulary, which is often preposterously antiquated, or in the elegant and consolatory historiographies of Howard Marraro and especially of Giovanni Schiavo),[6] the nurturing of identity was being developed while the actual cultural differences with mainstream America appeared to be slowly on the wane. The Italian community in search of identity had to face the threat of affluent society and its culture of suburbia.

Today, one should ask if, in our current, largely fragmented, and hypervirtual scenario, it is still possible to find a common thread uniting Italian American forms of the imaginary—now that identities, once a staple of community-building, have fallen prey to policy making and political correctness. There is no longer the need to turn a mirror toward a nonexistent motherland; the shared experience corresponds now, as for so many other strata or components of American society, to a constantly moving process that is capable of drastic and radical change, and oblivion is a very real possibility. And yet it is precisely in recent years that we have come to question the existence of an Italian American canon. This opens up other considerations and demands a different approach.

A poet, an artist, doesn't ask for permission to his or her public. He needs, first of all, to be true to himself: not to the reader, not to the critic; not to the existing, but invisible, structures of society. His life, and his urge to fulfill it by re-creating it, come first. The question about the existence or not of an emerging canon in Italian American literature suggests that we also ask ourselves why we have come to think in "canonical" terms, and what such a canon (if it exists at all) tells us about our position as scholars.

It is rather obvious, in my view, that a discourse on the canon (whatever its content) camouflages a desire to be accepted by the received wisdom of a majority. That has its perks. If you act according to a prevailing mindset, you are recognized, you are ushered in, and given a candy. You have behaved like a good boy, all the more because you have looked up to something or someone. A canon—or, rather, a canonical way of thinking—is the sweet harmony oozing out of the blissful spheres of Order. A good altar boy knows that: you sing in tune with someone else and acquiesce in the soothing sound of the organ. Call it the neo-Tomism of literary studies.

Take the mechanism a little further. Convince yourself. Not only that. Convince yourself of being able to see a canon, to teach it, and pass it on. Now you are on the way to turning into the chrysalis of an obedient scholar. You have learned to read the Books in their correct order. You will also be able to type in the correct order your credit card numbers and book a flight and a room for the next conference where a job is being searched. The parthenogenesis of higher learning requires an accurate tuning of your intellectual disposition.

The growing need for a canonical discourse in Italian American studies is then, more or less, an act of self-defense: be it Catholic, Machiavellian, or democratic in the American way. Inventing a tradition is a sign of distinction. Chanting the mantra in class, a proof of your reliability.

There is nothing wrong with an unquenchable thirst for acceptance. In a way, it reduplicates the assimilating rituals of the defamed melting pot. And one should point out, to its credit, that the canonical discourse requires a fair share of abstraction and inventiveness. It is binding in many ways, and it has the thin elegance of an airy formation, mesmerizing if you keep staring at it.

Fashioning a philology of immigrant writing means trying to ground the analysis of an epical, gigantic, historical phenomenon on its extant written traces: written words—*litterae*—or the staple of littera-ture. The histories of the "unsung heroes" (Rudolph Vecoli) largely belonging to the first immigrant generation allow us to get a much better picture of the birth of a nation, Italy. Being better acquainted with its past doesn't help us figure out the present, let alone the future, but can at least disabuse us and warn us against ossifying categories. It can help us being more open to possibilities.

The "fathers" of that literature—however wild and irreproducible—still release some great beams of light. Italian American literature was born with a Tuscan storyteller, a dime-novelist, the pulp-fiction writer Bernardino Ciambelli: his stories are crazy, but the thrust of his prose is contagious, and the maps of his dramas are far from naive; rather they are socially and ideologically revealing. Arturo Giovannitti was a giant soul, a poet divided, a cleft-poet of the proletariat: reading aloud his *Samnite Cradle Song*, in its Italian version, in the icy town-hall of his abandoned birthplace in Molise, at the end of the first international conference dedicated to him in 2005, was both a curse and a blessing, sending waves of recognition: such a poet could not be denied. Add Farfariello and his skits: in their marvelous studies, Haller and Bertellini have shown the semiotical and cultural depth that permeates this mask's diabolical comic art.[7] Migliaccio's scathing self-irony remains unsurpassed, linguistically and conceptually. And there are other, more occasional, points of reference: the rough-and-tumble fight against the goodfellas of NYPD cop Fiaschetti (from the Roman countryside, or *Terra di Lavoro*), armed with the weapons of irony: he defused and ridiculed Sopranos and sopranology before the fact—enough for a seat at the Pantheon; and Carlo Tresca spitting against capitalism and military intervention, a radical enemy of prevailing, eternal sanctimony.

No gods and no masters. And yet, in some unacknowledged, tense way, around those and other voices the first communities of immigrants from Italy managed to express their divisions and contradictions, their unremitting vitality. That literature functioned as a public forum. Its authors were the mouthpiece of a people. We have largely lost this collective, almost physical dimension.

I cannot see all of this as a lesson, or as anything "empowering": but those writers used their language to the brim, they filled their time and helped their readers to experience a respite—which, I think, was the most of harmony anyone could wrest under the circumstances. Unwitting canon-makers for their cushioned great-grandchildren, delivering messages difficult to fully grasp, written as they were in another language. And here is an obvious but necessary rediscovery: the roots of the canon grow obliquely and point toward the stratified and complex Italian tradition. The canon works canonically, and its origins are also in some way self-reflective. So much for the illiteracy of the first generation. No people is ever without a culture.

Chapter 6

Kings of Harlem

Garibaldi Lapolla and the "Grand" Gennaro

—What's his name?

—Garibaldi.

—What kind of name is that?

—Bernard Malamud, *The Assistant*

The intention of this essay is simply to pay well-deserved tribute to an Italian American writer of the early years, Garibaldi Mario Lapolla (b. 1888 in Rapolla, province of Potenza, d. 1954 in New York City),[1] author of three novels published in rapid succession at the beginning of the 1930s. The last of these, *The Grand Gennaro*, should unquestionably be considered one of the cornerstones of Italian emigration literature and one of the most convincing and absorbing narratives devoted to that epochal mass exodus. A work that is wide-ranging in scope, the culmination of unmistakable artistic maturity, *The Grand Gennaro* (published in 1935 by New York's Vanguard Press, publisher of Lapolla's two previous books) presents a powerful portrayal not only of the title's proletarian hero figure, but more generally of the entire local, domestic world of Southern Italy in its complex, troubled encounter with American modernity. The novel, which chronologically stands out as one of the earliest noteworthy endeavors in English originating within the Italian diaspora, may undoubtedly give the impression of looking backward in terms of narrative structure and writing style, relying on a realism certainly not unusual in American literature, much less in those works that at the beginning of the century had to all intents and purposes launched an "ethnic" literature (one is reminded of an Abraham Cahan).[2]

Although it did not pass unnoticed in the months immediately following its publication, *The Grand Gennaro* soon fell into oblivion.[3] As mentioned in one of the rare pieces written about Lapolla, the novel of the thirties had left behind that style of depicting the emigrant experience through broad ghetto frescoes: after the pomp and splendor of the turn of the century, the immigrant ghetto fiction, with its linearity, its mixture of minute description of surroundings and lurid characterization, in short its Balzac-like approach, had been marginalized by a literary milieu that had, on the one hand, veered toward experimentation and, on the other, justified its attention to social issues through increasingly distinct political positions.[4]

The fully drawn character of Calabrian Gennaro "the Grand," a tragic protagonist, a typical "manly" figure like no other at the center of an epic tale of ascent and sudden downfall, could to a certain extent be considered anachronistic. But it would be risky trying to explain at all costs such a heavy, unanimous silence. It is necessary to point it out, though, because in fact in the aftermath of his greatest book, Lapolla disappeared altogether from the literary scene, despite continuing his not insignificant publishing activities in the two specialized areas of textbooks and cookbooks.[5] The scope of Lapolla's reception is still more surprising when observed from the viewpoint of Italian and Italian American scholars: in Italy, unless I have missed something, the East Harlem novelist was mentioned only three times throughout the entire twentieth century. Nothing more, until the appearance in 2002 of the translation in Italian of an unpublished story, "Millie's Rebellion," which I retrieved from the Lapolla's papers in Philadelphia, and which became part of a small, precious volume of miscellaneous works edited by Francesco Durante.[6]

The ways in which this hidden presence nevertheless manifested itself are instructive. In 1934, in Turin's newspaper *Gazzetta del Popolo*, Giuseppe Prezzolini traced with absolute timeliness a very early panorama of Italian American prose, emphasizing among other things its composite nature and strong autobiographic foundation, well represented by the names of schoolteacher Angelo Patri and Ellis Island commissioner Edward Corsi. For narrative prose the names cited were those of Louis Forgione,

one of the most notable Italian American novelists writing in English in the twenties, Bernardino Ciambelli, journalist and author of endless appendices, and, of greater prominence, Lapolla, at this stage still the author of only two books: *The Fire in the Flesh* (1931) and *Miss Rollins in Love* (1932). Even within the limits of such recognition, the choice of these names is sufficient to attest to Prezzolini's critical intelligence, were there a need to do so. That such clarity could later be distorted by a broader albeit prejudiced and temperamental vision of an Italian culture outside its "natural" borders is a discussion that for now would lead us far afield from *The Grand Gennaro*—up to a certain point, however, because Lapolla's name reemerges in the *Trapiantati* (1963), the book that is the sum of Prezzolini's Italian American biased criticism, this time linked to his masterpiece and earning only a dismissive mention.[7]

Also associated with Prezzolini's name is the groundbreaking project brought to completion by his student Olga Peragallo (and, following her death, by her mother, Anita), who in the forties compiled the first alphabetical index of Italian American writers worthy of the name (in the overwhelming majority of cases, they were authors writing in the English language). Among the fifty-nine entries listed in this study, commendably positivistic for its exclusive attention to the facts, appears that of Garibaldi Lapolla, along with those of Mayor La Guardia and Jerre Mangione (rediscovered in the eighties by Sciascia, no less), names that at first glance might seem more prominent. And in the wake of Peragallo, with the rebirth of serious Italian American scholarship beginning in the seventies, others also at least indicated the existence of this work that meanwhile had been rendered more visible by the reprinting of *Fire in the Flesh* and *The Grand Gennaro* in 1975. Nevertheless, the few critical references made by outsiders, no matter how prestigious their names, do not seem to have encouraged a more long-lasting, contextualized interest. There are two notable exceptions: the pages devoted to Lapolla's best novel in 1985 by Robert Orsi, within his broad, magisterial ethnography of Italian Harlem, and several interpretive attempts by Robert Viscusi, who with remarkable critical intelligence has emphasized the mythical vividness of the Gennaro character. Among Italians, however, Alberto Traldi was essentially the only one to have shown any real interest, in 1976. But Traldi tends to observe emigration literature through the lens of contemporary journalistic criticism: the result is to diminish Lapolla's art, though he acknowledges the substance of the narrative and attentively traces its coordinates.[8] In short, Lapolla remained unheard-of, or nearly so, until the above-mentioned translation in Italian of a minor short story. And this while Italy, at least, experienced the rediscovery of John Fante from the end of the eighties and a rebirth of interest with respect to the history and culture of emigration.

But here we are back to where we started from, or almost. So let's adopt the confident, though short-lived, judgment of the early Prezzolini, who spoke of the "power and . . . keenness of the writer," and for a moment enter into Lapolla's fascinating creative workroom, conserved thanks to his wife's bequest to the Balch Institute. Not a location chosen by chance, if we consider the fact that the rather numerous documents of an Italian American colleague of Lapolla, Leonard Covello—educator and sociologist, a central figure of Italian Harlem—are also found in Philadelphia. Along with Covello, La Guardia, Corsi, and others, Lapolla was among the first descendants of Italian immigrants to emerge from the ghetto in every sense and earn higher education (in his case, a university degree) by attending courses at nearby Columbia University. Moreover, the themes of education, of acculturation in an American sense, and of the conquest of the citadel of New York knowledge return punctually in his three novels and constitute one of the pivotal points of the second, *Miss Rollins in Love*. Similarly, the main incidents of all three novels develop roughly in the thirty-year period ranging from the large migratory wave from Southern Italy in the 1890s to the crisis at the end of the twenties and the closing of American borders to lower-class peasants of Eastern and Mediterranean Europe, focusing on themes in the areas of family, work, and education. Just so, their author, having landed in New York as an infant in 1890, almost the same year as the sons of Gennaro Accuci, earns his university degrees very early, in 1910–1912, and becomes part of the city's life by making a career in the school world.

My intention is not, however, to trace a mechanical parallelism between the author's life and his works. It is true, though, that the profile of a true writer emerges from his unpublished papers. Lapolla, for instance, pursued the art of verse with perseverance and style and left a considerable number of poetic endeavors that varied widely in meter and subject, often of such an expressive confidence as to make the output not at all casual. Such seriousness of creative intent is confirmed by the existence of seven short stories set for the most part in Little Italy, though far from a purely descriptive approach. Rather, in their concision, they are rich in dramatic moments and in views at odds with the current mentality (to summarize briefly: a brilliant clerical career suddenly ended by an inexplicable fatal attraction between a head clerk and an immature, disturbing young woman; the failure of a proxy wedding between two immigrants that actually results in infanticide caused by lack of attention and indifference; and so on).

The existence of another unpublished novel (or perhaps two) is particularly striking: namely *Jerry*, a book that unfolds through the interaction of fifty or so characters duly listed in an introductory outline.⁹ At the center of attention, as elsewhere in this narrative, are the youths from the East River ghetto: and among the most successful pages are those whose setting is not far off from that of *Call It Sleep* (the same river, a few miles further south; the same young men, having come there from the Jewish ghetto downtown; the same time frame, even with regard to composition and publication). In a couple of pages attached to the typewritten manuscripts, Lapolla proposes at least three different endings for a story that would bring his readers back to already familiar places and situations: a school for orphans and maladjusted youths (the Juvenile Protective Asylum) and a relationship that can be perceived as almost incestuous between a young man and his benefactress.¹⁰

The world that we encounter in Lapolla's books and unpublished works is in large part one that is only apparently limited in its horizons and finds its justification, its etiology, in having abandoned the narrow, rural Italy of the South: an Italy dedicated to sheep farming, its perspectives brutally narrowed by a subsistence economy and suffocated by an atavistic respect for the customs and hierarchies that condition the relations between the sexes as well as social relations in general. That which results is the foundation, the κτίσις of the overseas colony, portrayed not only with skill and vividness, but, what's more important, with a very lucid, rigorous, layman's sense of its achievements and losses, its thousands of variations, contradictions and subtleties, its setbacks, its reversals (both geographic, as all the statistics on Italian emigration confirm, as well as emotional and irrational), and its unexpected turns, all portrayed on a canvas broad enough to take individual destinies into account. Lapolla leaves a powerful depiction of his own exodus, if you will, because he has the courage and feeling to go into personal details without hesitation: from the personal and the specific, he allows social issues to emerge.¹¹

From an outsider's standpoint, this is quite evident in his first two works, which at the time—as mentioned earlier—earned him the applause of a difficult Italian literary critic like Prezzolini, with definite, anti-rhetorical tastes: no small honor indeed. Looking back, thanks to a perspective made possible by the success of *The Grand Gennaro* and the consciousness of a not undistinguished production attested to by his unpublished writings, the first two works can only be considered as stages in his progressive literary development. Within the course taken by Lapolla, they perform the function of extensive sketches placed one on top of the other, in which the author lays out the figures and backgrounds to which he will give much greater prominence later on. Not that *The Fire in the Flesh* and *Miss Rollins in Love* are valuable solely as attempts or indefinite approximations: if anything, one notices a certain rigidity in them stemming from a desire to portray their respective themes with irrefutable clarity. They are novels of ideas, starting with their titles that define and summarize, which for that matter is a characteristic they have in common with the linchpin of this narrative triad.

A triad, rather than a cycle: one of the more obvious constants in Lapolla's narrative is the almost identical repetition of novelistic measure, both in general results (the three novels essentially have the same number of pages), as well as in the articulation of an internal rhythm, dictated by brief numbered paragraphs. Here too, however, *The Grand Gennaro* appears more ambitious in its sturdy, three-part division (*Gennaro*; *Rosaria*; *Carmela*) that suggests the existence of a more solid vaulting over the tumult of events; by contrast, *The Fire in the Flesh* and *Miss Rollins in Love* had been split up into approximately twenty brief chapters, to the detriment of an overall epic effect.

But the point is that reading through the first two novels, it is not at all difficult to discover in them compositional elements of the third, with respect to situations, ideologies (both the author's and those of the depicted surroundings), and character profiles. Everything in these novels proceeds from and continues to revolve continually around well-defined nuclei: strong, hot-blooded women attract both their male counterparts (that is, those who, though in difficulty, untiringly pursue their mission consistent with "making it in America," accumulating money and property or even merely maintaining their own distinct social status) as well as a heterogeneous group of different characters. Among the latter are those who, on the one hand, delude themselves that they are able to preserve a shaky, petit-bourgeois identity in the New World, often though not necessarily arriving at a painful undoing (they are figures of landlords and military men, priests and artists) and, on the other, those who, experiencing for themselves the transition between first and second generations, seek new paths to success in America, counting above all on education and their own creativity. This makes for interesting openings toward worlds that are parallel to those of manual labor and domestic intimacy: primarily a university and scholastic environment (a choice also motivated by Lapolla's biography). And alongside institutionalized instruction, the world of artistic apprenticeship: sculpture, painting, puppet theater, and female fashion. All of this, as may be easily understood, is the result of Lapolla's intent to pay scrupulous attention to the facts of the surrounding reality.

Beneath the large group of main characters then lies a bustling understory with specific features that essentially guarantees both continuity and a relatively peaceful day-to-day life, as well as a more respectable induction into "affluent" American society. Here we have an entire series of minor but representative characters: from the more traditional figures of priests, landlords or "boarders," and numerous "aunts" busy feeding everyone and straightening up the rooms; to the more "modern" figures of teachers, instructors of some specific art, exceedingly American do-gooders, or even directors of prison institutions.

The events narrated by Lapolla in a sweeping, expansive way are "small," meticulously individual incidents that rise to the level of typical case histories, representative in turn of a larger History, the dramatic culmination of a long period of social marginality and deprivation. For this reason, the two main agents of mediation between the individual and society can only be the home and family. Both are shown to be central to the development of the plots. Though they signify continuity of affections and preservation of customs, transplanted to such a different space and time, they also constitute a shell possibly open to renewal. To reconstitute the family and make a new home across the ocean in itself meant having the ability to accumulate capital. And therefore, in perspective, the ability to invest: to invest in the building of new houses (the centrality of the construction trade in Italian American society), to open the home to other individuals or families, and to expand therefore one's own contacts within the domestic walls themselves. All of this modified the internal arrangement of the traditional family even before young people became the bearers of new values, and herein lies the silent, poignant crisis of the wives-mothers who arrived from the Old World, often recalled after years of forced separation. Catarina in *The Fire in the Flesh*, Donna Angela in *Miss Rollins in Love*, Gennaro's wife Rosaria, and many others: they are women who suffer from maladjustment, between angry outbursts and hypochondriacal mute spells, or who fade away in sorrow. Sometimes, as in Rosaria's case, by turning their back on America and choosing a return that is literally equivalent to death (her daughter Elena will repeat the mother's fate by becoming a nun in a Calabrian convent).

A destroyed Verghian lair, half a century away and a continent apart. But it is the dizzying energy of change that occupies the forefront, more than bitterness (though it too is present): from beginning to end the objective remains focused on the home or family ties, in order to recount the changes that, in the span of a generation, will give birth to a new type of humanity. As for what will follow, Lapolla will not want to, or will not think he is able to recount it with as much meaningfulness. This is not the southern Italy of *The Leopard* but one in which, at long last, nothing remains as it was, beyond "cues" of a sentimental, folkloristic nature, and in which everything changes for real. But is it really and simply America that causes everything to change?

One of the "scandals" of Lapolla, perhaps one of the reasons why he was so little understood and read, is the very fact that he did not take refuge in a comfortable antimodernist, anti-American abhorrence in the name of popular, Catholic solidarity or individualistic vitalism, as was not infrequent in authors close to him. Passages in which characters dialectically discuss the advantages and disadvantages, the miseries and splendors, respectively, of their hometowns and a 'Merica discovered through sacrifice are not rare; but the dialectic has no resolution, even if it is understood that to turn one's back on America, and go back to the Apennines, undermines the very reason for the story at its foundations and jeopardizes not only the characters' destiny, but this literature itself. Lapolla is too human and too intelligent to suggest a historical-civil Manicheism. What makes the world go around, what brings about changes and transports families from one side of an ocean to another, is first and foremost the desire to put an end to poverty experienced as an unfathomable fate, and the equally insuppressible driving force of the senses. The first a masculine principle, the second feminine, though they are shared at times with different intensity by characters of both sexes: it is clear that these are the characters who really matter, the ones at the center of our attention and that of their author. Money and sex, to simplify further. These are the realities that, from one generation to another, from Calabria or Basilicata to Manhattan, challenge social conventions: especially that of marriage arranged by the family, forever bound to failure. On American soil, on the other hand, it was possible to start over again from zero, that is, very pragmatically without moral or material debts, as well as to marry by first of all heeding one's own intimate feelings.

The world of the past, that is, the Old World, reacts by expressing an atavistic violence, counteracting the initiative for success with the blackmail and abuses of an old Mafia-type gangsterism (as in *The Fire in the Flesh*, where the main character refuses to pay the protection money and sees her yards devastated by fire) and vindicating the role of honor and the use of force, knives included, against free unions based on passion. While pertaining to that world, Gennaro, though illiterate, is able to detach himself from it with full awareness: his novel originates as the result of a decision, formed in nearly total secrecy, to leave that world, explicitly rejecting the appeal of banditry. These and other ancestral traditions also function as the deus ex machina of a novelistic device that is ideologically courageous but not always immune to a certain predictability.

American modernity is not the deity solely responsible for this civil metamorphosis—a metamorphosis, among other things, that although tragic, appears inevitable to Lapolla and yet "progressive." America brings to fulfillment aspirations already present at the time of departure: this can be seen in those characters of a more solid mettle at least, while the fate of those transplanted against their will (wives and children) turns out to be much more unforeseeable.

From its incipit, *The Grand Gennaro* exhibits a narrative style that is fully mature and confident in its methods: this is evident in the rigorous unilaterality of the adopted viewpoint, in the splendid straightforwardness of the author's voice, in the virtuoso orchestration of events and individual characters, and in the consistent choice of an "ethnic" inflection of the language (that of the narrator, with its circumlocutions and syntactically heavy English, as well as that of those of his characters who express themselves in broken English).[12] The energy deriving from the protagonist, who oversees everything and towards whom everything converges, quickly penetrates the bloodstream of the story and sustains the narration. *The Grand Gennaro* is one of those novels that immediately wins over the reader, like a world apart that opens up, complete in itself and historically and geographically rooted (all the more so in its twofold nature, Italian and American); nearly organic, I would say, in its intense sensory charge that goes hand in hand with a psychological virtuosity applied to the lower, uncultured strata of the population. Cohesion and consistency are among the first words that come to mind, not only to try to explain the coarse fascination of this work, but also to do justice to what was not a slapdash, accidental outcome, but the result of protracted, masterly effort.

In *The Grand Gennaro*, then, Lapolla includes with a precise sense of rhythm the characters, situations and broad themes that we have already talked about: all revolving around the larger than life figure of the cafone Gennaro Accuci, a Calabrian peasant from Capomonte, who emigrated from Reggio at age thirty-two in the early 1880s, and whose experiences we follow step by step through the two economic recessions of the early 1890s and 1907, the arrival of his wife and three children at Ellis Island around 1890, and the Spanish-American war of 1898 (which claimed the life of his oldest son in Cuba). Gennaro makes it in America and reaps success without letting himself be held back by scruples. He does so with pride, intelligence, and an awareness of his limits, knowing how to hammer and push fortune: he deals in rags and discarded metal scraps that he collects, crushes, and resells to Jewish wholesalers downtown; over the course of the years he perfects his trade, mechanizes the warehouse and makes it more efficient, and becomes a modest boss who has to answer to the union and meet the requirements of his employees. He starts out from zero in a rented room shared with other people, then with a violent ploy he steals control of operations from a fellow countryman, Rocco. But the injustice is only the initial spurt that allows him to complete the leap toward true entrepreneurship. Soon Gennaro invests in the real estate market, acquiring a small house that will become the center of romantic and family intrigues. Meanwhile he never stops adapting to technological progress: in the early days, he carries his merchandise, covering on foot the long miles that separate him from downtown; later he uses horse-drawn wagons (the notorious, deafening elevated train of New York is reserved instead for individual transportation); by the end of the story, he supplies the company with motorized vans and electrical machinery and allows himself the luxury of riding in a car. He is always looking ahead, works constantly, and never allows himself a break; what's more, even in his private life (though this is a distinction superimposed by us because of a need to analyze) he sweeps over everything and tries to do and undo with his all-absorbing "masculine" energy. Success is not assured here, however; on the contrary. The four women who share his journey in different ways prove this to be so with splendid humanity: Nuora, the northern Italian landlady, will follow her husband, Bartolomeo, in his return to the homeland.[13] Dora Levin, the beautiful daughter of the Jewish merchant, boldly confesses her relations with younger men to Gennaro. His wife, Rosaria, by coming to join him, only makes plain the unbridgeable distance between them, and after ten years of painful estrangement, shattered by her failure and by her firstborn's death, finds the strength to turn her back on Gennaro and America and goes to live out her life in her native Calabria. And finally Carmela, who although she loves Gennaro dearly, is unable to give him a son, and indeed cannot resist a passion—though borne in silence, without betraying him—for his second born Emilio (a young, typical second-generation figure). At different times, in different ways, and for different reasons, all these women go away and leave Gennaro: nothing is stable, everything is mutable. But while this can be an incentive to progress in one's work and in society, it signifies loss, abandonment, and solitude in the sphere of affections. Not surprisingly, at a certain point Gennaro will turn to frequenting prostitutes with blind determination.

And the issue is not just one of erotic ties and domestic affections; interpersonal relations catalyzed by the two avatars of home and family reveal themselves to be equally problematic. Gennaro in fact forms a strong connection with the destinies of two other Southern Italian families, the Dauri and the Monterano families: father, mother, and numerous offspring engage Lapolla in additional efforts at characterization and plot (successful but undoubtedly laborious) and immobilize the protagonist in a generous but ultimately impossible inspection job. Beneficence succeeds if one's objectives are "traditional" and inanimate as it were: and here we have Gennaro allocating time and money in the construction of a church dedicated to the patron saint of his hometown, Saint Elena. But inside the walls of the little house in Harlem, within which surge the lives of three families and dozens of individuals, an odd accumulation of affections and interests, of modern and new, can only create imbalance, changes, and not a few tragedies (the Monterano couple will die, and the Dauri will decide to leave the city). So that one of the possible keys for reading the novel is one that underscores the generational and intrafamily contrasts between fathers and sons (Gennaro and Domenico, Gennaro and Emilio) or between mothers and daughters (Sofia and Carmela), with foreseeable supersensory interpretations of a psychological and social nature.

In any case, Gennaro is "grand" and a "man" even in his mistakes and defeats, such as the illusion of being able to maintain traditions in a totally changed context, or of being able to direct his passions toward assured, programmable goals:

> But he, he, the grand Gennaro, he had become a somebody [. . .]. And now that he had as his own such an accumulation that would put to shame the holdings of the baron of his Calabrian countryside, he, Gennaro Accuci, by his own right, was not Gennaro Accuci who had the farm at the foot of the hillslope but just plainly Gennaro Accuci, a man. (98)

Name and personal pronoun predominate even rhetorically in presentations like this one, forming a whole with the iteration of his successes. Further on, the strong centrality of the character will slowly begin to crumble: but even then his identity is never put into question. And clearly he is "grand" even in his death, which is both brutal and mechanical, bloody and silent, deserved but unexpected: after twenty years, his old coworker Rocco takes his revenge for the abuse he suffered at the start of their career by harpooning him in the neck with one of the new hooks in operation at the modernized warehouse. Gennaro, like a head of cattle, dies on the spot, spilling his blood on the bales of rags on which his wealth was founded.

Such a tragic end with all of its suggestiveness marks the end of a sweeping life span that, to be convincing, had to attract other destinies and other stories during its course, committing to and being open to new prospects. This simplicity within complexity is one of the keys of the novel and the element that, even at a first reading, makes it "grand" like its protagonist, all the more so after those that preceded it.

What's more, Lapolla builds up the coherence of the overall vision little by little, resorting to a series of effective stylistic constants. It is not only Gennaro's presence and the fascination radiating from his story that is convincing, but also the expressive maturity that has been attained. The fresco is painted with much greater assurance and fluidity with respect to the first two novels because the narrator has learned how to stand aside when required, letting the words of his characters act on their own and making objects speak. In this way the social portrayal gains immediacy and displays the elegance of a guided improvisation, one that is planned rather than extemporaneous. At the same time, thanks to a convincing use of language, it is as persuasive as something fully formed, like an instantaneous event we see happening before our eyes.

Of great effect, for example, is the precision with which Lapolla disconnects one scene from another, especially when dealing with irreversible, epochal changes in his characters' lives. These can certainly be foreseen and imagined by the reader, but they are not presented and prepared for in the narration, which tends to reveal them suddenly, in all their harshness. Gennaro knows that his wife, Rosaria, and their three children are finally arriving after a wait of nearly ten years; he arranges their journey and talks about it with his friends. Meanwhile, nothing is said to us about what is happening in Calabria. Then, all of a sudden: "Rosaria had landed. Gennaro first saw her through a grilled fence in the new immigrant station at Ellis Island" (94). A remark that is all the more powerful in that Lapolla deliberately buries it in the middle of a long paragraph, without giving it any importance. The arrival of Don Tomaso Dauri and his family later on is treated similarly: this time the personal and economic reasons governing their departure are being discussed when, all at once, in the New World, come the impact of reality and the unexpected end of illusions: "In New York he discovered very soon that the several thousand *scuti* he had realized on the sale of his possessions were not going to last any length of time" (123). More generally speaking, it is the appearance and vicissitudes of the Monterano and Dauri families within Gennaro's peripeteia that have a disconcertingly fulminating effect: as though the nature of that narrow microcommunity of three nuclei in the neighborhood was marked by a violent, unintentional destiny.

This is a world in which the materiality of existence leaps into the very forefront. Often, relationships between individuals are rendered explicit through the mediation of objects, and it may even be said that Lapolla's narrative style, late-Balzachian as it is, is all the more so to the extent that it relies on objective correlatives. The entire memorable scene of the end of Gennaro's relationship with the young Dora Levin revolves around mumbled words and a few things—a hat, a hair pin, a defective gas lamp—that slow down the verbal exchange and add a note of tension (67–68). Even more significant are the two gold earrings—handed down to Gennaro across generations—, that from beginning to end intensely express attachment to the roots, the character's pride, and—after a violent, unforeseen act forces him to part with them—his awareness of the distance he has come and of the metamorphosis and Americanization that have taken place. The earrings will reemerge in explicit form as the talisman-charm that Carmela gives to the last of the Accuci, Emilio.

Things but also, even more so, words. In *The Grand Gennaro*, much occurs in the degree to which something is said, articulated, during the frequent dialogues. Verbal exchanges that, given the social standing of the characters, are for the most part quick and essential, almost stichometrical. Dialogues abound, but real, full-fledged conversations are scarce. The tensions between the characters are all "told," expressed; but for the most part the task of reconstructing the psychological dynamics underlying them is left to the reader. Notable also is the presence (of no minor importance) of a middle zone between external, third-person narration and copious recourse to direct discourse. We might call it the "Verghian zone" of *The Grand Gennaro*, in which the discourse slips naturally from the narrator's consciousness to the thoughts and feelings of the characters, leading to fragments of interior monologue and unrestrained indirect discourse. So it is in the following passage, where the focus is on Rosaria's state of mind as she proposes to take her firstborn Domenico's side against her husband and Carmela's mother (Domenico is Carmela's rapist and as such forced to "make amends" by marriage):

> His mother had gone shopping deliberately. She had for the first time summoned enough courage to offer some kind of opposition to the dictates of her husband. She had spoken against the enforced marriage. Let women keep their daughters home. It was, after all, the mother's fault. Oh, Domenico had really done no harm. Certainly, it might have been a vicious attack. He had intended all the harm there could be, of course, of course. They were both young, however, babies both. To pummel the lad, beat him into a whimpering pitiful animal crying out for mercy—what for? (149)

Thanks to stratagems of this type, even characters on the brink of literacy, or unquestionably below the threshold, receive full dignity precisely because their intentions have a way of being expressed without always having to resort to the intermediation of the omniscient narrator. Moreover, they are figures who are themselves fully conscious of what they are doing, as well as being aware of their historical condition. The events of time shape their journey and change its features: the failure of the Bank of Naples, the memories of Garibaldi (the hero of the Two Worlds, not our author) wounded in Calabria on the mountains of the Aspromonte, the echoes of the defeat of Adua, the invasion of Cuba.

The Grand Gennaro, perhaps like no other work emerging from the culture of the Great Migration, rests solidly on two feet, from the

Mediterranean to the Atlantic. That was not the case with the serial novels produced in Italian in previous years; nor would it occur later on, not even with the finer names (Fante, di Donato, Mangione, Pagano, D'Agostino) whose Italian origins were taken for granted, a feature of their own diversity within a culture that was now different, in which one had in fact been included. For Lapolla, and for the "grand" Gennaro, on the other hand, Italy (Calabria, the "paese") is close by. First of all because it represents the goal of returning for many of his characters; not only that, but all of those who broke away from it know precisely what it is. They know it with passion: they suffer their origin; all of their actions are a direct, explicit consequence of it. Theirs is a nation that was newly created at the end of the nineteenth century, that has behind it a culture and deeply rooted customs: pizza, yes, arranged marriages, and devotion to patron saints; but also Dante, Leopardi, Manzoni, Giusti, remembered and read deliberately, not as mere ennobling labels. Italy here is not a nostalgic background, an empty cause for pride (and if it is, it is challenged and ridiculed as such): rather it is an ever present foundation, even at a distance.[14] From it, certainly, come contradictions and suffering: but also the potential for tragedy and heroism, resulting from a fractured identity that we observe in its making and unmaking, in its continual, day-to-day renegotiation. Profound reasons—artistic, historical, and cultural—that seem to compel a serious reading of this masterpiece and the discovery of its author.

Translated by Anne Milano Appel

Chapter 7

I Am(s)

Strategies of Acceptance and Denial

When in Rome, do as the Romans do. One usually tends to overlook the contribution that the Eternal City has played in the Great Migration, but still it wasn't by chance that Cesare Pascarella wrote *La scoperta de l'America* (1894) in *romanesco*, providing a model of sorts for future narratives of migration in the Roman dialect. Italians scattered *almost* everywhere from every part of the peninsula. I propose then to listen more closely to the Roman-American poetical voice of Alfredo Borgianini (Roma 1882–Trenton, New Jersey, 1955):

I

Roma mia bella che me stai lontano
tremila mija e più tra terra e mare,
tu m'aricordi tante cose care
da scrivece un romanzo sano sano.

Benché sto qui ner suolo Americano,
pure in certi momenti, embe', me pare
d'esse tornato tra le cose rare
che me fanno avanta' d'esse Romano.

Me pare da rivive in que l'ambiente
in do' so nato, in dove c'ho vissuto
venticinque anni spenzieratamente.

> Me pare da rivive in allegria
> tra li compagni che ce so cresciuto,
> me pare da riavecce Mamma mia. . .
>
> [. . .]
>
> ### IV
>
> E adesso ar dunque: Pe' 'na fantasia
> partii de botto senza amici intorno,
> e l'anni da quer giorno me passorno
> come passa quaggiù la ferrovia.
>
> Più er tempo corre e più la nostargia
> m'avvince, e penzo che si quarche giorno
> eguale ar Figliol Prodico ritorno,
> Roma mia bella nun me caccia' via.
>
> Perdoname si credi c'ho mancato
> co' l'imbarcamme e anna' tanto lontano,
> perdoname, nun dimme rinnegato.
>
> Nun me schifa', nun me guarda' in cagnesco.
> Vabbe' so' cittadino Americano,
> ma er core, er core è sempre Romanesco. . .[1]

I know all too well that poetry like this sounds and is amateurish and predictable. But it is not my intention to hail Borgianini as if he could soar to the unreachable heights of the giant Belli. What this self-taught poet deserves, though, is first of all that we evaluate his Muse by examining the cultural and historical context in which he lived and worked. Such a task is beyond the scope of the present contribution;[2] I just point out that, despite the mawkishness of these lines, in his volume *Sonetti e Poesie Romanesche* (1948) Borgianini shows a rather considerable variety of tones and flaunts a certain metrical and linguistic awareness. To pull back the curtain on this Roman vernacular intro, we should also bear in mind that the Roman question takes on very different colors in the memoirs of two other immigrants, the NYPD lieutenant Mike Fiaschetti

(*You Gotta Be Rough*, 1930), and the leftist activist Carl Marzani (*The Education of a Reluctant Radical*, 5 vols., 1992–2002).[3] Both Fiaschetti and Marzani wrote in English (although Fiaschetti's crime book also came out in a shorter Italian version, serialized in the popular daily *Corriere d'America*)—a fact that addresses the more substantial aspect of a general, and, I believe, more relevant, point: immigrant narratives comply with the dominant paradigms of their current country, which are reflected in their choice of language; immigrant literature reflects the country's cultural—and more specifically literary—history. And this is still mirrored in the way institutions of higher learning think and operate.

Not that I deny the role played by nations in shaping the curricula in the humanities. But the fact is that the culture lived by immigrants, the culture that the immigrant subjects produce and use in their interactions and in their more or less ethnic environments, and thus transmit to the following generations, this culture is, almost by nature, multifaceted, dialectic, and by necessity oriented toward a constant, grinding negotiation between its various components. This, in a nutshell, is why it is so very difficult for immigrants to fit in, and why it is problematic—to say the least—for scholars of immigrant cultures and history to find a home in university departments (and modes of thought) that remain defined, and confined, by strict national parameters.

As a scholar interested in Italian culture and with a specific competence in its literary—and more broadly, written—dimension, I have long focused on its exogenous aspects for the simple reason that I have always found them to be indicative of intellectual creativity, and more morally engaging than the usual suspects to be found in any required list of reading in your customary class of Letteratura italiana. This is not to say that immigrant cultures are per se innovative and not repetitious; but if as an Italian citizen I find it is my civic duty to make sense of the gigantic demographic fluxes affecting the peninsula, as an *italianista* by profession I do believe that first and foremost I have to open up the canon (to paraphrase Leslie Fiedler), if for no other reason than to reap new riches and explore new dimensions of a country notoriously keen on the dialogue between power and the arts.

The fact that Ariosto locates on the island of Lampedusa ("Lipadusa. / Una isoletta è questa, che dal mare / medesmo che li cinge, è circonfusa," OF 40, 55) one of the crucial duels of his poem—that of Orlando and two other Christian paladins against three Saracen Kings—is obviously a topos that today resonates well beyond the merely rhetorical level. Even if we limit ourselves to the pillars of the Western canon, it is always a question of approaching it without denying our current point of view.

On the other hand, even a cursory exploration of the intellectual and literary debate of the teeming Italian American "colony" of the early decades almost invariably produces discoveries that shed new light on the Italian cultural landscape. Take for instance a rare publication like *Ultra*, a 1934 collection of miscellaneous writings celebrating the fifteenth anniversary of Local 89 of the International Ladies' Garment Workers' Union (ILGWU). Alongside poems by Arturo Giovannitti, we read excerpts from Walt Whitman and Ignazio Silone, Petr Kropotkin and Arturo Labriola, but also contributions that for a number of ideological, cultural, and, yes, aesthetic reasons, one would be hard-pressed to come across in the Italian publications of the same time: a short but eloquent letter of congratulations, in parallel German and Italian, from Alfred Einstein; a special insert of exquisite full-page woodcuts showing New York (*La Città Incredibile*, by A. Scarpellini); and an article by Franz Boas debunking the *Mito ariano*.[4]

Or take into consideration the elaborate and creative ways in which, from Da Ponte to the Dante Club and *La Follia di New York*, and later to Gerard Malanga, Lawrence Ferlinghetti, Joseph Tusiani, John Ciardi, Nick Tosches, and Robert Viscusi, Italians and Italian Americans have contributed to the canonization of Dante in the United States.[5] Not only—and predictably—there is a discernible "Dantesque" element in Italian immigrant culture, but—on a narrower scale, which nonetheless reflects a heavy-handed symbolic predicament—Dante, and the inescapable classics, remain compulsory entries in the bibliography of any Italian literary scholar aspiring to a minimal degree of scientific and economic recognition.

This issue brings us to another aspect of the larger question, namely, the role of power structures in shaping cultural blueprints, and the hypostasis of the criterion of aesthetic excellence, whatever we mean by that. To put it bluntly—as an Italian American colleague once told me off the record: "early Italian American literature sucks." But at least he said it jokingly (although, from a certain point of view, I certainly see his point); Italian colleagues are so prejudiced that they dismiss such material out of hand. Even the innovative three-volume *Atlante della letteratura italiana* edited by Sergio Luzzatto and Gabriele Pedullà totally omits the culture of Italian emigration, with the customary exception of certain well-known political (usually anti-Fascist) exiles.⁶ On this topic, it would be too easy and self-indulgent to open up a can of anecdotes. We rightly bemoan the sorry state of Italian American studies in Italy, and at the same time the reluctance to deal with figures and cultural products of the "new" Italy shaped by recent waves of immigration to the peninsula. But—despite groundbreaking works such as the anthology edited by Luigi Bonaffini and Joseph Perricone⁷—the silence surrounding other destinations of the Italian diaspora is still puzzling, to say the least. In the case, for instance, of the contagiously funny, multilingual, and thought-provoking *Les Ritals*, by François Cavanna (arguably *the* masterpiece of the Italo-French experience),⁸ we should say that the refusal of *italianisti* and even more *francesisti* to accept it into their canon is actually *pénible*. Note that Cavanna, a second-generation Parisian artist of Italian descent and a legendary satirical illustrator and author, had been one of the founders of *Charlie Hebdo*: but academic disparagement is stronger than even curiosity. We have had mouthfuls of *Je suis Charlie* in the recent tragic past, but they don't seem to have reached certain ivory towers.

In fact, such analyses must neither be exclusively limited to the American (as in Italian American) field, nor, indeed, only to forms of written culture. If what I stated above wishes to be seriously taken into consideration, we ought to value the Italian immigrant and multigenerational epic as a worldwide phenomenon. Yet, while this is obvious historically, it is not recognized as an area worthy of study either by Italian Departments of History or even in the far larger field of the humanities.

One need only to peek out of the academic world to see that the topic of migration is arguably *the* political question of our time, and as such it is being passionately addressed in other sectors, starting with the publishing arena. The scholarly output is growing by the year, and it is particularly impressive outside Italy.⁹ And yet, despite the rising curve of essays and conferences, the institutional offering—especially in Italy—of courses dealing with the cultural aspects of migration remains notably scant.

Such timidity—to be nice—is clearly at odds with the overall media discourse and indeed with individual everyday life, where, at every turn, the tragedies, trials, and questions posed by migration have become the staple of public debate and concern. It is the organic dichotomy of a deeply traditional culture that oxymoronically both talks and keeps silent, depending on the venue. We do not need to resort to Bourdieu to propose that, in such lofty realms, considerations of prestige act as vicarious forms of class distinctions. It is the pervasive Italian *perbenismo*, applied to the field of academic hierarchies. Or, as a great scholar of Renaissance art once memorably asked me, "Do you *really* think this is interesting?" The end result is that today, in Italian universities, an *italianista* can well teach, from time to time, the literature of the Italian Great Migration, although nominally there is not any recognition of the dignity of the field per se.

This is why I am convinced that it is crucial, at this point, to try to win basic institutional recognition. By that I mean official teaching positions, linked to adequate hierarchical roles within the professorial roster. A direct consequence of the current situation is the impossibility of attracting students to this line of research. The functioning of academic life, in an Old World setting like the Italian, works along the lines of an elaborate metaphoric system that alludes to the reproductive mores of early modern family life. In effect, with both their field of research and their academic rigor disparaged, scholars of immigrant culture are treated as being underage and academically impotent. Ironically, this impotence is the equivalent, within our rather abstract profession, of the dire challenges faced at every step along the way by immigrants. And again, as an *italianista* I see myself as having the privilege and the responsibility of activating a critical reflection on a huge phenomenon that has affected, as we know, well over twenty million Italians in the aftermath of the so-called Unification, and that, conversely, after the fall of the Berlin Wall and the arrival in Bari of the Albanian cargo ship Vlora (August 1991)—to name just a couple of major instances—has changed the peninsula into a destination for migrants. If we are unable to perceive the nemesis in such a history and are not troubled by the difficulty of coming to terms with it, then I am afraid that all our venerable classical education has proved quite futile.

Not that this comes as a surprise. The prerequisite of philology is the attribution of value to a certain text. This often fixates scholarly research at the "genetic" phase. A respectable Italian philologist spends years trying to determine the date of composition of Dante's *Monarchia*, relying on the erudite reconstructions of the German polymath Karl Witte; but the fact that Hitler, seeking to inject cultural excellence into the Rome-Berlin Axis, brought Karl Witte's translation of the *Divine Comedy* as a gift to il Duce during his visit to Rome in 1938 is usually treated as a footnote. While Francesco Durante, Simone Cinotto, Stefano Luconi, Giorgio Bertellini, Marcella Bencivenni, Matteo Pretelli, Michele Presutto, a few others, and I have spent years going over the very rich columns of the Italian American press, a systematic exploration of the similar world of the ethnic, multilingual press in Italy today is still to come. We sorely need to work as a collective, making room for the collaboration of colleagues well-versed in the languages and cultures of the current migrations. And in Italy we need to push the agenda for the opening of our universities to the second generations and refugees. Look around in Italian college classrooms after high school and even after junior high, and you see an overwhelming majority of Italian white kids, which is dramatically out of sync with the demographics of Italy today.

My invitation is thus to start considering the importance of an institutionally sanctioned field of migration studies (and, to be more precise, of *Studi sull'emigrazione*), articulated if you will, at least provisionally, in two interrelated classes that I would tentatively name *Società e storia dell'emigrazione* and *Cultura e lingua dell'emigrazione*. I would also invite our institutions to consider the epistemological opportunity offered by the study of what I propose to call a *changing culture* predicament, which should be read at the same time both as a transitive action (changing one's culture) and a dynamic metamorphosis (a culture in the process of changing). A study of migrations must stress the sociohistorical and material component as well as the fact that we are dealing with a broader human condition of change and adaptability and the resulting necessity of pluralizing one's life in many different ways. If Donna Gabaccia has rightly bemoaned the "tyranny of the national," Peter Carravetta is now articulating these questions with what he calls a "post-identitarian" approach.[10] This is part of the intellectual framework I find currently relevant to this topic.

We cannot hide the fact that being accepted goes beyond the personal matter of having one's individual career recognized as valid. Administering the traditional cultural landscape (*l'amministrazione dell'esistente*) is only a step away—if I can indulge in the creative malapropism dear to Roman popular poetry—from *la ministrazione dell'ex-sistente*, a warming up of old soups, and at the same time a governmental imposition (a typically Italian "ministerial" *ukase*) of models long gone (the typical obsession of the Italian teacher for sticking to the phantasmatic *programma ministeriale*).

On the contrary, admitting migration and migrants in contemporary culture contradicts the *favola bella* of Italy's cultural-centrism. Culture, in Italian society, deftly functions as an equalizer, or as an enzyme, that makes the social imbalances acceptable. Culture (in the more common Italian meaning of "high," humanistic, "classical" code) provides an alibi for accepting the class divisions in our midst; it works as an element of self-assurance, a mirror that reflects the fairest of them all, *Italia felix*. It must be noted that most Italian American intellectuals of the early days concurred. In other words, migrations carry with them, and activate, a far-flung critique of received wisdom. The time has come to finally act on Abdelmalek Sayad's call to "institutionalize an autonomous discourse on emigration."[11] When the measure is full, the times are ripe. It is not by chance that a full critical recognition of the current, wide spectrum of italophone writing within the peninsula (Lecomte) occurs while an authoritative scholar of Italian studies in North America frames his analysis of Italian literature in the United States rightly speaking of "biculturalismo negato" (Tamburri).[12]

I would be tempted to paraphrase another great Roman writer, Ennio Flaiano, and say that *la situazione è grave ma non è seria*. Unfortunately, I am not sure that this could apply to our current predicament. I want to stress, though, that narratives of migration are not limited to mere tragedy. Because we are dealing with a life-changing experience, expressions take the most varied forms. Think only of the amazing richness of such diverse works as Robert Orsi's *The Madonna of 115th Street*, the collected essays on "Italian Folk," Sam Rodia's Watts Towers, and the needlework of Italian American women (the latter three edited respectively by Joseph Sciorra, Luisa Del Giudice, and again Sciorra and Edvige Giunta), and finally Sciorra's *Built with Faith*.[13]

But, closing the circle, let us go back to a short Italian American story that originates, again, with the Roman immigrant poet Alfredo Borgianini. This comes from a private letter sent jointly to Francesco Durante and me by one of his grandsons, Stephen Borgianini.

> I do want to pass on one funny story my Aunt Mable passed on to me. My grandfather was teaching a citizenship class in Trenton to recent Italian immigrants. He was teaching his students about the United States presidential line of succession and asked "If the president dies, who gets the job?" [. . .] after some discussion the answer given was "Gruerio's" the local funeral home in Trenton that did all the Italian funerals.[14]

This could be an easy start for exploring the trope of Italian American funerals, something that has already produced its share of bibliographies and filmographies. What I particularly treasure here, and find a source of provisional respite, is the black humor—an element that institutions are never properly equipped with. But irony is easier to accept if you are an insider. The problem is that the subjects and objects of migrations are all still treated as outsiders, and frankly, *that* has never been very funny.

Chapter 8

Reading Robert Viscusi

Breaking New Ground:
Robert Viscusi's *Buried Caesars*

As we grow older and we keep indulging in the wasteful practices of an intellectual life of any kind, one of the most treasured events is the unexpected finding of a vision that is as wide-ranging, articulate, all-encompassing, as it is expressed with a distinctly *human*, personal, lived-in accent: an interpretation of experience (of any kind of experience: existential, scientific, sociopolitical, artistic. . .) that ends up, more or less systematically, more or less intentionally, sweeping away the musty dust choking our eyes and tongues, and inviting us to a new way of using our dormant powers of investigation. I admit that *Buried Caesars* has meant for me one of those dangerous encounters. I have been in silent dialogue with this book ever since I read it voraciously and passionately when it first came out in 2006.[1] As a consequence primarily of Viscusi's book, I came to better understand some of the actual troubles, personal and scholarly, that had made my own explorations in Italian Americana an exhilarating chance to stumble into stolid misconceptions.

I am going to take some digressions. The first one could be titled *Taxonomy and taxidermy: a short note on the reception of Italian American studies*. Reality—you would think—is some big, visible entity. That doesn't apply very easily with things Italian American, at least with the way they are validated and thought of as worthy of some critical scrutiny. Consider those who study that reality, in a variety of forms, and are naturally eager to communicate it, not just to the sacrificial lambs—the students—but to those same environments that shaped our education a few decades ago. One would have thought, for instance, that the relative deluge of serious reexamination of the Italian colonial past would have sparked not only a persistent attention to what's new now in Italy in terms of cultural forms produced by the new immigrants (whose original languages, mores, and ideologies are by and large ignored), but at least some effort in trying to look back to what Italian immigrants had disseminated and how they had lived and survived abroad from the 1880s to the 1970s. Sure, there has been in recent years, especially at the publishing level, an impressive output of scholarly works: but they have remained outside the precincts, so to speak—and the sanctum of *italianità* has not been soiled—still cuddled and nurtured as it is, wary of any influence coming from the outside.

When forced to interpret an immigrant culture, "official" highbrow formulations proceed with a series of assumptions. The culture of the immigrants—according to the prevailing mindset—rooted in the life of the dispossessed, lower classes has reflected those popular roots; that is, its literature has been characterized by certain peculiar qualities: thematically, it couldn't but be folkloric, anthropologically demonstrative; genetically, it derived from the loose, improvisational, creative raw energies of the spoken languages and dialects (the redeeming emphasis on anything "oral"); a low level of authorship—almost as if it were the product of an anonymous, largely collective body; ideologically antagonistic. A close scrutiny of the forms of a distinct culture such as that of the Italians in North America points out, instead, that thematically it is more concerned with the clash with modernity than with its attempts to preserve ancient lores; that it relishes in its artsy qualities at any level and is as much oral as it is strongly formalized, written down, refined, and rerefined with an even tedious craftmanship; that it demands authorship (mostly by males) as proof of its dignity, seriousness, and accountability; that it is not overtly concerned with antagonism—but, rather, that it uses parody and self-parody to an extremely sophisticated degree, and in a way that is conducive to a large recognition; thus, it aims at success, and in doing so, no matter how parodistically, it expresses a distinct way of conformism. These could be some of the reasons why highbrows have found by and large problematic confronting their preconceptions (even their leftist, liberal preconceptions) with the results of a dispassionate research. I feel that the radicalism of some Italian American studies ends up at a similar dead end by adopting minoritarian events to a large, preconceived scheme of abstract righteousness. Highbrows deny legitimacy to Italian American culture by strength of taxonomy; do-gooders cover it up with straw to make it what they want it to be: taxidermy.

If we move now to an entirely Italian perspective, even there *Buried Caesars* really breaks new ground, and one would wish it could be appreciated and discussed enough to be considered a watershed in the much-needed effort of considering Italy as a moving cultural landscape, continuously breathing in a constant interplay with extra-peninsular languages, peoples, situations. By stressing how much deeply Italian, and even Roman, Italian American cultural artifacts are, Viscusi clearly implies, also, that Italian culture itself dramatically expanded, thus negating any rigid notion of confinement. The reciprocal opening up of the canons would not only be a scientific duty, but also the consequence of a new understanding of the notion of *tradition*. Such an epochal rethinking of Italian cultural dynamics could hardly be undervalued. *How to betray tradition without being caught* is, more or less, the gist of digression no. 2. Italian literary circles, conservative and progressive alike, usually cover up the unconscious sense of guilt that locks them like wild animals in a cage—gone crazy at the spectacle of their radical ineffectiveness and uselessness in society—by fashioning themselves as the ultimate dispensers of any good old Italian quality. Which also explains why, more and more in the last decades, Italian literature and literary criticism have decayed and belittled themselves so much. Tradition is treated as the stronghold, and the last bulwark, of a quixotic battle. There's even something sweet and romantic about this, were it not an alibi for the constant reproduction of a self-congratulatory circle of brahmins out of touch with reality. One of the ironies of this situation is that we have failed to appreciate precisely how organically tradition functioned across all levels of society, and how—to paraphrase Karl Polanyi's classic analysis—culture was embedded in the structure of society, not a master code functional to its interpretation.

Buried Caesars fundamentally challenges such a formulaic use of this notion of tradition. It posits that the grand cyclopes of the Italian venerable past were so much a part of the lived experiences of those who arrived steerage-class in the United States, that, *a.* their confrontation with the radically individualistic liberalism of American "economical" society produced a distinctive brand of anthropological malaise; and, *b.* that, as we try now to understand and explain what Italian American culture is and how it functions, starting from the mind of the individuals, we have to recognize how it grew around not exactly a void, or a black hole (the bereavement mode of old immigration studies), but rather something more embarrassing—something like the hazy eddy left behind by a mushroom drug gone sour, which has seeped through the cells of the individual and communal body.

Italian American culture stems out, or revolves around, this sense of empty grandeur. It starts with gigantism, and must come to terms with the more modest requirements of the American mosaic, where such monumental attitudes need to be curtailed. It might sound like an allegorical tale, built up of abstract metaphors: and Viscusi, who has a knack for semiotic analysis, tells it this way. But at the very same time, it's a totally realistic account of the DNA of a culture, issued from one of the most exquisite, sophisticated, articulate, and subdivided historical landscapes, and forced to unwittingly parochialize itself in the shape of an ethnic midget. And then you wonder where some Italian American tacky pomposity comes from. . .

This process has worked so fast that the presence of the Caesars has been overlooked. Viscusi makes clear that the avatars had not precisely been carried over like some old Roman spirit of the family house (the Lares and Penates of yore), but that they *were* part and parcel of the immigrants' consciousness and language. What happened was that in the course of one or two generations, those Caesars fell under the ground, where they are now buried. In Italy, one might probably point out similar results, obtained, though, with a somewhat reduced sense of trauma, which then, in turn, has softened a sense of recognition of what has happened, leaving a taste of Kevorkianesque oblivion.

Buried Caesars maps out a cultural territory exploring its origins, and the signs, the taints, the scars those beginnings have left on the big, glorious, contemporary body of a people tense with a sense of identity which has become too loose and familiar. It reads, in a way, like an attempt at a *Stones of Venice* of Italian Americana (evolutionally speaking, one might briefly wonder if it might actually inspire some future Italian American Proust). Viscusi has been trodding in an eerie mausoleum largely of his own making and has carefully listened to the words, the accents, the postures of the big masters (especially Pascal D'Angelo, Garibaldi Lapolla, Pietro di Donato, John Fante, Mario Puzo, and Helen Barolini). There is little doubt that he has a very strong idea of *writers*, which he interprets, literally and most deferentially, as those who live for writing, and for whom writing is living at its fullest: Caesars whose devotion to words is anything but gratuitous. In fact, both as a scholar and a writer, Viscusi himself is driven by a demiurgic vision of language—which is then what is at the core of his discourse. What language do the immigrants—and to a certain extent their descendants—speak? In a way, *Buried Caesars* provides a mantra instead of an answer—an intellectual chant of hope and disillusion, because that language, no matter how necessary, balks on the verge of impossibility—an "English as a Dialect of Italian," as Viscusi suggests in his amazing opening article.

But *Buried Caesars* is not, strictly speaking, a collection of essays by a straightforward literary historian. Apart from the actual writers, its ten thick, thoughtful essays analyze history, societies, and lives as different form of writings. All of them draw parallels between the writers' cogency to words, and the world's complex textuality—which can be visual, gestural, political-ideological, materialistic, psychological, and so forth (Viscusi, for instance, puts the right emphasis on the Risorgimento and its cultural aftermath, which should be an obvious, absolute must for any Italian American scholar). Literary works and cultural signs can, at times, appear being weakly motivated: but the interrelation between these two dimensions is hardly so, especially when it is constantly negotiated under the pressure of stereotypes and various forms of social conflict. This is why the keen analysis of Italian American texts, in Viscusi's essays, coexists with a masterly, although sketchy, interpretation of American and Italian cultures. Both literature and society are treated as the litmus test of one another.

Buried Caesars must be placed next to *Astoria* and to Viscusi's poetry. I stuffed and deformed it with the folded pages of the many newsletters written by the author in the 1990s and early 2000s for the Italian American Writers Association (IAWA). I consider those short, monthly manifestos one of the finest examples ever and anywhere of critical and political journalism. Not only the acumen and poignancy of those *Episodes* had been a feast of the mind: one could imagine, picking them up from the mailbox, that they were weaving an invisible fabric, that they were forging a community by igniting a dialogue that was branching way out of Academe. Likewise, and perhaps more deeply, more consistently, with *Buried Caesars* Viscusi shows the master essayist that he is: he is one, being a stylist in his writing—which is so clearly in line with the golden thread of that tradition, from Montaigne to the most representative Parisian intellectuals of post WWII, from the classics of nineteenth-century American literature to his beloved Beerbohm, and over. But his essayism is not a trait of mannerism: it represents Viscusi's own style as a thinker and—may I suggest it in passing—as a man (as much as it can be inferred from his oratorial exuberance). Viscusi is a mother goose who lays down ideas: he *tries* them, or *probes* them. Those ideas burn of an internal flame: they might be open to specific discussion on singular details—and yet what I find enthusing is the force of interpretation that they express. The added value to Viscusi's book lies in the fact that he is not only a superb cultural critic, but at the same time an acute psychoanalyst of his own culture. You understand his acuteness, and you feel his personal engagement with what he writes about.

His style and his ideological fertility are inextricably entwined: one mirrors the other. And the overall tone that is borne out of this nervous, almost baroque, twisted embrace is quite distinctly out of tune with what you read today on the scholarly *tapis roulant*. Viscusi tends to avoid the beaten paths and to shun the smart kudos. His urgency is deep; his words ring true and absolutely his. He is an original without being an eccentric (that is, seriously speaking; on a trivial level we might disagree, although just a little). He has got very little time for catchphrases, name-dropping, and faddish codes: *what* he is "essaying" is important, not the need to display ceremonial gestures to please his reader or to wink at colleagues. This is refreshing and inspirational in itself, as it befits a book that is masterly in both its analyses and its interpretive style, vibrant to the point of advocating the need of a new, wide cultural understanding.

The Substance of Chance:
Ellis Island, Robert Viscusi's Infinite Poem

It is easier for me to unite Italy than to write a sonnet

—Cavour

Ellis Island is Robert Viscusi's masterpiece: it is a life's work, one that defines a life, one that digs profoundly therein to recount it, to endow it with a sense of meaning by letting itself get carried away by ideas, images, and fantasies. At the same time, it is a work whose ambition is to be a sort of double of the author's life.[2] It is a far-reaching and, by today's standards, rare and unusual work, for it is truly an epic poem, as grand and majestic as those of yore that established the tradition.

Today, to read and, even more so, conceive and compose an epic poem is an invariably uncommon undertaking, something one could quite rightly define as anachronistic. In truth, however, between the United States and Italy, certain grand exemplars of this type of work have appeared in recent history—just think of the narrative poetical works by William Carlos Williams, Ed Sanders, and Attilio Bertolucci. Like these writers, the author of *Ellis Island*, too, came to port with full and heterogeneous load. Viscusi is not a newcomer to poetry. For years he performed, while playing the piano, a unique lyrical-poetic operetta (understood in the broadest of such terms), *An Oration Upon the Most Recent Death of Christopher Columbus* (1993). His activity extends into the critical realm as well where, over the course of at least three decades, he has published a great number of innovative essays steeped in original ideas, the thrust of them compiled into a masterful work on Italian culture as envisioned through different eyes, *Buried Caesars* (2006), a book still largely underappreciated. Viscusi's proper debut for broad American audiences, however, was an exquisitely postmodern novel, *Astoria* (1995), in which a passion for storytelling is enmeshed with a degree of autobiographical tension. A militant intellectual, Viscusi has, through the founding in 1991 of the Italian American Writers Association, facilitated more than anyone else the realization of an Italian American "Renaissance."

In short, Viscusi is a writer who shored up to the "island of tears"—the historical Ellis Island recalled by his grandparents from Campania and Abruzzo, as well as by millions of other Americans—having already refined, in his creative laboratory, many various forms of involvement with the literary word, his means of direct and explicit motivation for and intervention with the present. Even from a so-called "private" point of view (a highly inadequate, perhaps even paradoxical adjective given the nature of the work in question), Viscusi's choice of the epic form should readily dash any superficial impressions of haphazardly antiquated or exclusively hyperliterary work.

Ellis Island is indeed a courageously personal work. Yet it is also, on the whole, a stupefying, vertiginous machine of meanings and references, a factory of imagination. Viscusi (a well-defined poet-subject) has constructed a productive mechanism of signs and ideas that is also, at the same time, very human, indeed more than human. With the "simple" format of the sonnet, Viscusi breathes new life, in both geometrical and incantatory terms, into a structure at once semantically founded and civically responsible. The liberty-principle oxygenates the necessarily finite cells of the poetic organism and swells the epic poem into nearly impossible dimensions. By virtue of its insertion into a dialectical and expansive structure, the fragment of autobiographical reality becomes the fabric of a collective drama, a metaphor for a utopia. Such was already, in the earlier days of great American poetry, the dream of Whitman: "I contain multitudes." Likewise, Viscusi handles the verse—often long, metrically exceeding, and almost akin to prose—in such a way that he makes himself understood on a wide scale. Readability is a key for a poetry that aims at speaking to the multitudes, that is born out of a people from the past and reaches out to another, wholly contemporary one. Language, themes, rhythm itself collaborate in creating an atmosphere of stimulating communicativeness.

The title is explicitly preparatory. The reader will be thrust into an epic telling of the historic Great Migration to North America (from Europe, and from Italy in particular, but not only, as evidenced in sonnet 1.4). That event, itself a prolonged chronology brimming with millions of individual tales—each so chronically uncertain, undecided and quiet, or even sure of itself, fantasizing, in search of fortune and success—is entrusted, it would seem, to a lone voice, the voice of an heir and descendant who recounts, with observational acuity and attentive ears, its effects, from the most familiar to the most idiosyncratic and liberally associative, through 624 sonnets organized into 52 books, essentially twelve sonnets (168 lines) for each week (168 hours) of the year.

This basic structure can, in turn, be broken down into even more essential elements: all of the sonnets present an unusual distribution of four tercets and a couplet, which might bring to mind—however inadequately—Dante and Shelley. Further on in the book there appears, almost ironically, a group of memorable *terze rime* (10.4, 10.9, 10.11, 10.12, 43.4, 43.9). The basic structure gives life to a model of sequential narration, one that expresses an implicit, nearly mythic trust in a story characterized by a harmonious, tempered order. Moreover, already at this "linear" level, the story is made up of stories, the layered plot of a subject who speaks with generosity and urgency while leaving open spaces, nonetheless, for many other narrative presences.

Within the narrative, tensions are created and heightened in a number of different spheres: in conflicting opinions and views, in generational differences, in gender dynamics, in the changing perspectives and wavering doubts that occur with the passing of time. All of this, and a great deal more by way of allusion and suggestion, is activated on a second level of textual complexity in which each sonnet interacts with a corresponding one. The correspondences are regulated rhetorically by the figure of the chiasmus, or cross, and numerically resolved by the formula 53.13–y = x, where y is a given sonnet and x is the unknown sonnet that corresponds to it. To find the "mirror image" of sonnet 2.9, for example, one must look to the fourth sonnet of book 51. The correspondences are sometimes surprising or close; other times they are tangential and open to interpretation. This dynamic allows the perspectives to amplify, opening up the narration to varying types of fractures, contradictions, confusions, and contrasts. Indeed, contrasto and fuga are venerated modalities in poetic and musical language. Here, it is important to bear in mind that the dialectic is woven, intertwined around a structural trunk that is generally monological.

Up to this point, it seems one can rely on the solidity of certain Gutenbergian schemes in the work, on the geometry of a paper castle. Yet *Ellis Island*, conforming to its own oceanic genesis, aspires to something else as well. It contains, within itself, a "possible" or "virtual" structure related to purely mathematical combinations. This "factorial" structure is, indeed, also linguistically genetic, a model resembling *Cent mille milliards de poèmes*, by Raymond Queneau. It is an infinity expressed by the number 624^{14}, made possible thanks to a series of related structures: each verse is legible individually; rhymes are scarce; there are no enjambments; distinct graphic signs, such as capital letters, are eliminated, as is punctuation; and connective syntaxes are reduced to a minimum, particularly where verses begin and end. The price to pay for such a structure is, at least during a prolonged reading, an almost mechanical rhythm, a metallic sonorousness, an insidious monotony. To compensate, however, is an elaborated algorithm for the online version (www.ellisislandpoem.com) that can generate an essentially unlimited array of recombined verses—the sonnet count, to wit, reaches numbers featuring as many as thirty-nine zeroes. From this is born, or at least hypothesized, a form of "alien" narrative, at once possible and impossible, present almost exclusively in the minds of our computers. As such, it is a story propped up by the functions of our most modern but also our most quotidian and common technology, and one that exploits such functions as well. Moreover, it is a story that truly realizes the old modernist dream of infinite reproducibility, governed by the laws of chance and variation: a gargantuan throw of the dice, programmed and exhilarating, suggestive of the overwhelming unforeseeability of destinies consigned to history.

What one encounters, then, is the proposal—more than the effective composition—of a music not so much minimalist as "concrete," stochastic, yet "anchored" all the same. It is a music intelligent yet not cerebral, but also one of communicative necessity, one of great involvement. One must note the fact that in *Ellis Island* the diverse and variable narrative structures and forms live together, even if not in a reading, by intent of the poet, and perhaps by intent of the reader as well. Significantly, the reader—every one of us—is incorporated into the text to the greatest degree, by way of technology, through the internet-based "Random Sonnet Generator," making the work "a sort of public property" (32.1.6). It's as if the poet had set up, on that famed island at the mouth of the Hudson River, a telescopic periscope allowing him to envision all those who have passed through there, all their friends and relatives and the historically determined society that has resulted, not to mention the audience, both real and potential, that will read and recompose ad libitum all of those stories, however fragmentary or incoherent they might appear at first glance. The gigantic dimensions of the work in its entirety widen its temporal reach to embrace past, present, and future. Every emigration then becomes, in its own way, a form of creation, a thought process enacted before the event and later, in the context of the realities it eventually leads to, measured. A similar model of existential projection is reflected in *Ellis Island*: the poem's potential form precedes, from a logical and genetic point of view, its active form and steers its development. The poem is an idea, and has a body. Purity and reality, imagination and history.

The text, then, is an experimental one, one imbued with a profoundly, etymologically "poetic" sensitivity. It isn't limited, within itself, to just one story, for reverberating from that story are millions of others. The autobiographical I—written in lowercase, "i"—both implodes and explodes; the unknown mathematics then become an imaginable, calculable realization, not unlike the various unknowns that awaited the immigrants on the island of tears and that, more generally, await the readers. The periscope is pointed toward us, yet in a rather democratic sense we, too, can make use of it. The golem of the internet globalizes us without, however, allowing us to see it, to comprehend it: one never manages to exit from or regulate it. Here, however, one is oriented in a quite different, perhaps even liberating direction. We ourselves are made able, thanks to the author's input, to navigate, liberally and without foresight, each of us moving along trails that eventually cross paths with so many others. Viscusi's profound sentimental adhesion to his theme is accompanied by a scintillating, indeed an affectionate critical disposition. No wonder, then, that his style—which one might even call, given the text's premises, a hyper-style—is extremely personal, unmistakable.

Ellis Island, then, is a *possible* book, a book of possibility and possibilities. At the same time, it is a real epic poem. It is the epic of a man, an American of Italian origin, in an attempt to unravel himself through incessantly reconfiguring fragments of thoughts and memories. An entire life passes before him, complete with its requisite load of wishes and experiences, and he sings that life like a true "bard," fantasizing himself in the "hero's" clothes, a "colossal" hero insofar as he comes to embody the greatness of an entire populace. Alongside this drama of mythical proportions (one that is also at times de-dramatized, as when the bard and the hero actually encounter one another beneath the Brooklyn Bridge, 9.2) runs another drama, one more strictly biographical: the drama of a boy surrounded by relatives who, as a group of workers and dreamers pent up in the tumultuous neighborhoods of Queens, find themselves proud of il Duce, Mussolini; the drama of a young man who, in the sixties, goes to Rolling Stones concerts, seeks out girls, and finds creative brethren among New York School poets such as John Ashbery and Ted Berrigan; and the drama of a family man, one who is perennially in motion, fully engaged in his various obligations, career and research among them. A research, to be sure, into one's origins.

The poem contains the diagram of a progressively increasing awareness of ethnic identity. This identity is indeed a double duplicity and diversity that confronts, on the one hand, the toughness of American productivity and, on the other, the irritating condescension of "cousins" who, having remained in Italy, find themselves ill at ease with this return of a removed persona—or rather, in a more banal sense, with the "vulgar eloquence" of an Italian American whose studious pursuits contradict the usual stereotypes, all the more because he proclaims himself the brother of so many other sons of the infinite diaspora of work and oppression. The imaginative diagnosis that the poet proposes of the old Italian culture does not undo the tenacious ties that still, even with the remove of several generations, condition the Italian American sense of self. To recognize and loosen these binds (the "untying of knots" in 31.8.14, and again in 31.9–12) is one of the political imperatives of the work: it is a liberation of conscience that even contemporary Italians could, or should, make use of—not only those so nostalgically evoked in Ferlinghetti's memorable verses, but also those of us who, in a paradoxical reversal, have remained "on land," back on the other side of the Big Puddle.

The opposition between land and sea, between continental mass and oceanic vastness, is yet another of the work's great guiding forces, as the recurrence of the term "tide" readily indicates. It is thus also, in various ways, an epic of movement, of transformation, of passage. A "human wheel [is] turning" (2.7.1), the ocean divulges "teachings / that jesus himself had studied" (3.5.13–14), and not even the poet himself, as he says, knows "how to tell the story of changes by telling it" (4.12.3). Then, not far from the end of the work, appears the claim, "in this poem i have followed a great ellipse as a form of self study" (48.12.7). It is a traumatic arrival, nearly incomprehensible, followed by an entire series of continuous returns—attempted, failed, dreamed and late-coming. The admissions of weakness, of feeling downtrodden, of fear, are among the most touching moments of this work in which the "colossus" remains a compensatory myth quite disproportionate to the smallness of the individual. Even the real Ellis Island, having been transformed into a museum, risks being reduced to a cheap myth for the masses. The grandson of emigrants, in sum, has met his goal and can now save himself other voyages, other changes (16.8). The necessity of memory alternates with the inevitability of forgetting (44.7–8). In what direction does destiny face? Why punish oneself by pondering it so obsessively? What is the meaning of all this?

The reach of this epic poem, *Ellis Island*, extends far and wide. It is solemn, on the whole, yet continuously animated by so many currents of varying force and warmth. It resists being reduced to anything too simple as it mobilizes thoughts and feelings, all the while maintaining an awareness of its own flaws, imperfections at once mental, abstract, or even—in a few very emotional passages—of the body, one's own as well as those of others. Ancient trees, colorful parrots, Roman and Etruscan ruins, Canova and Ginsberg.

All this and much, much more in a fluidity of numbers, verses, and reflections.

Translated by Paul D'Agostino

Conclusion

As I move toward the end of this book, I find it instructive to recontextualize these explorations into the two-way interaction between American and Italian cultures within the coordinates of a past historiographical debate. And so, once again, I turn to Gramsci and his interpretation of the Risorgimento as a failed revolution, a "revolution without revolution" that did not involve the working class, but was rather a lofty patriotic goal advanced by the literate strata of society, who had no interest in bringing about a substantial change in land ownership and administration. Because of the lack of an agrarian revolution, the Risorgimento, according to Gramsci, had somehow repeated the "passivity" that in 1799 had rapidly caused the failure of the Neapolitan, French-leaning revolution. A line of thought inaugurated early on by Vincenzo Cuoco and variously articulated through the nineteenth century and well into the Novecento (Nievo, Pasquale Villari, Salvemini, to a certain extent Giustino Fortunato, and others). But while in Italy, in the post-WWII period, the debate has remained largely confined to scholars, in the United States and elsewhere, thanks to a freer and more dynamic approach to the Italian communist thinker, Gramsci's decontextualization has generated—interestingly—a rereading of his interpretation.

In *Astoria*—a postmodernist novel whose title contains multiple meanings—Robert Viscusi contends, for instance, that "The great migration was a revolution in which almost nothing had actually happened. . . The migration, even as it is remembered, included very few events that could give you any clear idea of what was in fact going on."[1] And further down,

> My head was full of revolution, I thought, when I arrived in Italy. *Was there an Italian revolution? Was the migration a*

revolution? These were the leading questions. . . What was the Risorgimento? My grandfather believed in it. He taught me its music, its poetry, his walls were covered with its Garibaldi and its Mazzini. But why then did he leave Italy? The Risorgimento was a revolution that emitted hungry exiles in the millions, was it?[2]

This was a revolution that, two generations later, at the time of the author's coming of age, was still expressing itself within the family with "the shimmering silences that occasionally appeared like sudden angels right in the middle of laughing, musical, stereotypical Sunday dinners."[3] Italy, then, had indeed experienced a revolution, but one that had driven millions of his subjects elsewhere. *Elsewhere* is the telling title of Richard Russo's intense memoir—a sorrowful exploration of his mother's silences—a second generation Sicilian-American.[4] That "silent" revolution had taken place beyond the borders of the motherland through emigration, with its baggage of displacements, adaptations, and trauma.

Should one forcefully take sides, here? Maybe not. One point is that Gramsci was so focused on the strategic importance of his analyses of the gap between intellectuals and people that—as we mentioned in the *Introduction*—he effectively overlooked the cultural relevance of the actual migratory phenomenon. Paradoxically, his critical acumen confirmed the very weakness that he was denouncing. Despite his analyses of "americanismo" and his interest in the popular exodus, he simply downplayed—like most Italian intellectuals—the existence of other forms of "Italian" societies outside the national borders. On the contrary, a much more confused thinker, the great turn-of-the-century poet Giovanni Pascoli (one of the few to devote some of his art to the plight of immigrants), had shown a considerable awareness of the decisive role played by the cultured elite in addressing and even directing such a crucial issue: "Our University [Messina], placed between the sea and lands offering so many lives to emigration [Sicily and Calabria], appears to me, more than any other, chosen by fate to fulfill, through its students, nomadic Italy's Reconquista."[5] Surely his early socialism was already moving toward nationalism and imperialism, and twelve years later he famously heralded in classicist tones the invasion of Libya as the right move for the *Grande Proletaria*, Italy. In his own way, though, Pascoli recognized that one had to confront emigration if one wanted to reflect on the deep popular identity of the new nation. Institutions of higher learning, and their students, had to be part of the debate.

More than a century later we are still faced with different narratives when it comes to making sense both of the epochal exodus and of the current, massive flux. Italian studies still strive to accept a wider and more mobile meaning of things Italian. You Shall Have No Other Italy Before Me seems to be the conscious and unconscious mantra expressing geographically and historiographically the difficulty in adopting a different approach. But such fixity is not confined to the field of Italian studies alone. American studies too—according to Jonathan Arac—despite the multicultural context within which they operate, are caught in a predicament where Americans are Many, or *Plural*, and yet America—as a cultural field—operates and is treated as One, or *Mono*, thanks to the late capitalist triumph of *Anglo-Globalism*.[6] Once again—but in different terms from those of nationalist Pascoli—a full recognition of the complex cultural interplay between nations set off by huge movements of people rests on an assumption of responsibilities on the part of intellectuals and scholars. Complicating and enriching migration studies implies reframing the role of the intellectual as a critical presence, not as the guarantor of an established order, which risks lifting the veil over the embarrassing weakness and disempowerment of the intellectual milieu in our current social hierarchy, on both sides of the Atlantic.

In fact, it is hard to point to a school of migration studies; the many stimulating contributions of the last thirty years or so seem not to have cohered in a clear "critical mass." Meanwhile, back on the peninsula, the huge question of a "new" Italy has arisen, placing itself alongside the never-resolved Southern question, another of Gramsci's main topics. Ports of departure have become ports of arrival. The Italian semiosphere is no more, simply—as it were—the home of sentimental adieus and mandolins, but an electric switch, activated and charged by currents moving in different directions. Cordiferro and Caruso's *Core 'Ngrato* (1911) has given way to the abrasive *Non pago affitto* (2016) by Italo-Ghanian rapper Bello Figo.

Two model writers of the huge exodus to Germany, Franco Biondi and Marisa Fenoglio, constructed cautionary tales around parables of return, where the main characters either move forward while coming back—returning from their return (Franco Biondi's, *Passavantis Rückkehr*, not by chance in German)—or reflect on the impossibility of return as they witness their birthplace, their offspring, and their mother tongue irretrievably become "other" from an origin more and more waning in memory (Marisa Fenoglio's *Il ritorno impossibile*).[7] In fact, in facing this layered impossibility, immigrant "narratives of return" often suggest, dialectically, a fuller acceptance of the "new" condition.[8]

But, as I said, the tables have turned. What Italy was forty years ago to Italo-German Franco Biondi—that is, a motherland to go back to, striving to overcome its call of nostalgia—Bosnia is today to Italo-Bosniac Elvira Mujčić, who almost miraculously created a black comedy out of her biography as a survivor of the massacre of Srebrenica, and narrated her return there from Italy with her grandmother's corpse to the hills where she last saw her father and her other relatives, butchered by the Serbian army of Ratko Mladić.[9] In this way, Italian parochial amnesia is forced to confront its decade-long strategy of sociocultural escapism and *perbenismo* and open its eyes wide to something different from *o' sole mio*. Mujčić's ultimate triumph consists of infusing a new life into one of the chief components of our imaginary. She does so straddling love and death, new and old generations, the blackest humor and tragedy, as well as languages and memories, and in so doing affirming a new, young and mature, way of being an Italian immigrant. As it often happens, fiction and art promote new ways of understanding a layered and difficult reality. Likewise, the studies in this book try to encourage a critical, historically and formally based examination of the Italian sign, in all its migrant mobility.

Notes

Introduction

1. Both Ojetti and Gramsci in Antonio Gramsci, *Letteratura e vita nazionale* (Roma: Editori Riuniti, 1971): 121–22.

2. Rose Basile Green, *The Italian-American Novel: A Document of the Interaction of Two Cultures* (Madison, NJ: Fairleigh Dickinson University Press, 1974).

3. Antonio Gramsci, *Gli intellettuali e l'organizzazione della cultura* (Roma: Editori Riuniti, 1977), 88.

4. Martino Marazzi, *Italexit: Saggi su Risorgimento e disunione nazionale* (Firenze: Franco Cesati, 2019).

5. Donna Gabaccia, "Juggling Jargons: 'Italians Everywhere,' Diaspora or Transnationalism?," *Traverse* 12 (2005): 49.

6. Ibid., 54.

7. Yiorgos Anagnostou, Review of Peter Carravetta, *After Identity: Migration, Critique, Italian American Culture* (New York: Bordighera Press, 2017), *The Italian American Review* 8, 2 (Summer 2018): 219.

8. Abdelmalek Sayad, *The Suffering of the Immigrant* (Malden, MA: Polity Press, 2004).

9. Robert Viscusi, *Ellis Island* (New York: Bordighera Press, 2013).

10. Luigi Pirandello, *I vecchi e i giovani*, 2 vols. (Milano: Treves, 1913; partially serialized in *Rassegna contemporanea* [Roma], 1909; American ed., *The Old and the Young*, trans. C. K. Scott-Moncrieff, New York: E.P. Dutton & Company, 1928).

11. Booker T. Washington, *The Man Farthest Down: A Record of Observation and Study in Europe*, with the collaboration of Robert E. Park (Garden City, NY: Doubleday, Page & Company, 1912).

12. Luigi Pirandello, *Le sorprese della scienza* (1905), in *Novelle per un anno: La mosca* (Firenze: Bemporad, 1923).

13. Charlotte Gower Chapman, *Milocca: A Sicilian Village* (Cambridge, MA: Schenkman, 1971 (but conceived in the late 1920s; *Milocca* is duly quoted by

Donna Gabaccia in her standard Sicilian works—see for instance *Militants and Migrants: Rural Sicilians Become American Workers* [New Brunswick, NJ: Rutgers University Press, 1988]).

14. Maria Occhipinti, *Una donna libera* (Palermo: Sellerio, 2004).

15. Just a couple of titles each: Joseph Sciorra, "'Why a Man Makes the Shoes?': Italian American Art and Philosophy in Sabato Rodia's Watts Towers," in *Sabato Rodia's Towers in Watts*, ed. Luisa Del Giudice (New York: Fordham University Press, 2014): 183–203; Sciorra, *Built with Faith: Italian American Imagination and Catholic Material Culture in New York City* (Knoxville: University of Tennessee Press, 2015); Simone Cinotto, *The Italian American Table: Food, Family, and Community in New York City* (Chicago: University of Illinois Press, 2013); Cinotto, *Making Italian America: Consumer Culture and the Production of Ethnic Identities*, ed. Simone Cinotto (New York: Fordham University Press, 2014).

16. Graziella Parati, *Migration Italy: The Art of Talking Back in a Destination Culture* (Toronto: University of Toronto Press, 2005).

17. Alessandro Leogrande, *La frontiera* (Milano: Feltrinelli, 2015).

18. For a thorough and insightful overview, see Jennifer Burns and Catherine Keen, "Italian Mobilities," *Italian Studies* 75, no. 2 (2020): 140–54.

Chapter 1

1. Margaret Fuller, *"These Sad But Glorious Days," Dispatches from Europe, 1846–1850*, ed. Larry J. Reynolds and Susan Belasco Smith (New Haven: Yale University Press, 1991), 176.

2. Ibid., *Dispatch* 19, 169–71; *Dispatch* 22, 203–5; *Dispatch* 23, 210; *Dispatch* 27, 248.

3. This is a point where I do not entirely concur with Paola Gemme's otherwise insightful analysis. See Paola Gemme, *An American Jeremiah in Rome: Margaret Fuller's* Tribune *Dispatches*, in *Domesticating Foreign Struggles: The Italian Risorgimento and Antebellum American Identity* (Athens: University of Georgia Press, 2005), 89–106.

4. Fuller, *"These Sad But Glorious Days," Dispatch* 17, 155.

5. Ibid., *Dispatch* 19, 173.

6. Ibid., *Dispatch* 23, 211.

7. Ibid.

8. Robert N. Hudspeth, ed., *The Letters of Margaret Fuller. Volume IV: 1845–47* (Ithaca: Cornell University Press, 1987), 271 (letter from Rome, May 7, 1847).

9. Robert N. Hudspeth, ed., *The Letters of Margaret Fuller: Volume V: 1848–49* (Ithaca: Cornell University Press, 1988), 86 (letter from Rieti, July 11, 1848).

10. Ibid., 168 (letter to Jane Tuckerman King, Rome, January 1849).

11. Fuller, *"These Sad But Glorious Days,"* Dispatch 17, 159.

12. Ibid., *Dispatch* 18, 165.

13. Margaret Fuller Family Papers, Houghton Library, Harvard Library, Harvard University, Series I, Vol. 11, General correspondence. In Fuller's original, the title is followed by "on l'accuse par le people / de faire rien. // Réponse de M. Belli Romain." Here is the version by Allen Andrews, retrieved thanks to Iuri Moscardi: "A *dog's life* // You say *his* life is idle, lazy bastards? / He never does a thing, the Pope, eh? Nothing? / By the same token you should be struck rigid, / The way he wears himself out day and night. // Who is it parleys with Almighty God? / Who gives so many whoresons absolutions? / Who circulates indulgences in dozens? / Who braves a carriage-ride to bless the people? // Who is there who will count his money for him? / Who helps him when he makes a cardinal? / Taxes, by God, aren't they his own creation? // He works as hard as any market-porter / All the year long, to tear up our petitions / To little scraps and dump them in the basket," in Giuseppe Gioachino Belli, *The People of Rome in 100 Sonnets* (Roma: Bardi, 1984), unnumbered page. The original can be read in Giuseppe Gioachino Belli, *I sonetti*, vol. 4, ed. Pietro Gibellini, Lucio Felici, Edoardo Ripari (Torino: Einaudi, 2018), 4583.

14. Margaret Fuller Family Papers, Houghton Library, Harvard Library, Harvard University, Series I, Vol. 11, General correspondence. Harold Norse's translation in New York "vernacular" goes like this: "*The sovrans of the old world* // Once there was a king who from his palace / Sent out among the people this edict: / "I am I, and you're nothing but shit, / A crowd of stinking rats, so shut up. // I make straight crooked and crooked straight: / I can sell you all at so much a bunch: / I, if I have you hanged, don't put you out, / 'Cause your life and all your stuff I rent to you. // Whoever lives in this world without a title / Either of Pope, or Emperor, or King, / Can never have a say in anything." // With this edict the executioner was sent / As messenger, probing the people on this view; / And they all replied: *It's true, it's true*.": in Damiano Abeni, Raffaella Bertazzoli, Cesare G. De Michelis, and Pietro Gibellini, eds., *Belli oltre frontiera: La fortuna di G.G. Belli nei saggi e nelle versioni di autori stranieri* (Roma: Bonacci, 1983), 245–46. For the original, see Belli, *I sonetti*, vol. 1, 857.

15. Marcello Teodonio, *Vita di Belli* (Roma-Bari: Laterza, 1993), 269–70; Nicola Di Nino, "Il Belli 'popolare' di Luigi Morandi (con lettere inedite all'editore Barbèra)," *Critica letteraria* 31, no. 4 (2003): 672.

16. Luigi Morandi, ed., *Duecento sonetti in dialetto romanesco di Giuseppe Gioachino Belli* (Firenze: Barbèra, 1870).

17. Teodonio, *Vita di Belli*, 211.

18. It must be remarked that this connection between Belli and Fuller was first pointed out by historian Emma Detti in her 1942 biography of the American author—the first of its kind in Italy—based on extensive archival

research in the United States and sponsored, during the war, by Giovanni Gentile: Emma Detti, *Margaret Fuller Ossoli e i suoi corrispondenti: Con lettere inedite di Giuseppe Mazzini, Costanza Arconati, Adam Mickiewicz, Lewis Cass, Jane Carlyle, Maria Mazzini, Benedetta Mazzini, Elizabeth Barrett Browning, Cristina Trivulzio di Belgioioso, Ralph Waldo Emerson* (Firenze: Le Monnier, 1942–XX). The elegant shape of the Mausoleo Ossario Garibaldino, hosting the remains of the young Republicans perished under French fire in 1849, had just been inaugurated on the Janiculum hill in November 1941. Passionate and lucid, Detti's essay can be read as the equivalent of that Fascist cult of the Risorgimento; but its function was also, quite obviously, that of keeping open a line of communication between the two countries. A similar dynamic has recently been studied by art historians Lorenzo Carletti and Cristiano Giometti in *Raffaello* on the road: *Rinascimento e propaganda fascista in America (1938–40)* (Roma: Carocci, 2016).

19. William Wetmore Story, *Roba di Roma* (London: Chapman and Hall, and New York: Appleton, 1863). For the following quotes I refer to the 8th edition: Boston: Houghton Mifflin, 1887.

20. Story, *Roba di Roma*, 198–99.

21. Angela Bianchini, *Voce donna* (Milano: Frassinelli, 1996), 222–23. ["The unique atmosphere of papist Rome, seen in her rituals, her habits, her colors, and in that class solidarity—that mixture of aristocracy and lower classes, of Romans and foreigners—that no one in Italy had ever bothered to document."]

22. "It summed up, with an extraordinary wealth of statement, with perpetual illustration and image, the incomparable *entertainment* of Rome, where almost everything alike, manners, customs, practices, processes, states of feeling, no less than objects, treasures, relics, ruins, partook of the special museum-quality [. . .] But I used to think, I remember, that the great challenge to envy was in the little evoked visions of that out-of-the-season Rome to which one had one's self to be a stranger, the Rome of the Romans only, of the picture-making populace, both in the city and the small hill-towns, who lead their lives as the sun gets low on the long summer days and the clear shade spreads like a tent above the narrow, sociable streets" (Henry James, *William Wetmore Story and His Friends: From Letters, Diaries, and Recollections*, 2 vols. [London: Thames & Hudson, 1903], 131–32). A later, and by now classic, treatment of both W. W. Story and Margaret Fuller is in Van Wyck Brooks, *The Dream of Arcadia: American Writers and Artists in Italy 1760–1915* (New York: E.P. Dutton & Co., 1958).

23. Notably, this ambivalence, or erasure, of modern Italy for the consumption of the American public has been the focus of a number of critical studies. See for instance, again, Paola Gemme (2005), and James Buzard, *The Beaten Track: European Tourism, Literature, and the Ways to "Culture," 1800–1918* (Oxford: Oxford University Press, 1993). I write from a slightly different perspective, emphasizing, so to speak, the writers' agency (when plausible) vis-à-vis

the migratory dynamics of popular cultures and the increasing modernization of media, with transnationalizing effects.

24. Jessie White Mario, *La miseria di Napoli* (Firenze: Le Monnier, 1877). Jessie White Mario, *The Poor in Naples*, in Robert Archey Woods et al., *The Poor in Great Cities: Their Problems and What Is Being Done to Solve Them* (New York: Charles Scribner's Sons, 1895), 300–38.

25. Nonetheless, the later article in English is accompanied by a number of intense, although rather stereotypical, illustrations by Ettore Tito.

26. White Mario, *La miseria di Napoli*, 5 ["Nowadays the nation has been created, the crops harvested and shared. The common people saw new taxes, higher prices for goods of prime necessity, a few schools for those who can afford shoes decent enough to wear. Nothing else [. . .]. But such a Christian patience cannot last for a long time"].

27. Ibid., 22 ["a land where the *camorra* rules"].

28. Ibid., 48 (in italics) ["*not even between slaves and whites in America*"].

29. Ibid. ["the deterioration of the race"].

30. Ibid., 281 (in italics) ["*Whites' freedom is founded on Blacks' slavery*"].

31. Jessie V.ª [sic] Mario, "Le miniere di zolfo in Sicilia," *Nuova Antologia* year 29, vol. 49, no. 3 (1 febbraio 1894): 441–66, and *Nuova Antologia* year 29, vol. 49, no. 4 (15 febbraio 1894): 719–43.

32. Jessie V.ª Mario, *Le miniere di zolfo*, 1 febbraio: 445 ["I observed them carefully: the youngest were like all the poor boys employed in the country: thin, frail, pale, and all with red and swollen eyes. As they grow, the effects of hard work become more visible. Their big and swollen knees are in strange contrast with their frail legs and with their arms, which are all skin and muscles. Some among them showed a crooked spine; some others a little hump on the left shoulder. And yet they were happy. . . ."].

33. Jessie V.ª Mario, *Le miniere di zolfo*, 15 febbraio: 722 ["It is clear that both physically and morally the job of the sulfur heavers is a form of slavery that exceeds that of the young Negroes"].

34. Booker T. Washington, *The Man Farthest Down: A Record of Observation and Study in Europe*, with the collaboration of Robert E. Park (Garden City, NY: Doubleday, Page & Company, 1912). "The Struggle of European Toilers" is the subtitle that appears on the cover—different from the one in the frontispiece.

35. Michel Huysseune, "'This Country, Where Many Things Are Strange and Hard to Understand': Booker T. Washington in Sicily," *RSA Journal* 25 (2014): 174, 177.

36. Washington, *The Man Farthest Down*, 181.

37. Ibid., 214.

38. Ibid., 175.

39. Ibid., 173.

40. Ibid., 214.

41. Ibid., 172–73.

42. Ibid., 122–23.

43. Il Turco di Ritorno, "Negri, Napoletani e Siciliani," *La Follia di New York*, 5 gennaio 1914, 4. Washington's position on the superiority of the black race had already been critiqued by the Italian American press in 1905 in the columns of San Francisco's *L'Italia*: see Lorella Viola and Jaap Verheul, "The Media Construction of Italian Identity: A Transatlantic, Digital Humanities Analysis of *italianità*, Ethnicity, and Whiteness, 1867–1920," *Identity* 19, no. 4 (2019): 308. I also find worthy of notice that in his masterly novel *I vecchi e i giovani* (serialized in 1909 and in volume in 1913) Luigi Pirandello, while treating at length the Sicilian revolt of the Fasci, makes absolutely no mention—deliberately, I would be inclined to think—of any investigative report on the working conditions in the sulfur mines, nor of the massive exodus from Sicily to the New World (a recurrent theme in many of his short stories).

44. The Italian original can be read, almost in its entirety, in Simona Frasca, Birds of Passage. *I musicisti napoletani a New York (1895–1940)* (Lucca: Libreria Musicale Italiana, 2010), 68 [American ed.: *Italian Birds of Passage: The Diaspora of Neapolitan Musicians in New York* (New York: Palgrave Macmillan, 2014), 209]. Frasca provides an insightful analysis from a socio-musicological point of view.

45. For a cogent discussion, see Joseph Sciorra, "Diasporic Musings on Veracity and Uncertainties of 'Core 'ngrato,'" in Goffredo Plastino and Joseph Sciorra, eds., *Neapolitan Postcards: The Canzone Napoletana as Transnational Subject* (Lanham: Rowman & Littlefield, 2016), 115–50.

46. Arturo Giovannitti, *Samnite Cradle-Song*, in *Arrows in the Gale*, intro. Helen Keller (Riverside, CT: Hillacre Bookhouse, 1914), 82–87.

47. Arthur M. Giovannitti, "The Brigandage of Tripoli," *The International Socialist Review* 12, no. 9 (March 1912): 572–76; Arturo Giovannitti, "The Walker," *The International Socialist Review* 13, no. 3 (September 1912): 201–4; and Giovannitti, *Arrows*, 21–27. Giovannitti's critical stance against the Italo-Turkish war in Lybia was all the more significant in light of the prevailing rhetoric couched in bombastic neo-Roman and emigrationist terms. See Giovanni Pascoli's 1911 famous speech *La grande Proletaria si è mossa*. . . (in English in Adriana M. Baranello, "Giovanni Pascoli's 'La grande proletaria si è mossa': A Translation and Critical Introduction," *California Italian Studies* 2, no. 1 (2011).

48. Sebastiano Martelli, *Tra militanza e letteratura*, in Norberto Lombardi, ed., *Il bardo della libertà: Arturo Giovannitti (1884–1959)* (Isernia: Cosmo Iannone, 2011), 245–50. A thorough examination of the Italian Whitman, from Carducci to Pavese via Pascoli and Ettore Ciccotti, is still to be written.

49. Giovannitti, "The Walker," in *Arrows*, 22–24. See also Arturo Giovannitti, *Parole e sangue*, ed. Martino Marazzi, with writings by Joseph Tusiani (Isernia: Cosmo Iannone, 2005), 129–31.

50. Clemens Spahr, *A Poetics of Global Solidarity: Modern American Poetry and Social Movements* (New York: Palgrave Macmillan, 2015). See 23ff. on Giovannitti and Sandburg.

51. Carl Sandburg, "Onion Days," in *Chicago Poems* (New York: Henry Holt and Company, 1916), 28.

52. Carl Sandburg, "Chicago," in *Chicago Poems* (New York: Henry Holt and Company, 1916), 3.

53. Arturo Giovannitti, *"O Labor of America: Heartbeat of Mankind,"* in Martino Marazzi, *Voices of Italian America: A History of Early Italian American Literature with a Critical Anthology* (Madison, NJ: Fairleigh Dickinson University Press, 2004): 217–18.

54. Louis Untermeyer, *The New Era in American Poetry* (New York: Henry Holt and Company, 1919). Giovannitti is at pages 183–99, tucked between Masters and Pound.

55. From the Official Bob Dylan Site: www.bobdylan.com/songs/hard-rains-gonna-fall/, according to which the song was first performed on September 20, 1962 (and a couple of days later at a legendary concert at Carnegie Hall in New York). Already back then, it used to be sung next to other ballads and blues. It should also be remembered that the young Dylan was a fervent admirer of Sandburg and aspired to be considered as an heir to his poetry.

56. Peter Burke famously praised the necessity of what he called—after Marc Bloch—a "regressive method" in studying European popular culture using sources from much later periods (see Peter Burke, *Popular Culture in Early Modern Europe* [New York: New York University Press, 1978], 81ff.).

57. Giovanni B. Bronzini, "Gli 'anelli intermedi' tra la ballata di *Lord Randal* e la canzone dell'*Avvelenato*," *Giornale italiano di filologia* 20 (1967): 53–70; *La canzone dell'Avvelenato nella tradizione popolare italiana*, in *Studi in onore di Carmelina Naselli*, vol. I (Catania: Università di Catania, Facoltà di Lettere e Filosofia, 1968), 39–74; *La ballata di "Lord Randal" e i suoi rapporti con la canzone dell' "Avvelenato,"* in *Studi di storia dell'arte bibliologia ed erudizione in onore di Alfredo Petrucci* (Milano: Carlo Bestetti-Edizioni d'Arte, 1969), 99–111. Phillips Barry, "The Ballad of Lord Randal in New England," *The Journal of American Folklore* 16, no. 63 (October-December 1903): 258–64.

58. For an in-depth analysis and interpretation, see Thomas Beebee, "Ballad of the Apocalypse: Another Look at Bob Dylan's 'Hard Rain,'" *Text and Performance Quarterly* 11 (1991): 18–34. An excellent comment is in Alessandro Carrera's Italian edition of Dylan's lyrics: Bob Dylan, *Lyrics 1961–1968*, ed. Alessandro Carrera (Milano: Feltrinelli, 2016), 475–76. Renato Giovannoli adds useful pieces of information on the biblical sources: Renato Giovannoli, *La Bibbia di Bob Dylan. Volume I: Dalle canzoni di protesta alla vigilia della conversione (1961–1978)*, with an essay by Alessandro Carrera (Milano: Àncora, 2017), 71–73.

59. I add as a title of curiosity that, at least up until late in the 1910s, Dylan's Hibbing had been the home to a sizable community of Italian American

miners, who had been socially and even poetically active. The Umbrian I.W.W. poet Efrem Bartoletti (a comrade of Giovannitti) had written most of his "proletarian nostalgias" (*Nostalgie proletarie: Raccolta di canti poetici e di inni rivoluzionari di Efrem Bartoletti* [Brooklyn, NY: Libreria editrice dei Lavoratori Industriali del Mondo–Italian I.W.W. Publishing Bureau, 1919]) while in Minnesota.

60. Nathaniel Hawthorne, *The Blithedale Romance* [1852] (Oxford: Oxford University Press, 1992), 223.

Chapter 2

1. David Pinski, *Arnold Levenberg* (New York: Simon and Schuster, 1928), 3.

2. Thomas S. Gladsky, *Princes, Peasants, and Other Polish Selves: Ethnicity in American Literature* (Amherst: University of Massachusetts Press, 1992), 2.

3. This is particularly true for George G. Foster. His many and insightful accounts of mid-nineteenth-century New York (which we could easily read today as the Ur-texts behind those by Joseph Mitchell, Luc Sante, Scorsese, etc.) are, to a good extent, the repository of most of what was to come next, save the ethnic subjectivity that would make all the difference. See now George G. Foster, *New York by Gas-Light and Other Urban Sketches*, ed. and intro. Stuart M. Blumin (Berkeley: University of California Press, 1990).

4. Mary Nolan, *The Transatlantic Century: Europe and America, 1890–2010* (Cambridge: Cambridge University Press, 2012).

5. Matthew F. Jacobson, *Special Sorrows: The Diasporic Imagination of Irish, Polish, and Jewish Immigrants in the United States* (Cambridge: Harvard University Press, 1995), 136.

6. Ross J. Wilson, *New York and the First World War: Shaping an American City* (Farnham: Ashgate, 2014), 34. For a dense discussion of the critical knot of Hellenism and emigration, see Ioanna Laliotou, *Transatlantic Subjects: Acts of Migration and Cultures of Transnationalism between Greece and America* (Chicago: University of Chicago Press, 2004).

7. Eric Homberger, "Immigrants, Politics, and the Popular Cultures of Tolerance," in *The Cambridge Companion to the Literature of New York*, ed. Cyrus R. K. Patell and Brian Waterman (Cambridge: Cambridge University Press, 2010), 139.

8. J. W. Sullivan, *Tenement Tales of New York* (New York: Henry Holt & Co., 1895). O'Connell points out that Sullivan tries "to portray the process of assimilation both with sympathy and with an understanding of the price it exacted from the immigrants" (Shaun O'Connell, *Remarkable, Unspeakable New York. A Literary History* [Boston: Beacon Press, 1995], 107).

9. See for instance R. W. Mueller, *Kegel-Reime, mit humoristischen Skizzen und Halbtonbildern*, Zweite Serie (New York: Lauter, 1891). On Nast and Keppler as ethnic brokers: Albert Bernhard Faust, *The German Element in the United States with Special Reference to Its Political, Moral, Social, and Educational Influence*, 2 vols. (Boston: Houghton Mifflin, 1909).

10. A classic reference study is David M. Fine, *The City, the Immigrant and American Fiction, 1880–1920* (Methuchen, NJ: The Scarecrow Press, 1977).

11. Peter Sloterdijk, *Stress and Freedom* (Cambridge: Polity Press, 2015).

12. Abraham Cahan, *The Rise of David Levinsky* (New York: The Modern Library, 2001 [1917]), 175.

13. Anzia Yezierska, "The Fat of the Land," *Century* 98 (August 1919): 466–79; Samuel Ornitz, *Haunch Paunch and Jowl: An Anonymous Autobiography* (New York: Boni and Liveright, 1923).

14. Anzia Yezierska, *Bread Givers* (Garden City, NY: Doubleday, Page & Co., 1925).

15. Garibaldi M. Lapolla, *The Grand Gennaro* (New York: The Vanguard Press, 1934).

16. Antonín Dvořák, "Music in America," *Harper's* 90, no. 537 (February 1895): 429–34; now in *Dvořák in America 1892–1895*, ed. John C. Tibbetts (Portland, OR: Amadeus Press, 1993), 370–80, where the composer's observation (together with his keen interest in African American and Native American music) is reiterated—see his 1893 *Letter to the Editor* of the *New York Herald*: 359–61; James Agee, *Brooklyn Is: Southeast of the Island, Travel Notes* (New York: Fordham University Press, 2005 [1968]).

17. Jean-Christophe Bailly, *La Phrase urbaine* (Paris: Seuil, 2013). A notable collection of essays on Italian American soundscapes is in a special issue of the *Italian American Review*, ed. John Gennari, 9, no. 1 (Winter 2019).

18. Edward Harrigan, *The Mulligans* (New York: G.W. Dillingham, 1901), 395–96.

19. Harrigan, *The Mulligans*, 137, 139. Similar descriptions punctuate German American literature. Barbara Lang (*The Process of Immigration in German-American Literature from 1850 to 1900: A Change in Ethnic Self-Description* [München: Wilhelm Fink, 1988]) brings attention, for instance, to Caspar Stürenburg's *Kleindeutschland: Bilder aus dem New Yorker Alltagsleben*, 1872, and to the many titles by Kathinka Sutro-Schücking. On the latter, see also Dorothea Diver Steucher, *Twice Removed: The Experience of German-American Women Writers in the Nineteenth Century* (New York: Peter Lang, 1990).

20. For instance, the Swiss German Oskar Kollbrunner dedicates a poem to telephone poles: *Telefonstangen* (in *Anthologie Deutschamerikanischer Dichtung* (New York: Association for Culture–Gemeinschaft für Kultur, 1925), 21ff. A superb sociohistorical analysis of ethnic gustatory practices in East Harlem is

Simone Cinotto's *The Italian American Table: Food, Family, and Community in New York City* (Champaign: University of Illinois Press, 2013).

21. Morris Rosenfeld, *Songs from the Ghetto*, with prose translation, glossary and introduction by L. Wiener (Boston: Copeland and Day, 1898), 3. The prose translation makes away with the metrical mold—here with a succession of octaves.

22. *A Treasury of Yiddish Stories*, ed. Irving Howe and Eliezer Greenberg (New York: Viking Press, 1954); *A Treasury of Yiddish Poetry*, ed. Irving Howe and Eliezer Greenberg (New York: Holt, Rinehart and Winston, 1969). The two volumes also hosted, as translators, a significant gathering of some of the best voices of the twentieth century, and especially post–Second World War American literature, from—among others—Ludwig Lewisohn to Saul Bellow and Alfred Kazin (in the selection of stories), and from Cynthia Ozick to Adrienne Rich, Allen Mandelbaum, Stanley Kunitz, James Wright, and W. S. Merwin (in the selection of poetry).

23. Leo Wiener, *The History of Yiddish Literature in the Nineteenth Century* (New York: Charles Scribner's Sons, 1899). Alexander Harkavy, *English-Yiddish Dictionary* (New York: Hebrew Publishing Co., 1891); Wiener, *Yidish-Englishes verterbukh: A Dictionary of the Yiddish Language, with a Treatise on Yiddish Reading, Orthography and Dialectal Variations* (New York: A. Harkavy, 1898); Hutchins Hapgood, *The Spirit of the Ghetto: Studies of the Jewish Quarter in New York* (New York: Funk & Wagnalls, 1902). Morris Rosenfeld is one of the four poets on whom Hapgood concentrates his attention, the other three being Eliakim Zunser (the *Badchen*), Menachem Dolitzki, and Abraham Wald (aka Lessin).

24. Moses Rischin, *The Promised City: New York's Jews, 1870–1914* (Cambridge: Harvard University Press, 1977).

25. Stefano Luconi, "La stampa in lingua italiana negli Stati Uniti dalle origini ai giorni nostri," *Studi Emigrazione* 46 (2009): 547–67; and Bénédicte Deschamps's wide-ranging monograph, *Histoire de la presse italo-américaine: Du Risorgimento à la Grande Guerre* (Paris: L'Harmattan, 2020).

26. Richard E. Helbig, *The Growth of the German American Collection of the New York Public Library During 1906–1907* (Philadelphia: The International Printing Co., 1908); Rudolf Cronau, *Drei Jahrhunderte Deutschen Lebens in Amerika: Eine Geschichte der Deutschen in der Vereinigten Staaten* (Berlin: Dietrich Reimer [Ernst Vohsen], 1909); James M. Bergquist, "The German-American Press," in *The Ethnic Press in the United States: A Historical Analysis and Handbook*, ed. Sally M. Miller (Westport, CT: Greenwood Press, 1987): 131–59; Peter Conolly-Smith, *Translating America: An Immigrant Press Visualizes American Popular Culture, 1895–1918* (Washington, DC: Smithsonian Books, 2004).

27. Anna D. Jaroszyńska-Kirchmann, *The Polish Hearst: Ameryka-Echo and the Public Role of the Immigrant Press* (Champaign: University of Illinois Press, 2015).

28. Andrew T. Kopan, "The Greek Press," in *The Ethnic Press*, 161–76.

29. Rischin, *The Promised City*, 133; Jacob Gordin, *The Jewish King Lear*, ed. Ruth Gay and Sophie Glazer (New Haven: Yale University Press, 2007) (first staged in Yiddish in 1892).

30. *Ethnic Theatre in the United States*, ed. Maxine Schwartz-Seller (Westport, CT: Greenwood Press, 1983).

31. *Other Witnesses: An Anthology of Literature of the German Americans, 1850–1914*, ed. Cora Lee Kluge (Madison, WI: Max Kade Institute for German-American Studies, University of Wisconsin, 2007), 149.

32. *A Bintel Brief: Sixty Years of Letters from the Lower East Side to the Jewish Daily Forward*, ed. and intro. Isaac Metzker, foreword and notes by Harry Golden (New York: Schocken Books, 1971).

33. Bernard Martin, "Yiddish Literature in the United States," *American Jewish Archives* 33, no. 2 (1981): 188.

34. Leo Wiener, *The History of Yiddish Literature in the Nineteenth Century* (New York: Charles Scribner's Sons, 1899), 218.

35. Rose Basile Green, *The Italian-American Novel: A Document of the Interaction of Two Cultures* (Rutherford, NJ: Fairleigh Dickinson University Press, 1974); Martino Marazzi, *Voices of Italian America: A History of Early Italian American Literature with a Critical Anthology* (Madison, NJ: Fairleigh Dickinson University Press, 2004); Francesco Durante, *Italoamericana: The Literature of the Great Migration, 1880–1943*, gen. ed. Robert Viscusi, trans. ed. Anthony Julian Tamburri, biblio. ed. James J. Periconi (New York: Fordham University Press, 2014).

36. Norman Duncan, "The Tenement Book and Reader," *Harper's* 107, no. 637 (June 1903): 102–3.

37. Henry Louis Mencken, *Appendix: Non-English Dialects in America*, in *The American Language: An Inquiry into the Development of English in the United States* (New York: Knopf, 1977), 616–97. (The *Appendix* first appeared in the fourth edition, 1936.)

38. Carl Schurz, *Lebenserinnerungen*, vols. 1–3 (Berlin: Reimer, 1906–1907); Schurz, *The Reminiscences of Carl Schurz*, vols. 1–3 (New York: The McClure Company, 1907–1908); Michael Boyden, "1869, March 4. Carl Schurz Is Sworn In as the First German-Born Senator of the United States, Representing Missouri: Reminiscences and Lebenserinnerungen," in *A New Literary History of America*, ed. Greil Marcus and Werner Sollors (Cambridge, MA: The Belknap Press of Harvard University Press, 2009), 344–48.

39. These are the two incipits: "Città senza storia e senza leggende, / città senza eroi e senza monumenti, / senza santuarii e senza fortificazioni, / Città senza porte, aperta a tutti i pedoni, / a tutti i romei del pane e dei pensieri importuni, / Città degli uomini comuni / che mangiano e bevono e dormono / e lavorano e generano senza altre ambizioni, / o Città incredibile, realtà senza visioni, / io ti saluto" ("La Città Incredibile," *Il Fuoco* [New York], 15 marzo 1915: 8). And

"City without history and without legends, / City without scaffolds and without monuments, / Ruinless, shrineless, gateless, open to all wayfarers, / To all the carriers of dreams, to all the burden bearers, / To all the seekers for bread and power and forbidden ken, / City of the Common Men, / Who work and eat and breed, without any other ambitions, / O incorruptible Force, / O Reality without visions, / What is between you and me?" (*New York and I*, in Arturo Giovannitti, *Parole e sangue*, ed. Martino Marazzi [Isernia: Iannone, 2005], 281).

40. Edward Bok, *The Americanization of Edward Bok: The Autobiography of a Dutch Boy Fifty Years After* (New York: Charles Scribner's Sons, 1920).

41. David Pinski, *The Generations of Noah Edon* (New York: The Macaulay Company, 1931).

42. Allen Guttmann, *The Jewish Writer in America: Assimilation and the Crisis of Identity* (New York: Oxford University Press, 1971), 101.

43. Ludwig Lewisohn, *The Island Within* (New York: Harper & Brothers, 1928), 187. For a larger discussion of the novel, see Yael Schacher, "1924, May 26. President Coolidge Signs the Johnson-Reed Act, Halting Mass Immigration to the United States. Americans All," in *A New Literary History of America*, 569–74.

44. A reference study in this sense is Dorothy Burton Skårdal, *The Divided Heart: Scandinavian Immigrant Experience through Literary Sources*, with a preface by Oscar Handlin (Oslo: Universitetforlaget, 1974).

45. Joseph Sciorra, "Diasporic Musings on Veracity and Uncertainties of 'Core 'ngrato,'" in *Neapolitan Postcards: The Canzone Napoletana as Transnational Subject*, ed. Goffredo Plastino and Joseph Sciorra (Lanham: Rowman & Littlefield, 2016), 115–50.

46. Martino Marazzi, "Raccontarsi bilingue: *Le Vie di New York* di Martino Iasoni," *Lingue Culture Mediazioni/Languages Cultures Mediation* 3, no. 1 (2016): 115–33.

47. Luigi Donato Ventura, *Peppino il lustrascarpe*, ed. Martino Marazzi (Milano: FrancoAngeli, 2007). (First original edition in French, 1885; in English, 1886; in Italian, with no date.) The English-language edition was published in the collection of short stories *Misfits and Remnants*, coauthored by Ventura and S. Shevitch (Boston: Ticknor and Company). On Shevitch, see Conolly-Smith, *Translating America*, 64.

48. Finley Peter Dunne, *Mr. Dooley's Philosophy* (New York: R.H. Russell, 1900); Dunne, *Mr. Dooley's Opinions* (New York: R.H. Russell, 1901); Dunne, *Observations by Mr. Dooley* (New York: R.H. Russell, 1902); Dunne, *Dissertations by Mr. Dooley* (New York: Harper & Brothers, 1906).

49. Conolly-Smith, *Translating America*, 61.

50. Sabine Haenni, "Constituting a Public: German Jewish Contact, German American Theater, and the Foundation of German American Ethnicity in the 1890s," in *German? American? Literature? New Directions in German-American Studies*, ed. Winfried Fluck and Werner Sollors (New York: Peter Lang, 2002), 217–48.

51. Conolly-Smith, *Translating America*, 156ff., 218ff.

52. Hermann Haller, *Tra Napoli e New York: Le macchiette italo-americane di Eduardo Migliaccio: Testi con introduzione e glossario* (Roma: Bulzoni, 2006). Interestingly enough, a "Migliaccio" (most likely the Italian American performer) is thanked in the Acknowledgments of a minor classic of New York urban anthropology like David Efron's *Gesture and Environment* (The Hague: Mouton and Co., 1941).

53. Karen Majewski, *Traitors and True Poles: Narrating a Polish-American Identity* (Athens: Ohio University Press, 2003), 129.

54. Myra Kelly, *Little Citizens: The Humours of School Life* (New York: McClure, Phillips & Co., 1904); Mike Gold, *Jews Without Money* (New York: Horace Liveright, 1930).

55. Edwin G. Burrows and Mike Wallace, *Gotham: A History of New York City to 1898* (New York: Oxford University Press, 1999); Mike Wallace, *Greater Gotham: A History of New York City from 1898 to 1919* (New York: Oxford University Press, 2017).

56. There are, of course, noticeable exceptions, for instance in the way skyscrapers are often used as signifiers of pride, strength, and modernity, as in the *Ballade von Woolworthturm, New York* by Oskar Kollbrunner (*Anthologie Deutschamerikanischer Dichtung*, 16–20). Sigurd Folkestad's *On the Suspension Bridge*, 1916, "points forward to Hart Crane": Orm Øverland, *The Western Home: A Literary History of Norwegian America* (n.p.: The Norwegian American Historical Association, 1996), 235.

57. "It's a 'scursion,'" comment the schoolkids, or rather, the "pilgrims from the East Side" of Myra Kelly's *Little Citizens* on the very special day of their trip to Central Park (Kelly, *Little Citizens*, 273, 264).

58. Mike Gold, "A Jewish Childhood in the New York Slums," in *Mike Gold: A Literary Anthology*, ed. Michael Folsom (New York: International Publishers, 1972), 292.

59. Even from the titles of some of the most incisive novels one notices the peculiar position of the Irish, lured by the temptation to merge, but at the cost of personal loss. See Maurice F. Egan's *The Disappearance of John Longworthy* (Notre Dame, IN: The Ave Maria, 1890), and John Talbot Smith's *The Art of Disappearing* (New York: William H. Yound & Company, 1902). Charles Fanning has shrewdly read F. Scott Fitzgerald's silence on his Irish origins through this perspective: Charles Fanning, *The Irish Voice in America: 250 Years of Irish-American Fiction*, 2nd ed. (Lexington, KY: University Press of Kentucky, 2000).

60. Henry Roth, *Call It Sleep* (New York: Robert O. Ballou, 1934); Daniel Fuchs, *Summer in Williamsburg* [1934], in *The Brooklyn Novels: Summer in Williamsburg, Homage to Blenholt, Low Company* (Boston: Black Sparrow Press, 2006).

61. Pietro di Donato, *Christ in Concrete* (Indianapolis: The Bobbs-Merrill Company, 1939).

62. Werner Sollors, "Immigrants and Other Americans," in *Columbia Literary History of the United States*, ed. Emory Elliott (New York: Columbia

University Press, 1988), 569–88; Sollors, *Multilingual America: Transnationalism, Ethnicity, and the Languages of American Literature*, ed. Werner Sollors (New York: New York University Press, 1998); Sollors, *Ethnic Modernism* (Cambridge, MA: Harvard University Press, 2008).

63. A dense and inspiring reflection on contemporary metropolises' self-representation is in Marco d'Eramo, *Il selfie del mondo. Indagine sull'età del turismo* (Milano: Feltrinelli, 2017).

64. Fuchs, *Summer in Williamsburg*, 337–38.

Chapter 3

1. On Dante in Longfellow, see especially J. Chesley Mathews, "An Historical Overview of American Writers' Interest in Dante (to about 1900)," in *Dante's Influence on American Writers 1776–1976*, ed. Anne Paolucci (New York: Griffon House, 1977), 19–20.

2. "I sell from the morn / Until the sun sets. / I'm selling words, that's right"; *Memorie di Lorenzo Da Ponte e scritti vari in prosa e poesia*, compendiate da Jacopo Bernardi (Firenze: Le Monnier, 1871), 385–86.

3. I thank Jim Periconi for having brought this rare Da Ponte to my attention.

4. "Those whom the turn of human things / then doomed to drag as victims / crust by crust their wretched lives, / drifters in exile"; Pietro D'Alessandro, *Monte Auburno* (Stati Uniti di America [sic], 1835), 6, lines 39–42.

5. Vincenzo Botta, *Dante as Philosopher, Patriot, and Poet: With an Analysis of the "Divina Commedia," Its Plot and Episodes* (New York: Scribner, 1865) [then as *Introduction to the Study of Dante* (London: Scribner, 1867 and 1887)].

6. Angelina La Piana, *Dante's American Pilgrimage: A Historical Survey of Dante Studies in the United States 1800–1944* (New Haven: Yale University Press, 1948), 136.

7. *Memorie della vita e delle peregrinazioni del fiorentino Filippo Mazzei, con documenti storici sulle sue missioni politiche come agente degli Stati Uniti d'America, e del re Stanislao di Polonia*, vol. 1 (Lugano: Tipografia della Svizzera italiana, 1845), 368.

8. Although Botta "refused to follow Rossetti in presenting Dante as a precursor of the Reformation" (La Piana, *Dante's American Pilgrimage*, 136).

9. "Dante Alighieri: 'To a Young Girl Dying: With a Gift of Fresh-Palm Leaves,'" *The Catholic World* 8, no. 44 (November 1868): 213–22. Angelina La Piana identifies the byline with the Italian priest Joseph Maria Finotti (La Piana, *Dante's American Pilgrimage*, 139).

10. See Giovanni Pascoli, *Odi e Inni. MDCCCXCVI-MCMXI* (Bologna: Zanichelli, 1953), 183–84.

11. The following articles all appeared in *La Follia di New York*: Pin, "Nella Colonia di Dante," July 30, 1911, 1; Cor., "Dante a New York," August 6, 1911 (with illustration by Onorio Ruotolo [aka Bayard]), 8; Corferreum, "Dante a New York: L'arrivo," August 13, 1911 (ill. Bayard), 8; Corferreum, "Dante a New York: Dante dinanzi ai Giudici Americani," August 20, 1911 (ill. Bayard), 8; Corferreum, "Dante a New York: Dante che visita la 'Dante,'" August 27, 1911 (ill. Bayard), 8; Pin, "Povero Dante!," September 10, 1911, 1; Pin, "Dante in acqua!," October 1, 1911, 1; Bayard (and ill.), "Dante a New York: L'Incontro del Poeta col Riformatore," October 1, 1911, 8; Eisenherz, "Dante a New York: Il soggiorno nella dogana," November 5, 1911 (ill. Bayard), 8.

12. This, incidentally, corresponds to historical reality. A first, monumental statue of Dante, shipped to New York from Italy, was at the center of an acrimonious debate in New York in 1911–12, and eventually rejected; it wasn't until 1921 that the current statue was effectively installed. See also Guy P. Raffa, *Dante's Bones: How a Poet Invented Italy* (Cambridge: The Belknap Press of Harvard University Press, 2020), 164–65.

13. "I, who am Italy's honor and pride / must lie here at the bottom of a steamer / after having always cried for more than a month /. . . ./ And so the prophet of our people / resigns himself to stay in Customs, / like a clandestine good shipped here"; Eisenherz, "Dante a New York. Il soggiorno nella dogana," *La Follia di New York*, November 5, 1911, 8.

14. See Giuseppe Prezzolini, *I trapiantati* (Milano: Longanesi, 1963), 332–36; Francesco Durante, *Italoamericana*, vol. 2 (Milano: Mondadori, 2005), 832, informs us that, in the 1910s, "'La Follia di New York' ospitava una rubrica fissa, 'La colonia di Dante,' dedicata alle peggiori castronerie segnalate dai lettori ['La Follia di New York' ran a regular column, 'La colonia di Dante,' dedicated to the most outrageous nonsense pointed out by its readers]."

15. "Here, the higher *morgheg* you have on *rialestèta* / the *isier* you become a *prominente*, / and the *isier* the Societies will make you / a president, the more you're illiterate. // With a big shot as friend, then, / a *politiscia*, a *bartenda* or a lawyer / you'll turn into a *bosso*, from being *Mistar so and so*; // and then they'll throw a banquet for you, just / like we do for a congressman, / and they'll put you on the paper's front page"; Prezzolini, 333–34.

16. "Dante is to no avail; nobody knows who he is. / Christopher Columbus is of little help. . . / Better Marconi! Radio-telephony!" (Prezzolini, *I trapiantati*, 331).

17. Efrem Bartoletti, *Nostalgie proletarie: Raccolta di Canti Poetici e di Inni Rivoluzionari* (Brooklyn: Libreria editrice dei Lavoratori Industriali del Mondo [Italian I.W.W. Bureau], 1919), 3, in Efrem Bartoletti, *Poesie: Alla scoperta delle nostre radici storiche* (Comune di Costacciaro, 2001), 5. The translations of these and subsequent verses by Bartoletti are by Ann Goldstein and me, in Martino Marazzi, *Voices of Italian America: A History of Early Italian American Literature*

with a Critical Anthology (Madison, NJ: Fairleigh Dickinson University Press, 2004), 232.

18. "To the narrow smoky hole, / sepulchre of the living, I walk / in pain and sadness. My wounded soul / laments its cruel, tragic destiny. / And I say: Here's the sad uncertain life / of the miner, who goes down in the morning / not knowing if he will come out at night!" (Efrem Bartoletti, *Nostalgie proletarie*, 110, in Efrem Bartoletti, *Poesie*, 112).

19. The same rhyme recurs at the beginning of the crucial second canto of *Purgatorio* (11–13).

20. "Vascello" is in Efrem Bartoletti, *Nostalgie proletarie*, 91–96 (and *Poesie*, 93–98); the manuscript of "La Ridda" can be read in the online Archivio Bartoletti (under the wrong heading *La bibbia delle ombre*): www.romanoguerra.it/efrem.php#poemipoesie.

21. "Per le nozze" is in Efrem Bartoletti, *Nostalgie proletarie*, 35 (in *Poesie*, 37); "Venticinque luglio" and "Morte" are in the later collection *Evocazioni e Ricordi* (*Poesie*, 335–38, 375–77); "Nel Sogno D'oltretomba [sic]" is now in *Poesie*, 190–230.

22. The former poem is in Efrem Bartoletti, *Nostalgie proletarie*, 45–47 (*Poesie*, 47–49); for the latter (signed with the pen name "Etrusco"), the online Archivio Bartoletti (www.romanoguerra.it/efrem.php#poemipoesie) provides the original manuscript; a ruined microfilm testifies to its partial publication in West Hoboken's *Avanti!* of November 5, 1921.

23. On a charming slip of paper at the private family archives (consulted thanks to the courtesy of the poet's grandson, David Giovannitti), Giovannitti copied in longhand the sonnet "Tanto gentile e tanto onesta pare" in an exercise of delicate calligraphy dedicated to his then-fiancée, Carrie (Caroline Zaikaner). This Dantesque billet-doux, adorned with a drawing of Dante staring at the sun, probably by Giovannitti himself, is part of the 1912 jail correspondence from the Essex County Jail, where Giovannitti was awaiting trial following the bread-and-roses strike in Lawrence, Massachusetts.

24. The 1938 original *Parole e sangue* (New York: The Labor Press) was a slender collection; its 2005 Italian edition (edited by Martino Marazzi, with essays by Joseph Tusiani [Isernia: Iannone]) reprints the much larger selection of Italian poems chosen by the author two years before his death in 1959, published under the title *Quando Canta il Gallo*. In *Parole e sangue* (2005) one finds "A mia madre" at pages 39–44; "Il cenacolo," 112–13; "Sogno del forzato," 121–24; "A Dante," 202–3.

25. Arturo Giovannitti, *The Collected Poems of Arturo Giovannitti*, intro. Norman Thomas (Chicago: Clemente, 1962), 131.

26. Ibid., 81.

27. Luigi Carnovale, *Esortazione ai Direttori dei Giornali Italo-Americani a gli Emigrati Italiani tutti per commemorare degnamente negli Stati Uniti d'America il Sesto Centenario della morte di Dante* (Chicago, 1921), 8–9.

28. "The Italians scattered around the United States of America, the exiled Italians, will celebrate religiously September 14, 1921, with an intense and austere recollection of their thought and soul; with the intimate, silent, but firm resolution always to be inspired and to conform, in every circumstance of life, to the purest and purifying virtues of him, the 'fugitive Ghibelline,' who, begging his life crust by crust, 'quite unbending against the blows of chance / and of his misfortune,' writing the divine poem and exhaling his rightly disdainful soul away from his *fair sheepfold*, made exile so sacred and glorious" (ibid., 13).

29. Carnovale's 1921 *Esortazione* was a slender pamphlet; three years later he published the redundant 747-page *Il Secentenario Dantesco 1321–1921 negli Stati Uniti d'America: Suprema purissima gloriosa imperitura affermazione di italianità intellettuale spirituale morale* (Chicago: Blakely-Oswald, 1924).

30. Gilbert F. Cunningham, *The Divine Comedy in English: A Critical Bibliography 1901–1966* (Edinburgh: Oliver and Boyd, 1966), 107–10.

31. V. A. Castellucci, *Le Avventure di Dante in America. Poemetto Satirico Umoristico* (New York: Vanni, 1935); Giuseppe Prezzolini (*I trapiantati*, 339–40) opines that "Castellucci" might be a pen name disguising the literary activity of a priest. Actually, the rare copy I was able to consult in the Harris Collection of American Poetry and Plays at the John Hay Library of Brown University (where I thank Jennifer Betts and Gayle Lynch) was a gift by the author, who inscribed it on the front page. A similar seal (but not an actual signature) is stamped on the copy in the Fondo Ragusa of the Biblioteca della Fondazione Spadolini in Florence (where I thank Silvia Forasiepi). That would seem to make it difficult to consider it a pseudonym; and as for his (or her?) profession, it may well be that Prezzolini was privy to information unavailable to us. Unless—given the peculiar degree of sophistication displayed by the literary irony suffusing the *poemetto*, and the circumstance of the connection with Olga Ragusa (a student of Prezzolini's and owner of the Vanni imprint)—we consider the possibility of Prezzolini as the author, deliberately and jokingly misleading the reader in a rather typical self-deprecating fashion. At this point, I would not rule out this hypothesis.

32. Ibid., 51: "unveiled so many mysteries / that the *ghenga* was seized by fright, / hastily abandoned those neighborhoods, / and went seeking fortune somewhere else."

33. Ibid., 15: "a little by handling the *sciabola* [shovel], a little by *pedolando* [peddling] his banana-cart, and a little by fixing *sciocchese* di *second-end* [second-hand showcases]." Here the "Italglish" adds peculiar meanings by playing on *double entendres*.

34. Ibid., 14: "Look . . . look how many people are queuing up for the breadline."

35. Ibid., 26.

36. Ibid., 43: "a son of Ethiopia (with golden teeth and a white jacket)." Note, of course, the timing of "Dante's" observation: it is 1935, the year of the Italian attack on Ethiopia.

37. Ibid., 66. "I'd like to cry: O depraved people, / a regal beauty was Beatrice indeed, / whose foot was short, whose teeth were perfect, / angelic her mien, inspiring / chaste virtues; the dresses / covering her matrix were not transparent; / how modest and immaculate, with her sweet accents!"

38. Ibid., 68–69: "*Tu-dei* women rightly don't adjust to / working as housemaids"; "one readies the electoral *fild*."

39. Ibid., 59. "It gets dark. New York, in the evening, shows the Poet an extraordinary sight, for the magical and surprising effect of its lights and its incredible colors, criss-crossing and shattering themselves with sparkles and prisms, stripes and twists; they burn, flame, twinkle in a luminous flicker made of letters."

40. Ibid., 73: "the paesano must remain 'paesano.'"

41. Garibaldi M. Lapolla, *The Grand Gennaro* (New York: Vanguard, 1935), 248 [new edition, ed. and intro. Steven J. Belluscio (New Brunswick: Rutgers University Press, 2009)].

42. "An unmistakably italochrome brilliance": Luigi Ballerini and Fredi Chiappelli, "Contributi espressivi delle scritture e parlate americo-italiane," in Vittore Branca et al., *L'espressivismo linguistico nella letteratura italiana (Roma, 16–18 gennaio 1984)* (Roma: Accademia Nazionale dei Lincei, 1985), 206.

43. Garibaldi M. Lapolla, *The Grand Gennaro*, 154.

44. See Stefano Albertini, "Dante in camicia nera: uso e abuso del divino poeta nell'Italia fascista," *The Italianist* 16 (1996): 117–42; and Luigi Scorrano, *Il Dante "fascista": Saggi, letture, note dantesche* (Ravenna: Longo, 2001).

45. "The Duce Benito Mussolini is presaged by the enigmatic number 666"; Bonifacio Grandillo, *Il messo di Dio: Mussolini profetizzato da San Giovanni il Divino e da Dante* (The Godsend: Mussolini prophesied by Saint John the Divine and by Dante) (New York: Vanni, 1936), 20.

46. "This 9, then, is Mussolini's auspicious number; indeed, we have: 9 letters in his family name Mussolini; 9 vowels in Duce Benito Mussolini; 9 letters in Predappio . . . . The words Italia, Impero, Romano, are made of six letters each, hence 6, 6, 6." Ibid., 40, 42.

47. Ibid., 38.

48. "Therefore, just as God made the world ready for the coming of Christ with the Roman Empire, so it might be that for the future He is preparing the world for Christ's return on earth, with the movement initiated by Mussolini. Will this be? Time and history will judge and bear witness." Ibid., 70.

49. I thank Paul Friedman of the NYPL.

50. Pietro di Donato, *Christ in Concrete* (New York: Signet, 1993 [1939]), 187.

51. *Farabutto* means "scoundrel," "rogue."

52. di Donato, *Christ in Concrete*, 198.

53. Joseph Tusiani, *The Age of Dante: An Anthology of Early Italian Poetry Translated into English Verse* (New York: Baroque, 1974).

54. Giuseppe Tusiani, *Dante in licenza* (Verona: Editrice Nigrizia, 1952); Joseph Tusiani, *Envoy from Heaven* (New York: Obolensky, 1965) [Italian translation: *Dal cielo "inviato speciale"* (Roma: Edizioni Presenza, 1966)].

55. Maria Carmela Fanciullo, "Il romanzo di Joseph Tusiani: dal *Dante in licenza* ad *Envoy from Heaven*," in *"Two Languages, Two Lands": L'opera letteraria di Joseph Tusiani*, ed. Cosma Siani (San Marco in Lamis: Quaderni del Sud, 2000), 127.

56. Joseph Tusiani, *Dante's Lyric Poems*, intro. Giuseppe C. Di Scipio, rev. ed. (Brooklyn: Legas, 1999 [1992]); Tusiani, *Dante's Divine Comedy: As Told for Young People* (Mineola: Legas, 2009 [2001])—which includes the previous *Dante's Inferno: As Told for Young People* (New York: Obolenski, 1965) and *Dante's Purgatorio: As Told for Young People* (New York: Astor-Honor, 1968).

57. Dante Alighieri, *The Inferno*, trans. John Ciardi, intro. Archibald T. MacAllister (New York: New American Library, 1954), 9–10.

58. See also, below, the often-quoted *The Old Italians Dying* by Ferlinghetti.

59. John Ciardi, *Selected Poems* (Fayetteville: University of Arkansas Press, 1984), 217.

60. John Ciardi, "Translator's Note," in Dante Alighieri, *The Divine Comedy: The Inferno, The Purgatorio, The Paradiso*, trans. John Ciardi (New York: New American Library, 2003 [1970]), xix.

61. John Ciardi, "The Relevance of the *Inferno*," in *Dante Alighieri: Three Lectures*, ed. J. Chesley Mathews, Francis Fergusson, and John Ciardi (Washington, DC: The Library of Congress, 1965), 35–53.

62. "He who is far from the living tongue of the homeland translates, whether he likes it or not, as if in a dream, touched by every new word that he learns, by every unpredicted and striking nuance of a language that is not his"; Giuseppe Tusiani, "Prefazione," in Nicola Testi, *Inferno: Da La Divina Commedia di Dante Alighieri in vernacolo pugliese* (Firenze: Vallecchi, 1958), 8. For an introduction to Testi's writings, see Francesco Durante, "Nicola Testi: una passeggiata nel sottobosco letterario italoamericano," in *Com'esuli pensieri: Giornate di studio sulla "Letteratura di confine." La Letteratura italoamericana*, ed. Ernesto L'Arab and Cosma Siani (Castelluccio dei Sauri: Edizioni Lampyris, 2014), 133–46.

63. Lawrence Ferlinghetti, *A Coney Island of the Mind* (New York: New Directions, 1958), 28.

64. Lawrence Ferlinghetti, "The Old Italians Dying," in *These Are My Rivers: New & Selected Poems 1955–1993* (New York: New Directions, 1994), 219–22.

65. Pietro di Donato, *Three Circles of Light* (New York: Messner, 1960), 2–3, and (with only slight variants), 245.

66. Matthew Diomede, *Pietro Di Donato, the Master Builder* (Lewisburg: Bucknell University Press, 1995), 146.

67. Pietro di Donato, *The American Gospels*, ed. Fred L. Gardaphé and Richard Alexander (New York: Bordighera, 2011), 25.

68. Ibid., 30.

69. Ibid., 95.

70. Ibid., 96.

71. Ibid., 136.

72. That great work by Don DeLillo, *Underworld* (London: Picador, 1999 [1997]), so rich in stimuli, voices, and layers, is well worth something more than a footnote. But smaller print is perhaps a more appropriate means of expressing doubts, or a caveat. The question of how and if, *Underworld* being the most "Italian American" among DeLillo's novels, a Dante theme can be detected, taken into consideration, and analyzed in it, has in fact already been addressed in various ways, and a number of interesting ideas have been put forward. See James J. Periconi, "DeLillo's *Underworld*: Toward a New Beginning for the Italian American Novel," *VIA: Voices in Italian Americana* 11, no. 1 (2000), 141–58; Ira Nadel, "The Baltimore Catechism; or Comedy in *Underworld*," in *UnderWords: Perspectives on Don DeLillo's* Underworld, ed. Joseph Dewey, Steven G. Kellmann, and Irving Malin (Newark: University of Delaware Press, 2002), 176–98; John Paul Russo, "Technology and the Mediterranean in DeLillo's *Underworld*," in *America and the Mediterranean*, ed. Massimo Bacigalupo and Pierangelo Castagnetto (Torino: Otto, 2003), 187–97; David L. Pike, "*Underworld* and the Architecture of the Urban Space," in *Don DeLillo: Mao II, Underworld, Falling Man*, ed. Stacey Olster (London: Continuum, 2011), 83–98. By dealing with the relevance in *Underworld* of the main character's Italian American roots and of the role played by the seemingly contrasting forces of Catholicism and of a fully developed technological landscape, and indeed by examining the crucial position occupied by waste vis-à-vis a search for structure, purity, and peace, these and other scholars have approached and occasionally focused on the issue of Dante's influence. And it is quite obvious that, among the multiple echoes that reverberate in the catchy title, one would be hard-pressed not to consider certain topical examples: the looming shadow of an underworld, nondescript as it may be; the recourse to a Virgilian pattern in the guise of a phantom limb (Albert Bronzini in relation to Nick Shay); the need for understanding and for a sort of spiritual cleansing; even—one might opine—the way the narrative's hyperrealist pronunciation grounds the mostly unpronounceable expression of the characters' inner beings, their sense of wonder and disillusion and loss. Elements such as these could well, I think, suggest some kind of Dantean impact. But I suspect one ought to value them ultimately as necessary but not sufficient evidence. Which, to be clear, is entirely to DeLillo's credit—to that of the daring maturity of his vision, both of fiction and of life's inexhaustible questions. The

question of Dante's presence in the grand arc of this narration risks hovering in the haze of academic self-referential prying for "intertextuality." Postmodernism, in an author like DeLillo, is no easy trinket; it is not a convoluted game to annihilate the past and its traditions. *That* would be too easy, and even a staple such as Dante would not be worth the effort.

73. Dan Brown, *Inferno* (New York: Doubleday, 2013); Matthew Pearl, *The Dante Club* (New York: Random House, 2003); David Fincher, *Seven* (Los Angeles: New Line Cinema, 1995), film.

74. See my *Danteum: Studi sul Dante imperiale del Novecento* (Firenze: Franco Cesati, 2015), 127–68.

75. Nick Tosches, *Power on Earth: Michele Sindona's Explosive Story* (New York: Arbor House, 1986); Tosches, *Dino: Living High in the Dirty Business of Dreams* (New York: Doubleday, 1992).

76. Nick Tosches, *In the Hand of Dante* (New York: Back Bay, 2003), 369.

77. Robert Viscusi, *Buried Caesars, and Others Secrets of Italian American Writing* (Albany, NY: State University of New York Press, 2006), 14.

78. Ibid., 25ff.

79. Ibid., 39ff.

80. Ibid., 22.

81. Robert Viscusi, *Ellis Island* (New York: Bordighera, 2013), 56, 257; 59, 254; 60.

82. Ibid., 60.

Chapter 4

1. Dante Alighieri, *Il Convivio/The Banquet*, trans. Richard Lansing (New York: Garland, 1990), 31 (I XIII 4). Here's the original: "Questo mio volgare fu congiungitore delli miei generanti, che con esso parlavano, sì come 'l fuoco è disponitore del ferro al fabro che fa lo coltello: per che manifesto è lui essere concorso alla mia generazione, e così essere alcuna cagione del mio essere" (Dante Alighieri, *Convivio. 2. Testo*, ed. Franca Brambilla Ageno [Firenze: Le Lettere, 1995], 56–57).

2. Quotation from Salvatore Scibona, *The End* (New York: Riverhead, 2009), 308.

3. These are the titles of, respectively, chapters 10 and 11 of Tore Janson's *Speak: A Short History of Languages* (Oxford: Oxford University Press, 2002).

4. In a convincing and deeply personal essay, the Italian Canadian poet Mary di Michele refers to the dense interrelation between language, landscape, and the sociocultural dimension of immigration as a *langscape*: Mary di Michele, "*Langscape*: Language, Landscape, and Memory, the Origins of a Poetics," *Literary Geographies* 3, no. 2 (2017).

5. *Circumstances* is, precisely, the title of the interesting play in one act copyrighted by Caterina Maria Avella in 1923 and now at the Library of Congress (*Catalogue of Copyright Entries*, Part 1: Books, Group 2, New Series, vol. 20, part 2 [Washington, DC: Government Printing Office, 1924], 171). Avella was one of the women writers whose Italian-language literature had been promoted by the nationalist-fascist monthly *Il Carroccio* in the 1920s (see her story "The Flapper" in my *Voices of Italian America: A History of Early Italian American Literature with a Critical Anthology* [Madison, NJ: Fairleigh Dickinson University Press, 2004], 78–91). One of the many telling examples of "creative" bilingualism. I thank Robin Masi Carlson for sharing the play with me and for the ongoing conversation about Avella.

6. Fred L. Gardaphe, "The Evolution of Italian American Autobiography," in *The Italian American Heritage: A Companion to Literature and Arts*, ed. Pellegrino D'Acierno (New York: Garland, 1999), 292.

7. Amy A. Bernardy, *America vissuta* (Torino: Fratelli Bocca, 1911), 316; Giuseppe Prezzolini, "La lingua della 'giobba,'" *Lingua Nostra* 1, no. 4 (agosto 1939): 121–22; Renzo Nissim, *In cerca del domani: Avventura autobiografica* (Livorno: Belforte, 1983). On the rhetoric of the ubiquitous ads of the Italian American press, see the incisive contribution by Sarah Salter, "Archival History and Forms of Surprise: Unraveling Italian American Newspaper Advertisements," *American Periodicals* 28, no. 1 (April 2018). For a more comprehensive account, see Martino Marazzi, *Lingua e letteratura nel contesto dell'emigrazione italiana. Preliminari*, in *Italexit. Saggi su Risorgimento e disunione nazionale* (Firenze: Franco Cesati, 2019), 205–32.

8. The exodus from the remote Alpine valleys of Canton Ticino has produced a real masterpiece, Plinio Martini's *Il fondo del sacco* (Bellinzona: Casagrande, 1970). A majestic scholarly nonfiction on this peculiar emigration is Renato Martinoni's *Il paradiso e l'inferno: Storie di emigrazione alpina* (Bellinzona: Salvioni, 2011).

9. A captivating starting point for the study of postcard rhetoric can be the Florida Atlantic University's website *Itamm—Italian American Memories*, https://itamm.omeka.net/, accessed July 12, 2021.

10. Eugenio Salvatore convincingly explains that the immigrants' "limited familiarity" (*scarsa dimestichezza*) with punctuation—in their letter-writings—is something "undoubtedly relevant, but at the same time not at all uncommon" (*dato senz'altro significativo, ma nient'affatto anomalo*): *Emigrazione e lingua italiana: Studi linguistici* (Ospedaletto: Pacini, 2017), 249ff.

11. Not far from the parents' birthplaces of such distinct Italian American personalities as novelist Mari Tomasi or politician and military officer Charles Poletti.

12. Marie H. Ets, *Rosa: The Life of an Italian Immigrant*, 2nd ed. (Madison, WI: University of Wisconsin Press, 1999 [1970]).

13. To be sure, this is a constant linguistic trait in the immigrant letters analyzed by Eugenio Salvatore (*Emigrazione e lingua italiana*, 141).

14. "Local Italian Theater Crowded Every Night," *The Brooklyn Daily Eagle*, December 3, 1899, 7.

15. Source: Giorgio Cheda, ed., *L'emigrazione ticinese in California*, Volume secondo, Epistolario II (Locarno: Dadò, 1981), 664–65.

16. Gardaphé has been advancing the concept of an Italian American "illiterature" based on his groundbreaking analyses of Italian immigrants' art and expressiveness, at the crossroads between literacy, illiteracy, and orality. Suffice it here to point to such reference studies as *Italian Signs, American Streets: The Evolution of Italian American Narrative* (Durham, NC: Duke University Press, 1996); *Dagoes Read: Tradition and the Italian/American Writer* (Toronto: Guernica, 1996). One should also add, as a case in point, his online presentation of the Augusto Lentricchia Collection, deposited in the Special Collections of Stony Brook University. Gardaphé kindly informed me about some of his conference presentations on the topic, among which is *Illiterary Acts: Barely Writing the Self*, at the MLA 2019 Chicago Conference.

17. See unnumbered colophon of Arturo Giovannitti's *The Cage* (Riverside, CT: Hillacre, 1914).

18. Simplicio, *Coraggio e avanti!*, in *Sgraffi* (Newark: Biblioteca de L'Adunata dei Refrattari, 1946), 93.

19. Act 3, Scene 3, 345–57.

20. A critical and most detailed overview of the "colonial" publishers is in James Periconi, *Italian American Book Publishing and Bookselling*, in *The Routledge History of Italian Americans*, ed. William J. Connell and Stanislao G. Pugliese (New York: Routledge, 2018), 252–67. See also *Strangers in a Strange Land: A Catalogue of an Exhibition on the History of Italian-language American Imprints (1830–1945). From the Collection of James J. Periconi, with a Bibliography of these and related works* (New York: The Grolier Club, 2012; paperback ed.: New York: Bordighera Press, 2013).

Chapter 5

1. The OED opts for the hyphenated form. In its online edition, the entry is dated March 2006.

2. My favorite is the least conspicuous, that is, the common misspelling of an Italian word in the 1873 entry from the *Boston Daily Globe*, which mentions the San Francisco Italian-language daily *La Voce del Populo*. Such minute misspellings, both by Italian Americans and non–Italian Americans, have indeed always been so pervasive that they would deserve a thorough in-depth analysis.

3. The volume, published by Random House, bore an Italian-language nonidentical twin brother: *Gli Italiani di New York*, versione italiana riveduta

ed ampliata da Alberto Cupelli (New York: Labor Press, 1939). A comparative analysis of the two books is, to my knowledge, still to be done.

4. Here is *Jerusalem Delivered*'s second stanza, in the historical (and notoriously free) translation by lord Fairfax: "O heavenly Muse, that not with adding bays / Deckest thy brow by the Heliconian spring, / But sittest crowned with stars' immortal rays / In Heaven, where legions of bright angels sing; / Inspire life in my wit, my thoughts upraise, / My verse ennoble, and forgive the thing, / If fictions light I mix with truth divine, / And fill these lines with other praise than thine" (Torquato Tasso, *Jerusalem Delivered: A Poem*, trans. Edward Fairfax, ed. Henry Morley [London: Routledge and Sons, 1890], 33). Andreoni's second stanza may be rendered with the following: "In my previous canto, friends, you heard my summer campaign; / the winter one have I now started; / you ought to listen to this one too, / and hear what I found / if you all take heed. / I shall tell all, as I can / and with the help of the eternal God." Andreoni's poem is in Maria Bendinelli Predelli and Antonio Andreoni, *Piccone e poesia: La cultura dell'ottava nel poema d'emigrazione di un contadino lucchese* (Lucca: n.p., 1997), 231–32.

5. Another example among many: *Polpetto*, an incisive and sour-mellow 1973 novel by Frank Mele (New York: Crown) is dedicated, among others, "to / Great-uncle Giovanni and laborer / Angelo Lezzi, my tutors, / who knew Dante, Tasso, and the / United States Constitution / by heart." The main aspect of Italian American art on which the story concentrates is a night of "macchiette" at a local theater in Rochester, New York.

6. See Stefano Luconi, "Whiteness and Ethnicity in Italian-American Historiography," in *The Status of Interpretation in Italian American Studies*, ed. Jerome Krase (Stony Brook, NY: Forum Italicum Publishing, 2011), 146–63.

7. Hermann W. Haller, *Tra Napoli e New York: Le macchiette italo-americane di Eduardo Migliaccio: Testi con introduzione e glossario* (Roma: Bulzoni, 2006); Giorgio Bertellini, *Italy in Early American Cinema: Race, Landscape, and the Picturesque* (Bloomington: Indiana University Press, 2010).

Chapter 6

1. Mario Garibaldino Lapolla, as recorded in the municipal birth records, was born on April 5, the son of Biagio Oreste, "age 31, occupation café owner" and Maria Nicola Buonvicino. He emigrated to the United States with his family at only two years of age, in 1890. The Lapollas settled almost immediately in the Italian section of East Harlem that is the setting for all of the author's novels. The variant "Marto," adopted as a middle name, is to be considered an editorial *lapsus calami*. The few biographical facts come in part from the

Garibaldi Mario Lapolla Papers (Mss. Group 64) preserved in Philadelphia at the Historical Society of Pennsylvania (formerly at the Balch Institute for Ethnic Studies), in part from the hometown municipality thanks to the courtesy of Donato Rapone. My thanks to Salvatore Salerno and Beagan Wilcox for their assistance in retrieving materials.

2. Finally, one can rely on a rigorous and much-deserved monograph: Steven J. Belluscio, *Garibaldi M. Lapolla: A Study of His Novels* (New York: Bordighera Press, 2017). Belluscio's study follows his highly laudable curatorial work, which has brought Lapolla's novels back to the readers' attention: *The Fire in the Flesh* (New York: Vanguard Press, 1931)—new edition, ed. and intro. Steven J. Belluscio (New York: Bordighera Press, 2012); *Miss Rollins in Love* (New York: Vanguard Press, 1932)—new edition, ed. and with a chronology, introduction and bibliography by Steven J. Belluscio (New York: Bordighera Press, 2016). *The Grand Gennaro* (New York: Vanguard Press, 1935)—new edition, ed. and intro. Steven J. Belluscio (New Brunswick, NJ: Rutgers University Press, 2009). In quoting from *The Grand Gennaro* and the other novels I use their first, Vanguard Press, editions.

3. It quickly received favorable mention, for example, in the columns of the *New York Times* (by Fred T. Marsh, "'The Grand Gennaro' and Some Other Recent Works of Fiction," *The New York Times*, September 1, 1935), and of the *New Republic* (by a friend such as Jerre Mangione, "'The Grand Gennaro,' by Garibaldi M. Lapolla," *The New Republic*, October 23, 1935).

4. Thus in part argues Richard A. Meckel, "A Reconsideration: The Not So Fundamental Sociology of Garibaldi Marto Lapolla," *MELUS* 14, nos. 3–4 (Fall–Winter 1987): 127–28, 138. With regard to political commitment, it is well to recall that in New York Lapolla, at the height of his most prolific season as a novelist, was a frontline militant of the Socialist Party (Elisabetta Vezzosi, *Il socialismo indifferente: Immigrati italiani e Socialist Party negli Stati Uniti del primo Novecento* [Roma: Edizioni Lavoro, 1991], 182).

5. Between 1929 and 1943 Lapolla authored a series of anthologies and English grammar texts for use in the schools (he was a teacher and principal his entire life, in Manhattan and Brooklyn), and the year before his death he wrote two cookbooks that were not without interest precisely because of their "ethnic" nature—see a title as suggestive as *Italian Cooking for the American Kitchen* (New York: Funk, 1953). The other book, *The Mushroom Cook Book* (New York: Funk, 1953) carried some illustrations by the author as well. Worthy of mention is the fact that *The Fire in the Flesh* (1931) contains what is perhaps one of the earliest descriptions of *pizza* (in italics in the text) in the United States: "a dough-cake flattened out and spread with anchovies, slices of tomato, and cheese, all seasoned spicily and baked on hot ashes" (67). More generally speaking, it is now possible to profitably place Lapolla's activity within the

framework of a social history of Italian American food: Simone Cinotto, *The Italian American Table: Food, Family and Community in New York City* (Chicago: University of Illinois Press, 2013).

6. La Ribellione di Millie, in *Figli di due mondi: Fante, Di Donato & C. Narratori italoamericani degli anni '30 e '40*, ed. Francesco Durante (Cava de' Tirreni: Avagliano, 2002).

7. Giuseppe Prezzolini, "Stati Uniti: autobiografia e romanzo," *Gazzetta del Popolo* [Torino], December 19, 1934; Prezzolini, *I trapiantati* (Milano: Longanesi, 1963).

8. Olga Peragallo, *Italian-American Authors and Their Contribution to American Literature*, ed. Anita Peragallo (New York: S.F. Vanni, 1949); Robert Anthony Orsi, *The Madonna of 115th Street: Faith and Community in Italian Harlem, 1880–1950* (New Haven: Yale University Press, 1985); Robert Viscusi, "The Text in the Dust: Writing Italy across America," *Studi Emigrazione* 19, no. 65 (March 1982); Viscusi, "Il Caso della Casa: Stories of Houses in Italian America," in Richard N. Juliani, ed., *The Family and Community Life of Italian Americans* (Staten Island, NY: American Italian Historical Association, 1983); Viscusi, "Gli dei: l'allegoria dell'America italiana," in Ignazio Baldelli and Bianca Maria Da Rif, eds., *Lingua e letteratura italiana nel mondo oggi* (Firenze: Olschki, 1991)—now in Robert Viscusi, *Buried Caesars, and Other Secrets of Italian American Writing* (Albany, NY: State University of New York Press, 2006); Alberto Traldi, "La tematica dell'emigrazione nella narrativa italo-americana," *Comunità* 30 (August 1976).

9. We possess three typewritten versions of *Jerry*, drafted between 1941 and 1954 (the one that appears most complete consists of 115 pages), and a manuscript contained in eighteen notebooks: the first eleven bearing the title *The Light That Never Was*, the last seven a different title: *The Journey Homeward*.

10. And that's not all. The archival documents contain, among other things, the typescripts of three theatrical works, part of the correspondence, and the most interesting testimonies regarding the profession of educator.

11. Thus, in those years, he replied to his sociologist friend Covello with the full awareness of experience: "You ask me to send you my manuscript of the novel I have been fortunate enough to find a publisher for and lo and behold you want it merely for a sociological document. Well, it ain't such a beast. It is just a yarn that happens to have the Italians living in Harlem doing a lot of things which they should not do and some they cannot help doing, and I am afraid of no more sociological interest than the numerous flies and bugs that infest Little Italy" (letter dated October 22, 1930, *Lapolla Papers*, Philadelphia). Lapolla is referring to his first novel, *The Fire in the Flesh*.

12. A first attempt at a strict linguistic analysis of Lapolla's prose and its contamination of American English and popular Italian is in the thesis of Sabrina Rivolta, *L'inglese degli italoamericani*: The Grand Gennaro di Garibaldi M. Lapolla (Università degli Studi di Milano, 2004–2005).

13. Lapolla puts in the mouth of this minor, but very well delineated, male character the most explicit condemnation of a society, like that of the United States, in which everything "seems upside down and crazy," in contrast to another in which "everyone knows his place and things are orderly and decent" (37): for this reason too, the choice of name makes one think of a possible homage paid to Bartolomeo Vanzetti.

14. See also the incisive essay by Stefania Dotti, "*Making America, Being Italian*. Le radici italiane di *The Grand Gennaro* di Garibaldi Lapolla," in Alberto Sorbini, ed., *Racconti dal mondo: Narrazioni, memorie e saggi delle migrazioni* (Foligno [Perugia]: Editoriale Umbra, 2017).

Chapter 7

1. Alfredo Borgianini, *A te, Roma mia 1921*, in *Sonetti e Poesie Romanesche* (Trenton, NJ: n.p., 1948), 86, 89.

2. A first monographic attempt is John Vincent Aquilecchia's BA thesis, *Alfredo Borgianini: Un poeta romanesco nel Nuovo Mondo* (Università degli Studi di Milano, a. a. 2013–2014).

3. Michael Fiaschetti, *You Gotta Be Rough: The Adventures of Detective Fiaschetti of the Italian Squad as Told to Prosper Buranelli by Michael Fiaschetti* (Garden City, NY: Doubleday, Doran & Company, 1930); Fiaschetti, *Gioco duro*, ed. Martino Marazzi (Cava de' Tirreni: Avagliano, 2003); Carl Marzani, *The Education of a Reluctant Radical*, Books 1–5 (New York: Topical Books, 1992–2002).

4. *Ultra*. Strenna commemorativa del XV anniversario della fondazione della Italian Dressmakers Union, Locale 89, I.L.G.W.U., New York, Italian Labor Education Bureau—Liberal Press, Inc., no date [but 1934].

5. See, above, *"Our Brother Dante": Dantesque Reappropriations in Italian America*. More in general, Martino Marazzi, *Danteum: Studi sul Dante imperiale del Novecento* (Firenze: Franco Cesati, 2015).

6. *Atlante della letteratura italiana*, ed. Sergio Luzzatto and Gabriele Pedullà, vols. 1–3 (Torino: Einaudi, 2010–2012).

7. Luigi Bonaffini and Joseph Perricone, eds., *Poets of the Italian Diaspora: A Bilingual Anthology* (New York: Fordham University Press, 2014).

8. François Cavanna, *Les Ritals* (Paris: Belfond, 1978). A reappraisal of Cavanna's masterpiece is in Teresa Fiore's *Pre-Occupied Spaces: Remapping Italy's Transnational Migrations and Colonial Legacies* (New York: Fordham University Press, 2017), 137–60.

9. For an updated overview, Franca Sinopoli, *Prospettiva transnazionale e ricerca di nuove politiche culturali nello studio della letteratura italiana contemporanea*, in *La Letteratura italiana nel mondo: Nuove prospettive*, ed. Luigi Bonaffini and Joseph Perricone (Isernia: Iannone, 2015), 29–39. An excellent critical introduction to the North American dimension is Edvige Giunta and Kathleen Zamboni

McCormick, eds., *Teaching Italian American Literature, Film, and Popular Culture* (New York: The Modern Language Association of America, 2010). An example of rigorous and in-depth analysis of the "new" Italian immigrant literature is Daniele Comberiati's *Scrivere nella lingua dell'altro: La letteratura degli immigrati in Italia (1989–2007)* (Bruxelles: Peter Lang, 2010).

10. Donna Gabaccia, "Is Everywhere Nowhere? Nomads, Nations, and the Immigrant Paradigm of United States History," *The Journal of American History* 86, no. 3 (December 1999): 1116; Peter Carravetta, *After Identity: Migration, Critique, Italian American Culture* (New York: Bordighera Press, 2016), 222.

11. I quote from Abdelmalek Sayad's *La doppia assenza: Dalla illusione dell'emigrato alla sofferenza dell'immigrato*, ed. Salvatore Palidda (Milano: Cortina, 2002), 169 [the original French edition came out in 1999]).

12. Mia Lecomte, *Di un poetico altrove: Poesia transnazionale italofona (1960–2016)* (Firenze: Franco Cesati, 2018); Anthony Julian Tamburri, *Un biculturalismo negato: La letteratura italiana negli Stati Uniti* (Firenze: Franco Cesati, 2018).

13. Robert A. Orsi, *The Madonna of 115th Street: Faith and Community in Italian Harlem, 1880–1950*, 3rd ed. (New Haven: Yale University Press, 2010 [first ed.: 1985]); Joseph Sciorra, ed., *Italian Folk: Vernacular Culture in Italian-American Lives* (New York: Fordham University Press, 2010); Luisa Del Giudice, ed., *Sabato Rodia's Towers in Watts: Art, Migrations, Development* (New York: Fordham University Press, 2014); Edvige Giunta and Joseph Sciorra, eds., *Embroidered Stories: Interpreting Women's Domestic Needlework from the Italian Diaspora* (Jackson, MS: University Press of Mississippi, 2014); Joseph Sciorra, *Built with Faith: Italian American Imagination and Catholic Material Culture in New York City* (Knoxville, TN: University of Tennessee Press, 2015).

14. Email from Stephen A. Borgianini to Francesco Durante and me, ca. January 2012.

Chapter 8

1. Robert Viscusi, *Buried Caesars, and Other Secrets of Italian American Writing* (Albany, NY: State University of New York Press, 2006).

2. Robert Viscusi, *Ellis Island* (New York: Bordighera Press, 2013); and www.ellisislandpoem.com.

Conclusion

1. Robert Viscusi, *Astoria* (Toronto: Guernica, 1995), 22.

2. Viscusi, *Astoria*. . . : 216.

3. Viscusi, *Astoria*. . . : 23.

4. Richard Russo, *Elsewhere* (New York: Knopf, 2012).

5. "La nostra Università, collocata sul mare e fra terre che danno tante vite all'emigrazione, a me par destinata più d'ogni altra a compiere, col mezzo dei suoi alunni, la riconquista dell'Italia nomade." Giovanni Pascoli, *Una sagra* [1900], in *Prose: Volume primo. Pensieri di varia umanità*, ed. Augusto Vicinelli (Milano: Mondadori, 1946), 180.

6. Jonathan Arac, "Are Americans Plural but America Mono?," *ADFL Bulletin* 43, no. 2 (2015): 34–36; Arac, "Anglo-Globalism?," *New Left Review* 16 (July–August 2002): 35–45.

7. Franco Biondi, *Passavantis Rückkehr: Erzählungen* (Fischerhude: Verlag Atelier im Bauernhaus, 1982); Marisa Fenoglio, *Il ritorno impossibile* (Roma: Nutrimenti, 2012).

8. Michela Baldo, *Italian-Canadian Narratives of Return: Analysing Cultural Translation in Diasporic Writing* (London: Palgrave Macmillan, 2019).

9. Elvira Mujčić, *Dieci prugne ai fascisti* (Roma: Elliott, 2016).

Bibliography

Abeni, Damiano, Raffaella Bertazzoli, Cesare G. De Michelis, and Pietro Gibellini, eds. *Belli oltre frontiera: La fortuna di G.G. Belli nei saggi e nelle versioni di autori stranieri*. Roma: Bonacci, 1983.
Agee, James. *Brooklyn Is: Southeast of the Island, Travel Notes*. New York: Fordham University Press, 2005.
Albertini, Stefano. "Dante in camicia nera: uso e abuso del divino poeta nell'Italia fascista." *The Italianist* 16 (1996): 117–42.
Alighieri, Dante. *Il Convivio/The Banquet*. Translated by Richard Lansing. New York: Garland, 1990.
———. *Convivio. 2. Testo*. Edited by Franca Brambilla Ageno. Firenze: Le Lettere, 1995.
———. *The Divine Comedy: The Inferno, The Purgatorio, The Paradiso*. Translated by John Ciardi. New York: New American Library, 2003.
———. *The Inferno*. Translated by John Ciardi, introduction by Archibald T. MacAllister. New York: New American Library, 1954.
Anagnostou, Yiorgos. [Review of Peter Carravetta, *After Identity: Migration, Critique, Italian American Culture* (New York: Bordighera Press, 2017)]. *The Italian American Review* 8, no. 2 (Summer 2018): 212–19.
Anthologie Deutschamerikanischer Dichtung. New York: Association for Culture-Gemeinschaft für Kultur, 1925.
Aquilecchia, John Vincent. *Alfredo Borgianini: Un poeta romanesco nel Nuovo Mondo*. BA thesis, Università degli Studi di Milano, 2013–2014.
Arac, Jonathan. "Anglo-Globalism?" *New Left Review* 16 (July–August 2002): 35–45.
———. "Are Americans Plural but America Mono?" *ADFL Bulletin* 43, no. 2 (2015): 34–36.
Atlante della letteratura italiana. Vols. 1–3. Edited by Sergio Luzzatto and Gabriele Pedullà. Torino: Einaudi, 2010–2012.
Bailly, Jean-Christophe. *La Phrase urbaine*. Paris: Seuil, 2013.

Baldo, Michela. *Italian-Canadian Narratives of Return: Analysing Cultural Translation in Diasporic Writing.* London: Palgrave Macmillan, 2019.
Ballerini, Luigi, and Fredi Chiappelli. "Contributi espressivi delle scritture e parlate americo-italiane." In Vittore Branca et al., *L'espressivismo linguistico nella letteratura italiana (Roma, 16–18 gennaio 1984).* Roma: Accademia Nazionale dei Lincei, 1985.
Baranello, Adriana M. "Giovanni Pascoli's 'La grande proletaria si è mossa': A Translation and Critical Introduction." *California Italian Studies* 2, no. 1 (2011): n.p.
Barry, Phillips. "The Ballad of Lord Randal in New England." *The Journal of American Folklore* 16, no. 63 (October–December 1903): 258–64.
Bartoletti, Efrem. *Nostalgie proletarie: Raccolta di canti poetici e di inni rivoluzionari di Efrem Bartoletti.* Brooklyn, NY: Libreria editrice dei Lavoratori Industriali del Mondo–Italian I.W.W. Publishing Bureau, 1919.
Basile Green, Rose. *The Italian-American Novel: A Document of the Interaction of Two Cultures.* Madison, NJ: Fairleigh Dickinson University Press, 1974.
Bayard [aka Onorio Ruotolo]. "Dante a New York: L'Incontro del Poeta col Riformatore." *La Follia di New York*, October 1, 1911, 8.
Beebee, Thomas. "Ballad of the Apocalypse: Another Look at Bob Dylan's 'Hard Rain.'" *Text and Performance Quarterly* 11 (1991): 18–34.
Belli, Giuseppe Gioachino. *The People of Rome in 100 Sonnets.* Roma: Bardi, 1984.
Belli, Giuseppe Gioachino. *I sonetti*, vols. 1–4. Edited by Pietro Gibellini, Lucio Felici, and Edoardo Ripari. Torino: Einaudi, 2018.
Belluscio, Steven J. *Garibaldi M. Lapolla: A Study of His Novels.* New York: Bordighera Press, 2017.
Bendinelli Predelli, Maria, and Antonio Andreoni. *Piccone e poesia: La cultura dell'ottava nel poema d'emigrazione di un contadino lucchese.* Lucca: n.p., 1997.
Bergquist, James M. "The German-American Press." In *The Ethnic Press in the United States: A Historical Analysis and Handbook*, edited by Sally M. Miller, 131–59. Westport, CT: Greenwood Press, 1987.
Bernardy, Amy A. *America vissuta.* Torino: Fratelli Bocca, 1911.
Bertellini, Giorgio. *Italy in Early American Cinema: Race, Landscape, and the Picturesque.* Bloomington: Indiana University Press, 2010.
Bianchini, Angela. *Voce donna.* Milano: Frassinelli, 1996.
Biondi, Franco. *Passavantis Rückkehr: Erzählungen.* Fischerhude: Verlag Atelier im Bauernhaus, 1982.
Bok, Edward. *The Americanization of Edward Bok: The Autobiography of a Dutch Boy Fifty Years After.* New York: Charles Scribner's Sons, 1920.
Bonaffini, Luigi, and Joseph Perricone, eds. *Poets of the Italian Diaspora: A Bilingual Anthology.* New York: Fordham University Press, 2014.
Borgianini, Alfredo. *Sonetti e Poesie Romanesche.* Trenton, NJ: n.p., 1948.
Botta, Vincenzo. *Dante as Philosopher, Patriot, and Poet: With an Analysis of the "Divina Commedia," Its Plot and Episodes.* New York: Scribner, 1865.

Boyden, Michael. "1869, March 4. Carl Schurz Is Sworn in as the First German-Born Senator of the United States, Representing Missouri. Reminiscences and Lebenserinnerungen." In *A New Literary History of America*, edited by Greil Marcus and Werner Sollors, 344–48. Cambridge, MA: The Belknap Press of Harvard University Press, 2009.

Bronzini, Giovanni B. "Gli 'anelli intermedi' tra la ballata di *Lord Randal* e la canzone dell'*Avvelenato*." *Giornale italiano di filologia* 20 (1967): 53–70.

———. *La ballata di "Lord Randal" e i suoi rapporti con la canzone dell' "Avvelenato."* In *Studi di storia dell'arte bibliologia ed erudizione in onore di Alfredo Petrucci*, 99–111. Milano: Carlo Bestetti–Edizioni d'Arte, 1969.

———. *La canzone dell'Avvelenato nella tradizione popolare italiana*. In *Studi in onore di Carmelina Naselli*. Vol. I, 39–74. Catania: Università di Catania, Facoltà di Lettere e Filosofia, 1968.

Brooks, Van Wyck. *The Dream of Arcadia: American Writers and Artists in Italy 1760–1915*. New York: E.P. Dutton & Co., 1958.

Brown, Dan. *Inferno*. New York: Doubleday, 2013.

Burke, Peter. *Popular Culture in Early Modern Europe*. New York: New York University Press, 1978.

Burns, Jennifer, and Catherine Keen. "Italian Mobilities." *Italian Studies* 75, no. 2 (2020): 140–54.

Burrows, Edwin G., and Mike Wallace. *Gotham: A History of New York City to 1898*. New York: Oxford University Press, 1999.

Buzard, James. *The Beaten Track: European Tourism, Literature, and the Ways to "Culture," 1800–1918*. Oxford: Oxford University Press, 1993.

Cahan, Abraham. *The Rise of David Levinsky*. New York: The Modern Library, 2001.

Carletti, Lorenzo, and Cristiano Giometti. *Raffaello on the Road: Rinascimento e propaganda fascista in America (1938–40)*. Roma: Carocci, 2016.

Carnovale, Luigi. *Esortazione ai Direttori dei Giornali Italo-Americani a gli Emigrati Italiani tutti per commemorare degnamente negli Stati Uniti d'America il Sesto Centenario della morte di Dante*. Chicago: n. p., 1921.

———. *Il Secentenario Dantesco 1321–1921 negli Stati Uniti d'America: Suprema purissima gloriosa imperitura affermazione di italianità intellettuale spirituale morale*. Chicago: Blakely-Oswald, 1924.

Carravetta, Peter. *After Identity: Migration, Critique, Italian American Culture*. New York: Bordighera Press, 2016.

Castellucci, V. A. *Le Avventure di Dante in America: Poemetto Satirico Umoristico*. New York: Vanni, 1935.

Cavanna, François. *Les Ritals*. Paris: Belfond, 1978.

Chapman, Charlotte Gower. *Milocca: A Sicilian Village*. Cambridge, MA: Schenkman, 1971.

Cheda, Giorgio, ed. *L'emigrazione ticinese in California. Volume secondo. Epistolario II*. Locarno: Dadò, 1981.

Ciardi, John. "The Relevance of the *Inferno*." In *Dante Alighieri: Three Lectures*, ed. J. Chesley Mathews, Francis Fergusson, and John Ciardi, 35–53. Washington, DC: The Library of Congress, 1965.

———. *Selected Poems*. Fayetteville: University of Arkansas Press, 1984.

———. Translator's Note. In Dante Alighieri, *The Divine Comedy: The Inferno, the Purgatorio, the Paradiso*, translated by John Ciardi, XIX–XXV. New York: New American Library, 2003.

Cinotto, Simone. *The Italian American Table: Food, Family, and Community in New York City*. Champaign: University of Illinois Press, 2013.

———. *Making Italian America: Consumer Culture and the Production of Ethnic Identities*, edited by Simone Cinotto. New York: Fordham University Press, 2014.

Comberiati, Daniele. *Scrivere nella lingua dell'altro: La letteratura degli immigrati in Italia (1989–2007)*. Bruxelles: Peter Lang, 2010.

Conolly-Smith, Peter. *Translating America: An Immigrant Press Visualizes American Popular Culture, 1895–1918*. Washington, DC: Smithsonian Books, 2004.

Cor. [aka Riccardo Cordiferro]. "Dante a New York." *La Follia di New York*. August 6, 1911, 8.

Corferreum [aka Riccardo Cordiferro]. "Dante a New York: L'arrivo." *La Follia di New York*. August 13, 1911, 8.

———. "Dante a New York: Dante che visita la 'Dante.'" *La Follia di New York*. August 27, 1911, 8.

———. "Dante a New York: Dante dinanzi ai Giudici Americani." *La Follia di New York*. August 20, 1911, 8.

Cronau, Rudolf. *Drei Jahrhunderte Deutschen Lebens in Amerika: Eine Geschichte der Deutschen in der Vereinigten Staaten*. Berlin: Dietrich Reimer (Ernst Vohsen), 1909.

Cunningham, Gilbert F. *The Divine Comedy in English: A Critical Bibliography 1901–1966*. Edinburgh: Oliver and Boyd, 1966.

Da Ponte, Lorenzo. *Memorie di Lorenzo Da Ponte e scritti vari in prosa e poesia, compendiate da Jacopo Bernardi*. Firenze: Le Monnier, 1871.

D'Alessandro, Pietro. *Monte Auburno*. Stati Uniti di America [sic], 1835.

Del Giudice, Luisa, ed. *Sabato Rodia's Towers in Watts: Art, Migrations, Development*. New York: Fordham University Press, 2014.

DeLillo, Don. *Underworld*. London: Picador, 1999.

d'Eramo, Marco. *Il selfie del mondo: Indagine sull'età del turismo*. Milano: Feltrinelli, 2017.

Deschamps, Bénédicte. *Histoire de la presse italo-américaine: Du Risorgimento à la Grande Guerre*. Paris: L'Harmattan, 2020.

Detti, Emma. *Margaret Fuller Ossoli e i suoi corrispondenti: Con lettere inedite di Giuseppe Mazzini, Costanza Arconati, Adam Mickiewicz, Lewis Cass, Jane Carlyle, Maria Mazzini, Benedetta Mazzini, Elizabeth Barrett Browning, Cristina Trivulzio di Belgioioso, Ralph Waldo Emerson*. Firenze: Le Monnier, 1942.

di Donato, Pietro. *The American Gospels*. Edited by Fred L. Gardaphé and Richard Alexander. New York: Bordighera Press, 2011.
———. *Christ in Concrete*. Indianapolis: The Bobbs-Merrill Company, 1939.
———. *Three Circles of Light*. New York: Messner, 1960.
di Michele, Mary. "*Langscape*: Language, Landscape, and Memory, the Origins of a Poetics." *Literary Geographies* 3, no. 2 (2017): 125–38.
Di Nino, Nicola. "Il Belli 'popolare' di Luigi Morandi (con lettere inedite all'editore Barbèra)." *Critica letteraria* 31, no. 4 (2003): 671–98.
Diomede, Matthew. *Pietro Di Donato, the Master Builder*. Lewisburg: Bucknell University Press, 1995.
Diver Steucher, Dorothea. *Twice Removed: The Experience of German-American Women Writers in the Nineteenth Century*. New York: Peter Lang, 1990.
Dotti, Stefania. "*Making America, Being Italian*: Le radici italiane di *The Grand Gennaro* di Garibaldi Lapolla." In *Racconti dal mondo: Narrazioni, memorie e saggi delle migrazioni*, edited by Alberto Sorbini, 305–24. Foligno: Editoriale Umbra, 2017.
Duncan, Norman. "The Tenement Book and Reader." *Harper's* 107, no. 637 (June 1903): 100–6.
Dunne, Finley Peter. *Dissertations by Mr. Dooley*. New York: Harper & Brothers, 1906.
———. *Mr. Dooley's Opinions*. New York: R.H. Russell, 1901.
———. *Mr. Dooley's Philosophy*. New York: R.H. Russell, 1900.
———. *Observations by Mr. Dooley*. New York: R.H. Russell, 1902.
Durante, Francesco. *Italoamericana*. Vol. 2. Milano: Mondadori, 2005.
———. *Italoamericana: The Literature of the Great Migration, 1880–1943*. Edited by Robert Viscusi, Anthony Julian Tamburri, and James J. Periconi. New York: Fordham University Press, 2014.
———. "Nicola Testi: una passeggiata nel sottobosco letterario italoamericano." In *Com'esuli pensieri: Giornate di studio sulla "Letteratura di confine." La Letteratura italoamericana*, edited by Ernesto L'Arab and Cosma Siani, 133–44. Castelluccio dei Sauri: Edizioni Lampyris, 2014.
Dvořák, Antonín. "Music in America." *Harper's* 90, no. 537 (February 1895): 429–34.
Dylan, Bob. *Lyrics 1961–1968*. Edited by Alessandro Carrera. Milano: Feltrinelli, 2016.
Efron, David. *Gesture and Environment: A Tentative Study of Some of the Spatio-Temporal and "Linguistic" Aspects of the Gestural Behavior of Eastern Jews and Southern Italians in New York City, Living under Similar as Well as Different Environmental Conditions*. The Hague: Mouton and Co., 1941.
Egan, Maurice F. *The Disappearance of John Longworthy*. Notre Dame, IN: The Ave Maria, 1890.
Eisenherz [aka Riccardo Cordiferro]. "Dante a New York: Il soggiorno nella dogana." *La Follia di New York*. November 5, 1911, 8.

Ets, Marie H. *Rosa: The Life of an Italian Immigrant*. 2nd ed. Madison, WI: University of Wisconsin Press, 1999.
Fanciullo, Maria Carmela. "Il romanzo di Joseph Tusiani: dal *Dante in licenza ad Envoy from Heaven*." In *"Two Languages, Two Lands": L'opera letteraria di Joseph Tusiani*, edited by Cosma Siani, 127–42. San Marco in Lamis: Quaderni del Sud, 2000.
Fanning, Charles. *The Irish Voice in America: 250 Years of Irish-American Fiction*. 2nd ed. Lexington, KY: The University Press of Kentucky, 2000.
Faust, Albert Bernhard. *The German Element in the United States with Special Reference to Its Political, Moral, Social, and Educational Influence*. 2 vols. Boston: Houghton Mifflin, 1909.
Fenoglio, Marisa. *Il ritorno impossibile*. Roma: Nutrimenti, 2012.
Ferlinghetti, Lawrence. *A Coney Island of the Mind*. New York: New Directions, 1958.
———. *These Are My Rivers: New & Selected Poems 1955–1993*. New York: New Directions, 1994.
Fiaschetti, Michael. *Gioco duro*. Edited by Martino Marazzi. Cava de' Tirreni: Avagliano, 2003.
———. *You Gotta Be Rough: The Adventures of Detective Fiaschetti of the Italian Squad as told to Prosper Buranelli by Michael Fiaschetti*. Garden City, NY: Doubleday, Doran & Company, 1930.
Fine, David M. *The City, the Immigrant and American Fiction, 1880–1920*. Metuchen, NJ: The Scarecrow Press, 1977.
[Finotti, Joseph Maria?]. "Dante Alighieri: 'To a Young Girl Dying: With a Gift of Fresh-Palm Leaves.'" *The Catholic World* 8, no. 44 (November 1868): 213–22.
Fiore, Teresa. *Pre-Occupied Spaces: Remapping Italy's Transnational Migrations and Colonial Legacies*. New York: Fordham University Press, 2017.
Foster, George G. *New York by Gas-Light and Other Urban Sketches*. Edited and with an introduction by Stuart M. Blumin. Berkeley: University of California Press, 1990.
Frasca, Simona. *Birds of Passage. I musicisti napoletani a New York (1895–1940)*. Lucca: Libreria Musicale Italiana, 2010 [American edition, *Italian Birds of Passage: The Diaspora of Neapolitan Musicians in New York*. New York: Palgrave Macmillan, 2014].
Fuchs, Daniel. *Summer in Williamsburg*. In *The Brooklyn Novels. Summer in Williamsburg. Homage to Blenholt. Low Company*. Boston: Black Sparrow Press, 2006.
Fuller, Margaret. *"These Sad But Glorious Days": Dispatches from Europe, 1846–1850*. Edited by Larry J. Reynolds and Susan Belasco Smith. New Haven: Yale University Press, 1991.
Gabaccia, Donna. "Is Everywhere Nowhere? Nomads, Nations, and the Immigrant Paradigm of United States History." *The Journal of American History* 86, no. 3 (December 1999): 1115–34.

———. "Juggling Jargons: 'Italians Everywhere,' Diaspora or Transnationalism?" *Traverse* 12 (2005): 49–64.

———. *Militants and Migrants: Rural Sicilians Become American Workers*. New Brunswick, NJ: Rutgers University Press, 1988.

Gardaphe, Fred L. *Dagoes Read: Tradition and the Italian/American Writer*. Toronto: Guernica, 1996.

———. "The Evolution of Italian American Autobiography." In *The Italian American Heritage: A Companion to Literature and Arts*, edited by Pellegrino D'Acierno, 289–321. New York: Garland, 1999.

———. *Italian Signs, American Streets: The Evolution of Italian American Narrative*. Durham, NC: Duke University Press, 1996.

Gemme, Paola. 2005. *Domesticating Foreign Struggles: The Italian Risorgimento and Antebellum American Identity*. Athens: University of Georgia Press, 2005.

Gennari, John, ed. "Special Issue: Listening to Italian America." *Italian American Review* 9, no. 1 (Winter 2019): 1–130.

Giovannitti, Arthur M. "The Brigandage of Tripoli." *The International Socialist Review* 12, no. 9 (March 1912): 572–76.

Giovannitti, Arturo. *Arrows in the Gale*. Introduction by Helen Keller. Riverside, CT: Hillacre Bookhouse, 1914.

———. *The Cage*. Riverside, CT: Hillacre, 1914.

———. "La Città Incredibile." *Il Fuoco* [New York], 15 marzo 1915, 8.

———. *The Collected Poems of Arturo Giovannitti*. Introduction by Norman Thomas. Chicago: Clemente, 1962.

———. *Parole e sangue*. New York: The Labor Press, 1938.

———. *Parole e sangue*. Edited by Martino Marazzi, with writings by Joseph Tusiani. Isernia: Cosmo Iannone, 2005.

———. *Quando Canta il Gallo*. Introduzione del dr. Carmelo Zito. Chicago: Clemente, 1957.

———. "The Walker." *The International Socialist Review* 13, no. 3 (September 1912): 201–4.

Giovannoli, Renato. *La Bibbia di Bob Dylan. Volume I. Dalle canzoni di protesta alla vigilia della conversione (1961–1978)*. With an essay by Alessandro Carrera. Milano: Àncora, 2017.

Giunta, Edvige, and Kathleen Zamboni McCormick, eds. *Teaching Italian American Literature, Film, and Popular Culture*. New York: The Modern Language Association of America, 2010.

———, and Joseph Sciorra, eds. *Embroidered Stories: Interpreting Women's Domestic Needlework from the Italian Diaspora*. Jackson, MS: University Press of Mississippi, 2014.

Gladsky. Thomas S. *Princes, Peasants, and Other Polish Selves: Ethnicity in American Literature*. Amherst: University of Massachusetts Press, 1992.

Gli Italiani di New York. Versione italiana riveduta ed ampliata da Alberto Cupelli. New York: Labor Press, 1939.

Gold, Mike. "A Jewish Childhood in the New York Slums." In *Mike Gold: A Literary Anthology*, edited by Michael Folsom, 292–319. New York: International Publishers, 1972.

———. *Jews Without Money*. New York: Horace Liveright, 1930.

Gordin, Jacob. *The Jewish King Lear*. Edited by Ruth Gay and Sophie Glazer. New Haven: Yale University Press, 2007.

Gramsci, Antonio. *Gli intellettuali e l'organizzazione della cultura*. Roma: Editori Riuniti, 1977.

———. *Letteratura e vita nazionale*. Roma: Editori Riuniti, 1971.

Grandillo, Bonifacio. 1936. *Il messo di Dio: Mussolini profetizzato da San Giovanni il Divino e da Dante*. New York: Vanni, 1936.

Guttmann, Allen. *The Jewish Writer in America: Assimilation and the Crisis of Identity*. New York: Oxford University Press, 1971.

Haenni, Sabine. "Constituting a Public: German Jewish Contact, German American Theater, and the Foundation of German American Ethnicity in the 1890s." In *German? American? Literature? New Directions in German-American Studies*, edited by Winfried Fluck and Werner Sollors, 217–48. New York: Peter Lang, 2002.

Haller, Hermann. *Tra Napoli e New York: Le macchiette italo-americane di Eduardo Migliaccio: Testi con introduzione e glossario*. Roma: Bulzoni, 2006.

Hapgood, Hutchins. *The Spirit of the Ghetto: Studies of the Jewish Quarter in New York*. New York: Funk & Wagnalls, 1902.

Harkavy, Alexander. *English-Yiddish Dictionary*. New York: Hebrew Publishing Co., 1891.

Harrigan, Edward. *The Mulligans*. New York: G.W. Dillingham, 1901.

Hawthorne, Nathaniel. *The Blithedale Romance*. Oxford: Oxford University Press, 1992.

Helbig, Richard E. *The Growth of the German American Collection of the New York Public Library During 1906–1907*. Philadelphia: The International Printing Co., 1908.

Homberger, Eric. "Immigrants, Politics, and the Popular Cultures of Tolerance." In *The Cambridge Companion to the Literature of New York*, edited by Cyrus R. K. Patell and Brian Waterman, 134–45. Cambridge: Cambridge University Press, 2010.

Howe, Irving, and Eliezer Greenberg, eds. *A Treasury of Yiddish Poetry*. New York: Holt, Rinehart and Winston, 1969.

———, and Eliezer Greenberg, eds. *A Treasury of Yiddish Stories*. New York: Viking Press, 1954.

Hudspeth, Robert N., ed. *The Letters of Margaret Fuller. Volume IV: 1845–47*. Ithaca: Cornell University Press, 1987.

———. *The Letters of Margaret Fuller. Volume V: 1848–49*. Ithaca: Cornell University Press, 1988.

Huysseune, Michel. "'This Country, Where Many Things Are Strange and Hard to Understand': Booker T. Washington in Sicily." *RSA Journal* 25 (2014): 173–90.

Jacobson, Matthew F. *Special Sorrows: The Diasporic Imagination of Irish, Polish, and Jewish Immigrants in the United States*. Cambridge: Harvard University Press, 1995.

James, Henry. *William Wetmore Story and His Friends: From Letters, Diaries, and Recollections*. 2 vols. London: Thames & Hudson, 1903.

Janson, Tore. *Speak: A Short History of Languages*. Oxford: Oxford University Press, 2002.

Jaroszyńska-Kirchmann, Anna D. *The Polish Hearst: Ameryka-Echo and the Public Role of the Immigrant Press*. Champaign: University of Illinois Press, 2015.

Kelly, Myra. *Little Citizens: The Humours of School Life*. New York: McClure, Phillips & Co., 1904.

Kluge, Cora Lee, ed. *Other Witnesses. An Anthology of Literature of the German Americans, 1850–1914*. Madison, WI: Max Kade Institute for German-American Studies, University of Wisconsin, 2007.

Kopan, Andrew T. *The Greek Press*. In *The Ethnic Press in the United States: A Historical Analysis and Handbook*, edited by Sally M. Miller, 161–76. Westport, CT: Greenwood Press, 1987.

La Piana, Angelina. *Dante's American Pilgrimage: A Historical Survey of Dante Studies in the United States 1800–1944*. New Haven: Yale University Press, 1948.

Laliotou, Ioanna. *Transatlantic Subjects: Acts of Migration and Cultures of Transnationalism between Greece and America*. Chicago: University of Chicago Press, 2004.

Lang, Barbara. *The Process of Immigration in German-American Literature from 1850 to 1900: A Change in Ethnic Self-Description*. München: Wilhelm Fink, 1988.

Lapolla, Garibaldi M. *The Fire in the Flesh*. New York: Vanguard Press, 1931 [new edition, Steven J. Belluscio, ed. New York: Bordighera Press, 2012].

———. *The Grand Gennaro*. New York: The Vanguard Press, 1934 [new edition, Steven J. Belluscio, ed. New Brunswick: Rutgers University Press, 2009].

———. *Italian Cooking for the American Kitchen*. New York: Funk, 1953.

———. *Miss Rollins in Love*. New York: Vanguard Press, 1932 [new edition, Steven J. Belluscio, ed. New York: Bordighera Press, 2016].

———. *The Mushroom Cook Book*. New York: Funk, 1953.

———. *La Ribellione di Millie*. In *Figli di due mondi. Fante, Di Donato & C. Narratori italoamericani degli anni '30 e '40*, edited by Francesco Durante, 147–54. Cava de' Tirreni: Avagliano, 2002.

Lecomte, Mia. *Di un poetico altrove: Poesia transnazionale italofona (1960–2016)*. Firenze: Franco Cesati, 2018.

Leogrande, Alessandro. *La frontiera*. Milano: Feltrinelli, 2015.

Lewisohn, Ludwig. *The Island Within*. New York: Harper & Brothers, 1928.

"Local Italian Theater Crowded Every Night." *The Brooklyn Daily Eagle*, December 3, 1899, 7.

Luconi, Stefano. "La stampa in lingua italiana negli Stati Uniti dalle origini ai giorni nostri." *Studi Emigrazione* 46 (2009): 547–67.

———. "Whiteness and Ethnicity in Italian-American Historiography." In *The Status of Interpretation in Italian American Studies*, edited by Jerome Krase, 146–63. Stony Brook, NY: Forum Italicum Publishing, 2011.

Majewski, Karen. *Traitors and True Poles: Narrating a Polish-American Identity*. Athens: Ohio University Press, 2003.

Mangione, Jerre. "'The Grand Gennaro,' by Garibaldi M. Lapolla." *The New Republic*, October 23, 1935, 313.

Marazzi, Martino. *Danteum: Studi sul Dante imperiale del Novecento*. Firenze: Franco Cesati, 2015.

———. *Italexit: Saggi su Risorgimento e disunione nazionale*. Firenze: Franco Cesati, 2019.

———. "Raccontarsi bilingue: *Le Vie di New York* di Martino Iasoni." *Lingue Culture Mediazioni/Languages Cultures Mediation* 3, no. 1 (2016): 115–33.

———. *Voices of Italian America: A History of Early Italian American Literature with a Critical Anthology*. Madison, NJ: Fairleigh Dickinson University Press, 2004.

Mario, Jessie White. "Le miniere di zolfo in Sicilia." *Nuova Antologia* year 29, vol. 49, no. 3 (1 febbraio 1894): 441–66.

———. "Le miniere di zolfo in Sicilia." *Nuova Antologia* year 29, vol. 49, no. 4 (15 febbraio 1894): 719–43.

———. *La miseria di Napoli*. Firenze: Le Monnier, 1877.

———. The Poor in Naples. In *The Poor in Great Cities: Their Problems and What Is Being Done to Solve Them*, by Robert Archey Woods, William Thaddeus Elsing, Jacob A. Riis, Willard Parsons, Evert Jansen Wendell, William Jewett Tucker, Joseph Kirkland, Walter Besant, Edmund R. Spearman, Jessie White Mario, Oscar Craig, and Ernest Flagg, 300–38. New York: Charles Scribner's Sons, 1895.

Marsh, Fred T. "'*The Grand Gennaro*' and Some Other Recent Works of Fiction." *The New York Times*, September 1, 1935, BR6.

Martelli, Sebastiano. Tra militanza e letteratura. In *Il bardo della libertà: Arturo Giovannitti (1884–1959)*, edited by Norberto Lombardi, 245–50. Isernia: Cosmo Iannone, 2011.

Martin, Bernard. "Yiddish Literature in the United States." *American Jewish Archives* 33, no. 2 (1981): 184–209.

Martini, Plinio. *Il fondo del sacco*. Bellinzona: Casagrande, 1970.

Martinoni, Renato. *Il paradiso e l'inferno: Storie di emigrazione alpina*. Bellinzona: Salvioni, 2011.

Marzani, Carl. *The Education of a Reluctant Radical*, Books 1–5. New York: Topical Books, 1992–2002.

Mathews, J. Chesley. "An Historical Overview of American Writers' Interest in Dante (to about 1900)." In *Dante's Influence on American Writers 1776–1976*, edited by Anne Paolucci, 13–21. New York: Griffon House, 1977.

Meckel, Richard A. "A Reconsideration: The Not So Fundamental Sociology of Garibaldi Marto Lapolla." *MELUS* 14, nos. 3–4 (Fall–Winter 1987): 127–39.

Mele, Frank. *Polpetto*. New York: Crown, 1973.

Memorie della vita e delle peregrinazioni del fiorentino Filippo Mazzei, con documenti storici sulle sue missioni politiche come agente degli Stati Uniti d'America, e del re Stanislao di Polonia. Vol. 1. Lugano: Tipografia della Svizzera italiana, 1845.

Mencken, Henry Louis. *The American Language: An Inquiry into the Development of English in the United States*. New York: Knopf, 1977.

Metzker, Isaac, ed. *A Bintel Brief: Sixty Years of Letters from the Lower East Side to the Jewish Daily Forward*. Foreword and notes by Harry Golden. New York: Schocken Books, 1971.

Morandi, Luigi, ed. *Duecento sonetti in dialetto romanesco di Giuseppe Gioachino Belli*. Firenze: Barbèra, 1870.

Mueller, R. W. *Kegel-Reime, mit humoristischen Skizzen und Halbtonbildern*, Zweite Serie. New York: Lauter, 1891.

Mujčić, Elvira. *Dieci prugne ai fascisti*. Roma: Elliott, 2016.

Nadel, Ira. "The Baltimore Catechism; or Comedy in *Underworld*." In *Under-Words: Perspectives on Don DeLillo's Underworld*, edited by Joseph Dewey, Steven G. Kellmann, and Irving Malin, 176–98. Newark: University of Delaware Press, 2002.

Nissim, Renzo. *In cerca del domani. Avventura autobiografica*. Livorno: Belforte, 1983.

Nolan, Mary. *The Transatlantic Century. Europe and America, 1890–2010*. Cambridge: Cambridge University Press, 2012.

Occhipinti, Maria. *Una donna libera*. Palermo: Sellerio, 2004.

O'Connell, Shaun. *Remarkable, Unspeakable New York. A Literary History*. Boston: Beacon Press, 1995.

Ornitz, Samuel. *Haunch Paunch and Jowl: An Anonymous Autobiography*. New York: Boni and Liveright, 1923.

Orsi, Robert Anthony. *The Madonna of 115th Street: Faith and Community in Italian Harlem, 1880–1950*. New Haven: Yale University Press, 1985.

Øverland, Orm. *The Western Home: A Literary History of Norwegian America*. n.p.: The Norwegian American Historical Association, 1996.

Parati, Graziella. *Migration Italy: The Art of Talking Back in a Destination Culture*. Toronto: University of Toronto Press, 2005.

Pascoli, Giovanni. *Odi e Inni. MDCCCXCVI–MCMXI*. Bologna: Zanichelli, 1953.

———. *Prose: Volume primo: Pensieri di varia umanità*. Edited by Augusto Vicinelli. Milano: Mondadori, 1946.

Pearl, Matthew. *The Dante Club*. New York: Random House, 2003.

Peragallo, Olga. *Italian-American Authors and Their Contribution to American Literature*. Edited by Anita Peragallo. New York: S.F. Vanni, 1949.
Periconi, James J. "DeLillo's *Underworld*: Toward a New Beginning for the Italian American Novel." *VIA: Voices in Italian Americana* 11, no. 1 (2000): 141–58.
———. Italian American Book Publishing and Bookselling. In *The Routledge History of Italian Americans*, edited by William J. Connell and Stanislao G. Pugliese, 252–67. New York: Routledge, 2018.
Pike, David L. "*Underworld* and the Architecture of the Urban Space." In *Don DeLillo: Mao II, Underworld, Falling Man*, edited by Stacey Olster, 83–98. London: Continuum, 2011.
Pin. "Dante in acqua!" *La Follia di New York*, October 1, 1911, 1.
———. "Nella Colonia di Dante." *La Follia di New York*, July 30, 1911, 1.
———. "Povero Dante!" *La Follia di New York*, September 10, 1911, 1.
Pinski, David. *Arnold Levenberg*. New York: Simon and Schuster, 1928.
———. *The Generations of Noah Edon*. New York: The Macaulay Company, 1931.
Pirandello, Luigi. *I vecchi e i giovani*. 2 vols. Milano: Treves, 1913 [American edition, *The Old and the Young*, trans. C. K. Scott-Moncrieff. New York: E.P. Dutton & Company, 1928].
———. *Le sorprese della scienza*. In *Novelle per un anno. La mosca*. Firenze: Bemporad, 1923.
Prezzolini, Giuseppe. "La lingua della 'giobba.'" *Lingua Nostra* 1, no. 4 (agosto 1939): 121–22.
———. "Stati Uniti: autobiografia e romanzo." *Gazzetta del Popolo* [Torino], December 19, 1934, 3ff.
———. *I trapiantati*. Milano: Longanesi, 1963.
Raffa, Guy P. *Dante's Bones: How a Poet Invented Italy*. Cambridge, MA: The Belknap Press of Harvard University Press, 2020.
Rischin, Moses. *The Promised City: New York's Jews, 1870–1914*. Cambridge: Harvard University Press, 1977.
Rivolta, Sabrina. *L'inglese degli italoamericani*. The Grand Gennaro *di Garibaldi M. Lapolla*. BA thesis, Università degli Studi di Milano, 2004–2005.
Rosenfeld, Morris. *Songs from the Ghetto*. With prose translation, glossary, and introduction by L. Wiener. Boston: Copeland and Day, 1898.
Roth, Henry. *Call It Sleep*. New York: Robert O. Ballou, 1934.
Russo, John Paul. "Technology and the Mediterranean in DeLillo's *Underworld*." In *America and the Mediterranean*, edited by Massimo Bacigalupo and Pierangelo Castagnetto, 187–97. Torino: Otto, 2003.
Russo, Richard. *Elsewhere*. New York: Knopf, 2012.
Salter, Sarah. "Archival History and Forms of Surprise: Unraveling Italian American Newspaper Advertisements." *American Periodicals* 28, no. 1 (April 2018): 56–72.

Salvatore, Eugenio. *Emigrazione e lingua italiana: Studi linguistici*. Ospedaletto: Pacini, 2017.

Sandburg, Carl. *Chicago Poems*. New York: Henry Holt and Company, 1916.

Sayad, Abdelmalek. *The Suffering of the Immigrant*. Malden, MA: Polity Press, 2004 [Italian edition. *La doppia assenza: Dalla illusione dell'emigrato alla sofferenza dell'immigrato*, edited by Salvatore Palidda. Milano: Cortina, 2002].

Schacher, Yael. "1924, May 26. President Coolidge Signs the Johnson-Reed Act, Halting Mass Immigration to the United States. Americans All." In *A New Literary History of America*, edited by Greil Marcus and Werner Sollors, 569–74. Cambridge, MA: The Belknap Press of Harvard University Press, 2009.

Schurz, Carl. *Lebenserinnerungen*. Vols. 1–3. Berlin: Reimer, 1906–1907.

———. *The Reminiscences of Carl Schurz*. Vols. 1–3. New York: The McClure Company, 1907–1908.

Schwartz-Seller, Maxine, ed. *Ethnic Theatre in the United States*. Westport, CT: Greenwood Press, 1983.

Scibona, Salvatore. *The End*. New York: Riverhead, 2009.

Sciorra, Joseph, ed. *Built with Faith: Italian American Imagination and Catholic Material Culture in New York City*. Knoxville: University of Tennessee Press, 2015.

———. "Diasporic Musings on Veracity and Uncertainties of 'Core 'ngrato.'" In *Neapolitan Postcards: The Canzone Napoletana as Transnational Subject*, edited by Goffredo Plastino and Joseph Sciorra, 115–50. Lanham: Rowman & Littlefield, 2016.

———. *Italian Folk: Vernacular Culture in Italian-American Lives*. New York: Fordham University Press, 2010.

———. "'Why a Man Makes the Shoes?': Italian American Art and Philosophy in Sabato Rodia's Watts Towers." In *Sabato Rodia's Towers in Watts*, edited by Luisa Del Giudice, 183–203. New York: Fordham University Press, 2014.

Scorrano, Luigi. *Il Dante "fascista": Saggi, letture, note dantesche*. Ravenna: Longo, 2001.

Simplicio [aka Gigi Damiani]. *Sgraffi*. Newark: Biblioteca de L'Adunata dei Refrattari, 1946.

Sinopoli, Franca. *Prospettiva transnazionale e ricerca di nuove politiche culturali nello studio della letteratura italiana contemporanea*. In *La Letteratura italiana nel mondo: Nuove prospettive*, edited by Luigi Bonaffini and Joseph Perricone, 29–39. Isernia: Cosmo Iannone, 2015.

Skårdal, Dorothy Burton. *The Divided Heart: Scandinavian Immigrant Experience through Literary Sources*, with a preface by Oscar Handlin. Oslo: Universitetforlaget, 1974.

Sloterdijk, Peter. *Stress and Freedom*. Cambridge: Polity Press, 2015.

Smith, John Talbot. *The Art of Disappearing*. New York: William H. Yound & Company, 1902.
Sollors, Werner. *Ethnic Modernism*. Cambridge, MA: Harvard University Press, 2008.
———. "Immigrants and Other Americans." In *Columbia Literary History of the United States*, edited by Emory Elliott, 569–88. New York: Columbia University Press, 1988.
———. *Multilingual America: Transnationalism, Ethnicity, and the Languages of American Literature*, edited by Werner Sollors. New York: New York University Press, 1998.
Spahr, Clemens. *A Poetics of Global Solidarity: Modern American Poetry and Social Movements*. New York: Palgrave Macmillan, 2015.
Steucher, Dorothea Diver. *Twice Removed: The Experience of German-American Women Writers in the Nineteenth Century*. New York: Peter Lang, 1990.
Story, William Wetmore. *Roba di Roma*. London: Chapman and Hall; and New York: Appleton, 1863.
Strangers in a Strange Land: A Catalogue of an Exhibition on the History of Italian-language American Imprints (1830–1945). From the Collection of James J. Periconi, with a Bibliography of These and Related Works. New York: The Grolier Club, 2012.
Sullivan, J. W. *Tenement Tales of New York*. New York: Henry Holt & Co., 1895.
Tamburri, Anthony Julian. *Un biculturalismo negato: La letteratura italiana negli Stati Uniti*. Firenze: Franco Cesati, 2018.
Tasso, Torquato. *Jerusalem Delivered: A Poem*. Translated by Edward Fairfax, edited by Henry Morley. London: Routledge and Sons, 1890.
Teodonio, Marcello. *Vita di Belli*. Roma: Laterza, 1993.
Tibbetts, John C., ed. *Dvořák in America 1892–1895*. Portland, OR: Amadeus Press, 1993.
Tosches, Nick. *Dino: Living High in the Dirty Business of Dreams*. New York: Doubleday, 1992.
———. *In the Hand of Dante*. New York: Back Bay, 2003.
———. *Power on Earth: Michele Sindona's Explosive Story*. New York: Arbor House, 1986.
Traldi, Alberto. "La tematica dell'emigrazione nella narrativa italo-americana." *Comunità* 30 (August 1976): 245–72.
Il Turco di Ritorno [aka Riccardo Cordiferro]. "Negri, Napoletani e Siciliani." *La Follia di New York*, 5 gennaio 1914, 4.
Tusiani, Joseph. *The Age of Dante: An Anthology of Early Italian Poetry Translated into English Verse*. New York: Baroque, 1974.
———. *Dante's Divine Comedy: As Told for Young People*. Mineola: Legas, 2009.
———. *Dante's Inferno: As Told for Young People*. New York: Obolenski, 1965.
———. *Dante in licenza*. Verona: Editrice Nigrizia, 1952.

———. *Dante's Lyric Poems*. Introduction by Giuseppe C. Di Scipio. Brooklyn: Legas, 1999.

———. *Dante's Purgatorio: As Told for Young People*. New York: Astor-Honor, 1968.

———. *Envoy from Heaven*. New York: Obolensky, 1965 [Italian translation. *Dal cielo "inviato speciale."* Roma: Edizioni Presenza, 1966].

———. "Prefazione." In *Inferno: Da La Divina Commedia di Dante Alighieri in vernacolo pugliese*, by Nicola Testi, 7–10. Firenze: Vallecchi, 1958.

Ultra. Strenna commemorativa del XV anniversario della fondazione della Italian Dressmakers Union, Locale 89, I.L.G.W.U. New York: Italian Labor Education Bureau–Liberal Press, Inc., no date [but 1934].

Untermeyer, Louis. *The New Era in American Poetry*. New York: Henry Holt and Company, 1919.

Ventura, Luigi Donato, and S. Shevitch. *Misfits and Remnants*. Boston: Ticknor and Company, 1886.

———. *Peppino il lustrascarpe*. Edited by Martino Marazzi. Milano: FrancoAngeli, 2007.

Vezzosi, Elisabetta. *Il socialismo indifferente: Immigrati italiani e Socialist Party negli Stati Uniti del primo Novecento*. Roma: Edizioni Lavoro, 1991.

Viola, Lorella, and Jaap Verheul. "The Media Construction of Italian Identity: A Transatlantic, Digital Humanities Analysis of *italianità*, Ethnicity, and Whiteness, 1867–1920." *Identity* 19, no. 4 (2019): 294–312.

Viscusi, Robert. *Astoria*. Toronto: Guernica, 1995.

———. *Buried Caesars, and Others Secrets of Italian American Writing*. Albany, NY: State University of New York Press, 2006.

———. *Ellis Island*. New York: Bordighera Press, 2013.

Wallace, Mike. *Greater Gotham: A History of New York City from 1898 to 1919*. New York: Oxford University Press, 2017.

Washington, Booker T. *The Man Farthest Down: A Record of Observation and Study in Europe*. With the collaboration of Robert E. Park. Garden City, NY: Doubleday, Page & Company, 1912.

Wiener, Leo. *The History of Yiddish Literature in the Nineteenth Century*. New York: Charles Scribner's Sons, 1899.

———. *Yidish-Englishes verterbukh: A Dictionary of the Yiddish Language, with a Treatise on Yiddish Reading, Orthography and Dialectal Variations*. New York: A. Harkavy, 1898.

Wilson, Ross J. *New York and the First World War: Shaping an American City*. Farnham: Ashgate, 2014.

Yezierska, Anzia. *Bread Givers*. Garden City, NY: Doubleday, Page & Co., 1925.

———. "The Fat of the Land." *Century* 98 (August 1919): 466–79.

Index

Abeni, Damiano, 147n14
Aberdeen, lord George Hamilton Gordon, 18
Agee, James, 35, 153n16
Albertini, Stefano, 162n44
Alexander, Richard, 164n67
Alighieri, Dante, 3, 45–75, 79, 81, 117, 122, 124, 136, 158n1, 158n8, 159n12, 160n23, 163n57, 163n60, 164–65n72, 165n1
    fascist and nationalist interpretation of, 55–56, 59–61, 162nn44–48
    Italian American satires of, 49–50, 56–58, 159n11
Alighieri, Gemma, 72
Almerini, Achille, 50, 53
Anagnostou, Yiorgos, 2, 145n7
Andreoni, Antonio, 98–99, 168n4
Andrews, Allen, 147n13
Aquilecchia, John Vincent, 171n2
Arac, Jonathan, 143, 173n6
Ariosto, Ludovico, 121
Aristotle, 71
Ashbery, John, 139
Atlantís, 38
Avella, Caterina Maria, 166n5

Bachi, Pietro, 46–47
Bacigalupo, Massimo, 164n72

Bailly, Jean-Christophe, 35, 153n17
Baldelli, Ignazio, 170n8
Baldo, Michela, 173n8
ballad, 17, 24–25, 27–30, 151n55, 151nn57–58
Ballerini, Luigi, 59, 162n42
Bandini, Albert R., 56
Baranello, Adriana M., 150n47
Barlow, Henry Clark, 48
Barolini, Helen, 132
Barry, Phillips, 151n57
Bartoletti, Efrem, 51–53, 152n59, 159n17, 160n18, 160nn20–22
Barzini, Luigi sr., 57
Basile Green, Rose, 1, 145n2, 155n35
Bayard. *See* Ruotolo, Onorio
Beebee, Thomas, 151n58
Beerbohm, Max, 133
Belletristiches Journal, Der, 39
Belli, Giuseppe Gioachino, 14–16, 23, 30, 120, 147nn13–14, 147n18
Bello Figo, 143
Bellow, Saul, 154n22
Belluscio, Stephen J., 162n41, 169n2
Bencivenni, Marcella, 125
Bendinelli Predelli, Maria, 168n4
Bergquist, James M., 154n26
Bernardi, Jacopo, 158n2

Bernardy, Amy A., 81, 166n7
Berrigan, Ted, 139
Bertazzoli, Raffaella, 147n14
Bertellini, Giorgio, 102, 125, 168n7
Bertolucci, Attilio, 135
Betteloni, Vittorio, 156
Betts, Jennifer, 161n31
Bianchini, Angela, 148n21
bi- and multilingualism, 24–25,
    40–41, 44, 58, 65, 85, 94, 96,
    123, 125, 155–56n39, 156nn46–
    47, 157n62, 165n4, 166n5,
    171n7
Biondi, Franco, 143–44, 173n7
Bloch, Marc, 151n56
Blumin, Stuart M., 152n3
Boas, Franz, 122
Boito, Arrigo, 19, 94–95
Bok, Edward, 40, 156n40
Bonaffini, Luigi, 123, 171n7, 171n9
Borgianini, Alfredo, 67, 119–20, 126,
    171n1
Borgianini, Stephen A., 172n14
Botta, Vincenzo, 46–48, 158n5,
    158n8
Bourdieu, Pierre, 123
Boyden, Michael, 155n38
Brachvogel, Udo, 39
Brambilla Ageno, Franca, 165n1
Branca, Vittore, 162n42
Bravi, Adrián, 7
Brazil, 19
Bresci, Gaetano, 24
Bronzini, Giovanni, 28, 151n57
Brooks, Van Wyck, 148n22
Brown, Dan, 71, 165n73
Buenos Aires, 85
Buonvicino, Maria Nicola, 168n1
Burke, Peter, 151n56
Burns, Jennifer, 146n18
Burrows, Edwin G., 42, 157n55
Buzard, James, 148n23

Cabrini (Mother), 64
Cahan, Abraham, 34, 38–40, 104,
    153n12
Calhoun, John, 19
California, 85–86, 88–89, 94
Camaiti, Venturino, 57
Canada, 19
Canova, Antonio, 140
Carducci, Giosue, 56, 150n48
Carletti, Lorenzo, 148n18
Carnovale, Luigi, 55–56, 160n27,
    161n29
Carravetta, Peter, 125, 145n7, 172n10
Carrera, Alessandro, 151n58
Carroccio, Il, 94, 166n5
Caruso, Enrico, 40, 99, 143
Cary, Henry Francis, 48
Cassettari, Rosa, 85
Castagnetto, Pierangelo, 164n72
Castellucci, V. A., 56–58, 161n31
Cavalieri, Enea, 20
Cavanna, François, 123, 171n8
Cavour, Camillo Benso, 48, 134
Cellini, Benvenuto, 62
changing culture, 3, 7, 31–44, 125
Channing, William, 13
Chapman, Charlotte Gower, 5, 145n13
Cheda, Giorgio, 167n15
Chiappelli, Fredi, 59, 162n42
Christians, Rudolf, 41
Ciambelli, Bernardino, 39, 49, 57,
    101, 105, 159n11
Ciardi, John, 63
    and Dante, 65–67, 163n57,
    163nn59–61
Ciccotti, Ettore, 150n48
Cinotto, Simone, 6, 124, 146n15,
    154n20, 170n5
city-self, 34, 37, 43
Columbus, Christopher, 53, 135,
    159n16
Comberiati, Daniele, 172n9

Connell, William J., 167n20
Conolly-Smith, Peter, 154n26, 156n47, 156n49, 156n51
Cor. *See* Cordiferro, Riccardo
Cordiferro, Riccardo, 22–23, 49, 143, 159n11, 159n13
Corferreum. *See* Cordiferro, Riccardo
Corriere d'America, 38, 57, 96, 121
Corsi, Edward, 104, 106
Covello, Leonard, 106, 170n11
Crane, Hart, 157n56
Crispi, Francesco, 20
Crocetti, Dino Paul. *See* Martin, Dean
Cronau, Rudolf, 154n26
Cunningham, Gilbert F., 161n30
Cuoco, Vincenzo, 141
Cupelli, Alberto, 168n3

Da Ponte, Lorenzo, 46–47, 122, 158nn2–3
Da Rif, Bianca Maria, 170n8
D'Acierno, Pellegrino, 166n6
D'Agostino, Guido, 117
D'Agostino, Paul, 140
D'Alessandro, Pietro, 46–47, 158n4
Damiani, Gigi, 94, 167n18
D'Angelo, Pascal, 94, 132
D'Annunzio, Gabriele, 40, 53, 56
Dante Club, 46, 71, 122, 165n73
De Boni, Filippo, 15
De Michelis, Cesare G., 147n14
Del Giudice, Luisa, 126, 146n15, 172n13
DeLillo, Don, 164–65n72
d'Eramo, Marco, 158n63
Deschamps, Bénédicte, 154n25
Detti, Emma, 147–48n18
Dewey, Joseph, 164n72
di Donato, Pietro, 43, 58, 68, 117, 132, 157n61, 162n50, 162n52, 163n65, 164n67
  and Dante, 61–63, 69–71, 74

di Michele, Mary, 165n4
Di Nino, Nicola, 147n15
Di Scipio, Giuseppe C., 163n56
diasporic Italian culture, 7, 123, 141–44
Diomede, Matthew, 164n66
Divagando, 96
Diver Steucher, Dorothea, 153n19
divided modes, 40–42, 102
Dolitzki, Menachem, 154n23
Dones, Elvira, 7
Dotti, Stefania, 171n14
double presence, 3
Doyle, Arthur Conan, 99
Duncan, Norman, 39
Dunne, Finley Peter, 41, 156n48
Durante, Francesco, 4, 104, 124, 126, 155n35, 159n14, 163n62, 170n6, 172n14
Dvořák, Antonín, 35, 153n16
Dylan, Bob, 28–29, 151n55, 151nn58–59

Efron, David, 157n52
Egan, Maurice F., 157n59
Einstein, Alfred, 122
Eisenherz. *See* Cordiferro, Riccardo
Eliot, Thomas Stearns, 49
Elliott, Emory, 157n62
Emerson, Ralph Waldo, 13
epistolary writing, 82–88, 166nn9–10, 167n13
Epoca, 96
ethnic modernism, 43
Ethnikós Kýrix, 38
Etrusco. *See* Bartoletti, Efrem
Ets, Marie Hall, 85

Fairfax, lord Edward, 168n4
Fanciullo, Maria Carmela, 163n55
Fanning, Charles, 157n59
Fante, John, 106, 117, 132

Farfariello (Eduardo Migliaccio), 41, 94, 96, 102, 157n52
Faust, Albert Bernhard, 153n9
Felici, Lucio, 147n13
Fenoglio, Marisa, 143–44, 173n7
Fergusson, Francis, 67, 163n61
Ferlinghetti, Lawrence, 68, 122, 140, 163n58, 163nn63–64
Fiaschetti, Michael, 102, 120–21, 171n3
Fiedler, Leslie, 121
Fincher, David, 72, 165n73
Fine, David M., 153n10
Finotti, Joseph Maria, 158n9
Fiore, Teresa, 171n8
Fitzgerald, Francis Scott, 157n59
Flaiano, Ennio, 126
Fluck, Winfried, 156n50
Folkestad, Sigurd, 157n56
Follia di New York, La, 22, 39, 49, 99, 122, 150n43, 159n11, 159nn13–14
Forasiepi, Silvia, 161n31
foreign-language journalism, 38–39
Forgione, Louis, 104
Fortunato, Giustino, 141
Foscolo, Ugo, 47–48, 93
Foster, George G., 152n3
Fourier, Charles, 13
Frasca, Simona, 150n44
Freccero, John, 65
Friedman, Paul, 162n49
Frost, Robert, 28, 94
Frugone & Balletto (publisher), 95
Fuchs, Daniel, 43, 157n60, 158n64
Fuller, Margaret, 11–17, 21, 23, 30, 146nn1–7, 147nn11–14, 148n22
  and Belli's Roman sonnets, 14–16, 147nn13–14

Gabaccia, Donna, 2, 125, 145n5, 146n13, 172n10
Gamberale, Luigi, 25
Gardaphé, Fred, 94, 164n67, 166n6, 167n16
Garibaldi, Giuseppe, 12, 103, 116, 142
Gay, Ruth, 155n29
Gemme, Paola, 146n3
Gennari, John, 153n17
Gentile, Giovanni, 148n18
German immigrant literature, 39, 153n19, 154n26, 155n31, 155n38
Gibellini, Pietro, 147nn13–14
Ginsberg, Allen, 140
Giolitti, Giovanni, 49
Giometti, Cristiano, 148n18
Giovannitti, Arturo, 23–29, 40, 51, 53–54, 94, 96, 102, 122, 150nn46–49, 151n50, 151nn53–54, 152n59, 156n39, 160nn23–26, 167n17
  Nenia Sannita, 24
  The Walker, 25–27
Giovannitti, David, 160n23
Giovannoli, Renato, 151n58
Giunta, Edvige, 126, 171n9, 172n13
Giusti, Giuseppe, 56, 117
Gladsky, Thomas S., 152n2
Gladstone, William Ewart, 18
Glazer, Sophie, 155n29
Gold, Mike, 42, 157n54, 157n58
Golden, Harry, 155n32
Goldstein, Ann, 159n17
Gordin, Jacob, 38, 155n29
Gramsci, Antonio, 1–2, 141–43, 145n1, 145n3
Grandillo, Bonifacio, 59, 162nn45–48
Greek immigrant literature, 38, 154n28
Greenberg, Eliezer, 38, 154n22
Guttmann, Allen, 40, 156n42

Haenni, Sabine, 156n50

Haller, Hermann W., 102, 157n52, 168n7
Handlin, Oscar, 156n44
Hapgood, Hutchins, 38, 154n23
Harding, Warren, 55
Harkavy, Alexander, 38, 154n23
Harrigan, Edward, 36, 153nn18–19
Hawthorne, Nathaniel, 30, 152n60
H. D. (Hilda Doolittle), 28
Helbig, Richard E., 154n26
Hoepli (publisher), 55
Homberger, Eric, 152n7
Howe, Irving, 38, 154n22
Hudspeth, Robert N., 146nn8–9, 147n10
Huysseune, Michel, 20, 149n35

Iasoni, Martino, 41, 156n46
illiteracy and "illiterature," 62, 79–94, 102, 111, 116, 159n15, 167n16
immigrant literacy, 79–94, 98–99
immigrant poetry, 24–29, 37–38, 40, 47, 49–54, 56–58, 89–95, 98–99, 119–20
inscriptions and street signs, 81–82
International Socialist Review, The, 25
Irish immigrant literature, 33–34, 36, 41–42, 157n59
Italian American literary canon, 100–102
Italian American Writers Association (IAWA), 133, 135
Italian Book Company (publisher), 95

Jacobson, Matthew F., 152n5
James, Henry, 17, 148n22
Janeczek, Helena, 7
Janson, Tore, 165n3
Jaroszyńska-Kirchmann, Anna D., 154n27

Jeffers, Robinson, 94
Jefferson, Teddy, ix
Jesus Christ, 44, 54, 61, 70–71, 140, 162n48
Jewish Daily Forward, The, 38–39, 155n32
Johnson-Reed Act, 32, 156n43
Juliani, Richard N., 170n8

Kafka, Franz, 3
Kazin, Alfred, 154n22
Keen, Catherine, 146n18
Kellman, Steven G., 164n72
Kelly, Myra, 42, 157n54, 157n57
Keppler, Joseph, 34, 153n9
Kluge, Cora Lee, 155n31
Koch, Theodore, 55
Kollbrunner, Oskar, 153n20, 157n56
Kopan, Andrew T., 154n28
Krase, Jerome, 168n6
Kropotkin, Petr, 122
Kunitz, Stanley, 154n22

La Guardia, Fiorello, 58, 105–106
La Piana, Angelina, 158n6, 158nn8–9
Labriola, Arturo, 122
Lakhous, Amara, 7
Laliotou, Ioanna, 152n6
Lang, Barbara, 153n19
Lansing, Richard, 165n1
Lapolla, Biagio Oreste, 168n1
Lapolla, Garibaldi M., 35, 58, 103–17, 132, 153n15, 162n41, 162n43, 168n1, 169nn2–5, 170n11, 171n13
L'Arab, Ernesto, 163n62
Lecomte, Mia, 126, 172n12
Lentricchia, Augusto, 167n16
Leogrande, Alessandro, 7, 146n17
Leoni, Giuseppe, 81
Leopardi, Giacomo, 93, 117

Lessin. *See* Wald, Abraham
Lewisohn, Ludwig, 40, 154n22, 156n43
Lezzi, Angelo, 168n5
Life, 96
Lima, 1
Lindsay, Vachel, 28
Lombardi, Norberto, 150n48
Long, Huey Pierce, 52
Longfellow, Henry Wadsworth, 47, 67, 158n1
Lowell, Amy, 28
Luconi, Stefano, 125, 154n25, 168n6
Luzzatto, Sergio, 122, 171n6
Lybia, 23, 25, 150n47
Lynch, Gayle, 31

MacAllister, Archibald T., 163n57
Machiavelli, Niccolò, 64
Majewski, Karen, 42, 157n43
Malamud, Bernard, 103
Malanga, Gerard, 122
Malin, Irving, 164n72
Mandelbaum, Allen, 154n22
Mangione, Jerre, 105, 117, 169n3
Manzoni, Alessandro, 117
Marazzi, Martino, 145n4, 150n49, 151n53, 155n35, 156n39, 156nn46–47, 159n17, 160n24, 166n7, 171n3, 171n5
Marconi, Guglielmo, 50
Marcus, Greil, 155n38
Marraro, Howard, 100
Marseille, 1
Marsh, Fred T., 169n3
Martelli, Sebastiano, 25, 150n48
Martin, Bernard, 39, 155n33
Martin, Dean, 72
Martini, Plinio, 166n8
Martinoni, Renato, 166n8
Marzani, Carl, 121, 171n3
Masi Carlson, Robin, 166n5

Masters, Edgar Lee, 28
Mastriani, Francesco, 18
Mathews, J. Chesley, 67, 158n1, 163n61
Matteotti, Giacomo, 52
Mazzei, Filippo, 48, 158n7
Mazzini, Giuseppe, 12, 15, 19, 48, 142, 148n18
McKenzie, Kenneth, 55
Meckel, Richard A., 169n4
Melbourne, 1
Mele, Frank, 168n5
Mencken, Henry Louis, 40, 155n37
Merwin, W. S., 154n22
Metzker, Isaac, 155n32
Michelangelo, 62, 64
Migliaccio, Eduardo. *See* Farfariello
Milano Appel, Anne, 117
Miller, Henry, 2
Miller, Sally M., 154n26
Mitchell, Joseph, 152n3
Mladić, Ratko, 144
Moffa, Ettore, 97–98
Monti, Luigi, 46–47
Monti, Vincenzo, 52, 56
Morandi, Luigi, 16, 147nn15–16
Morgen Journal, Der, 38
Morley, Henry, 168n4
Moscardi, Iuri, 147n13
Mueller, R. W., 153n9
Mujčić, Elvira, 7, 144, 173n9
multilingualism. *See* bilingualism
Mussolini, Benito, 58–60, 124, 139, 162nn45–46, 162n 48

Nadel, Ira, 164n72
Naples, 18, 20, 23, 116
Nast, Thomas, 34, 153n9
Nation, The, 94
New York, 31–44, 95–97, 122, 152n3, 152n6, 157n52
Nievo, Ippolito, 141

Nissim, Renzo, 81, 166n7
Nolan, Mary, 152n4
Norse, Harold, 147n14

Occhipinti, Maria, 6, 146n14
O'Connell, Shaun, 152n8
Ojetti, Ugo, 1, 145n1
Olster, Stacey, 164n72
Ornitz, Samuel, 35, 153n13
Orsi, Robert Anthony, 105, 126, 170n8, 172n13
Ossoli (family), 16
Øverland, Orm, 157n56
Ozick, Cynthia, 154n22

Pagano, Jo, 117
Paglia, Camille, 98
Palidda, Salvatore, 172n11
Pallavicini, Paolo, 94
Paolucci, Anne, 158n1
Papini, Giovanni, 56
Parati, Graziella, 146n16
Parini, Giuseppe, 47, 93
Park, Robert Ezra, 20, 145n11, 149n34
Parsons, Thomas W., 47–48
Pascarella, Cesare, 119
Pascoli, Giovanni, 23, 49–50, 52–53, 142–43, 150nn47–48, 158n10, 173n5
Patell, Cyrus R. K., 152n7
Patri, Angelo, 104
Pavese, Cesare, 150n48
Pearl, Matthew, 71, 165n73
Pedullà, Gabriele, 122, 171n6
Peragallo, Anita, 170n8
Peragallo, Olga, 105, 170n8
Periconi, James J., 155n35, 158n3, 164n72, 167n20
Perricone, Joseph, 123, 171n7, 171n9
Petrosino, Joe, 21
Pfeijffer, Ilja Leonard, 7

Philipp, Adolf, 41
Pike, David L., 164n72
Pin. *See* Ciambelli, Bernardino
Pinski, David, 32, 40, 152n1, 156n41
Pirandello, Luigi, 5–6, 19, 56, 145n10, 145n12, 150n43
Pius IX, 16
Pius XI, 59
Plastino, Goffredo, 150n45, 156n45
Polanyi, Karl, 131
Poletti, Charles, 166n11
Polish immigrant literature, 38, 42, 154n27, 157n53
Polish Morning World, The, 38
Pound, Ezra, 28, 49, 151n54
Presutto, Michele, 125
Pretelli, Matteo, 125
Prezzolini, Giuseppe, 50, 81, 104–107, 159nn14–16, 161n31, 166n7, 170n7
Progresso Italo-Americano, Il, 38, 95
Proletario, Il, 24
Puccini, Giacomo, 99
Pugliese, Stanislao G., 167n20
Puzo, Mario, 132

Queneau, Raymond, 137

Raffa, Guy P., 159n12
Ragusa, Olga, 161n31
Raphael, 62
Rapone, Donato, 169n1
Renan, Ernest, 48
return, 24, 82, 99, 110, 112–13, 117, 140, 143–44, 173n8
Reynolds, Larry J., 146n1
Rich, Adrienne, 154n22
Righetti, Dante, 89
Righetti, Pompeo, 89, 93
Riis, Jacob A., 18
Rio de Janeiro, 1
Ripari, Edoardo, 147n13

Rischin, Moses, 154n24, 155n29
Risorgimento, 11, 16, 46, 48, 96, 133, 141–42, 148n18
  and disunity, 2, 17–19
Rivolta, Sabrina, 170n12
Rodia, Sam, 126
Rolling Stones (band), 139
Rome, 11–17, 60, 63, 119–20
Rosenfeld, Morris, 37–38, 154n21, 154n23
Rossetti, Dante Gabriel, 48, 158n8
Rossi, E. (store), 95
Roth, Henry, 43, 157n60
Roy, 86–87
Ruotolo, Onorio, 159n11
Russo, John Paul, 164n72
Russo, Richard, 142, 173n4

Salerno, Salvatore, 169n1
Salter, Sarah, 166n7
Salvatore, Eugenio, 166n10, 167n13
Salvemini, Gaetano, 141
San Francisco, 1, 32, 56, 68–69, 85, 94–95, 150n43, 167n2
Sandburg, Carl, 27–28, 151nn50–52, 151n55
Sanders, Ed, 135
Sante, Luc, 152n3
Sayad, Abdelmalek, 3, 126, 145n8, 172n11
Sayers, Dorothy, 67
Scarpellini, A., 122
Scartazzini, Giovanni Andrea, 56
Schacher, Yael, 156n43
Schiavo, Giovanni Ermenegildo, 100
Schliemann, Heinrich, 4
Schurz, Carl, 40, 155n38
Schwartz-Seller, Maxine, 155n30
Sciascia, Leonardo, 105
Scibona, Salvatore, 79, 165n2
Sciorra, Joseph, 6, 126, 146n15, 150n45, 156n45, 172n13
Scorrano, Luigi, 162n44

Scorsese, Martin, 152n3
Scott-Moncrieff, C. K., 145n10
Secchi de Casali, Giovanni, 12
Severo, 83–85
Shakespeare, William, 94
Shelley, Percy Bysshe, 136
Shevitch, S., 156n47
Siani, Cosma, 163n55, 163n62
Sicilian sulfur mines, 5, 17, 19–21, 149n33, 150n43
Sicily, 5–6, 20–21, 73, 142, 145n13, 150n43
Silone, Ignazio, 122
Simplicio. *See* Damiani, Gigi
Sindona, Michele, 72
Singleton, Charles, 63
Sinopoli, Franca, 171n9
Sisca (family), 39
Sisca, Alessandro. *See* Cordiferro, Riccardo
Skårdal, Dorothy Burton, 156n44
Sloterdijk, Peter, 34, 153n11
Smith, John Talbot, 157n59
Smith, Susan Belasco, 146n1
Sollors, Werner, 43, 155n38, 156n50, 157–58n62
Sorbini, Alberto, 171n14
Spahr, Clemens, 151n50
Staats-Zeitung, Die, 38
Stanco, Italo. *See* Moffa, Ettore
Story, William Wetmore, 23, 148n22
  Roba di Roma, 16–17, 148nn19–20
Stürenburg, Caspar, 153n19
Sue, Eugène, 99
Sullivan, James W., 33, 152n8
Sutro-Schücking, Kathinka, 153n19

Tageblatt, Das, 38
Tamburri, Anthony Julian, 126, 155n35, 172n12
Tasso, Bernardo, 89
Tasso, Torquato, 56, 89, 98, 168nn4–5
Teodonio, Marcello, 147n15, 147n17

Testi, Nicola, 163n62
Thomas Aquinas, 64
Tibbetts, John C., 153n16
Ticknor, W. D. (publisher), 47
Tito, Ettore, 149n25
Tomasi, Mari, 166n11
Tosches, Nick, 71, 122, 165n75
 In the Hand of Dante, 72–73, 75, 165n76
Traldi, Alberto, 105, 170n8
Tresca, Carlo, 96, 102
Tuckerman King, Jane, 147n10
Tunis, 1
Turco di Ritorno, Il. See Cordiferro, Riccardo
Turner, Frederick Jackson, 7
Tusiani, Joseph, 68, 73, 122, 150n49, 160n24, 163n62
 and Dante, 63–65, 163nn53–56

Umberto I, King of Italy, 24
Untermeyer, Louis, 28, 151n54

Vallecchi (publisher), 67
Vanguard Press, 103
Vanni, S. F. (publisher), 60–61, 161n31
Vanzetti, Bartolomeo, 171n13
Vecoli, Rudolph, 101
Ventura, Luigi Donato, 41, 156n47
Verdi, Giuseppe, 94–95, 99
Verga, Giovanni, 5, 19
Verheul, Jaap, 150n43
Vezzosi, Elisabetta, 169n4
Vicinelli, Augusto, 173n5
Villari, Pasquale, 18, 141
Viola, Lorella, 150n43
Virgil, 56–58, 94
Viscusi, Robert, 4, 71–72, 105, 141, 155n35, 170n8, 172nn1–3
 and Dante, 74–75, 122

Buried Caesars, 129–34, 165nn77–80, 172n1
Ellis Island, 134–40, 145n9, 165nn81–82, 172n2
Vlora (cargo ship), 124
Voce del Popolo, La, 95
Volkszeitung, Die, 38

Wahrheit, Die, 38
Wald, Abraham, 154n23
Wallace, Mike, 42, 157n55
Washington, Booker T., 150n43
 The Man Farthest Down, 5, 20–23, 145n11, 149n34, 149nn36–39, 150nn40–42
Waterman, Brian, 152n7
White Mario, Jessie, 17–21, 23, 149n24, 149nn26–33
Whitman, Walt, 25, 29, 122, 136, 150n48
Wiener, Leo, 38–39, 154n21, 154n23, 155n34
Wilcox, Beagan, 169n1
Wilkins, Ernest Hatch, 55
Williams, William Carlos, 135
Wilson, Ross J., 152n6
Witte, Karl, 124
Woods, Robert Archey, 149n24
Wright, James, 154n22

Yezierska, Anzia, 35, 153nn13–14
Yiddish literature, 34–35, 37–39, 154nn22–23, 155n29, 155nn33–34

Zaikaner, Caroline, 160n23
Zamboni McCormick, Kathleen, 171n9
Zatti, Florinda, 83–85
Zocchi, Cesare, 49
Zunser, Eliakim, 154n23

www.ingramcontent.com/pod-product-compliance
Lightning Source LLC
Chambersburg PA
CBHW030653230426
43665CB00011B/1076